ADVANCE PRAISE

"I was hesitant at first to read *Speaking Out: Families of LGBTQ+ Advance the Dialogue* because so often, stories that include family members end up overshadowing our own stories and wellbeing, as though we only exist in terms of how we affect others. At best they tend to be cookie cutter in nature. But Esther Schwartz-McKinzie produced instead a rare gem of sincere, complex, and respectful interviews of both family members and LGBTQ people with a warmth and intimacy that makes it very clear her whole heart is engaged with this work and with our community. I look forward to re-reading it many times."

—Robin Lombard, MoCo Pride Center

"These paired accounts represent a sea change in acceptance of sexual diversities, an encouraging multi-generational cheer. Wishing my parents had been able to read this book when I was growing up and glad to have this compelling resource for all of us now."

—Loraine Hutchins,
co-editor, *Bi Any Other Name: Bisexual People Speak Out*

Speaking Out

Families of LGBTQ+ Advance the Dialogue

edited by Esther Schwartz-McKinzie

Gival Press

Arlington, Virginia

Publication of this project is supported in part by Montgomery College.

Published by Gival Press, an imprint of Gival Press, LLC.
For information please write:
Gival Press, LLC
P. O. Box 3812
Arlington, VA 22203
www.givalpress.com

First edition
ISBN: 978-1-940724-27-0
eISBN: 978-1-940724-26-7
Library of Congress Control Number: 2022944497

Cover art: © Lazyllama.
Internal art: © Brainstormoff.
Book Design by Ken Schellenberg

This book is dedicated to the families

*who speak out here, with admiration for their
courage,*

and to readers who find connection.

Stories can break the dignity of a people. But stories can also repair that broken dignity.

Chimamanda Ngozi Adichie,

"The Danger of a Single Story"

DON'T BURY THEM

bring your broken pieces, jagged edges at your feet,
don't, don't, don't bury them

share your broken pieces shattered hopes and weary dreams,
don't, don't, don't bury them

spread them out upon on the ground
when loves light shines down—many treasures can be found,
don't bury them

bring your deepest secrets, the hurt and anger locked inside,
don't, don't, don't bury them

share your well-kept secrets, the ones they wanted you to hide,
don't, don't, don't bury them,

lay them out upon the ground when love's light shines down,
there is healing to be found
oh, don't you bury them

from all the textures & colors, a mosaic starts to form
from so many fragments, new creations are born,
don't, don't, don't bury them

bring your sparkling pieces, the ones that make you who you are,
don't, don't, don't bury them

share your shimmering pieces, even our dust is made of stars,
don't, don't, don't bury them

lay them out upon the ground, when loves light shines down
many treasures can be found, many treasures can be found,
don't, don't, don't bury them

by K.K. Capps

TABLE OF CONTENTS

INTRODUCTION

"What is more important than an attempt at understanding a different corner of human experience than the one you inhabit? What is more life-giving than an affirmation that people like you can live?"

After I asked my daughter to read this book, she replied with these questions; since she is my inspiration, I gladly give the opening words to her.

Mac recently returned from her first year of college and is suspicious of labels that never quite convey the right import for beings as complex as humans. The closest fit for her, she says, is cisgender lesbian.

When she, as a small but mighty 11-year old, declared (to us, and then to her entire school) that she was lesbian, we did not know a lot about what that meant. Could a child, at that age, know what they were talking about? We did not know how to counsel her, and we did not know how to navigate family, school and friendship situations that can become challenging very quickly when children do not conform to heteronormative appearance and behavior.

We did know that we loved this child, and that if we did not have a map, we would have to make one.

It soon became clear that she did not want our guidance: she wanted us to hurry up and get on board.

I have since learned that this is the experience of many parents of LGBTQ+ children and adults. According to the American Academy of Pediatrics (AAAP), children typically have a stable understanding of their gender identity, whether that is congruent with the sex assigned at birth or not, by age four (Rafferty). Mayo Clinic asserts that "children categorize their own gender by age three years, but that "because gender stereotypes are reinforced, some children learn to behave in ways that bring them the most reward, despite their authentic gender identity" ("Children").

In other words, by the time a child (particularly an adult child) comes out, they have likely known and been struggling for a long time with the dissonance between their identity and the cultural expectation of gender conformity.

Moreover, they may have been navigating a complicated calculus of loss: who will stop loving me if I reveal myself? How will I be hurt? Or even, *where will I sleep?*

Parents, especially cisgender heterosexual parents who do not already have ties to LGBTQ+ communities, find themselves needing to catch up in an environment that is both politically hostile and rife with information that is scary, wrong, or both.

Analysis of data from the Centers for Disease Control's 2019 Youth Risk Behavior Surveillance survey recently led the Human Rights Campaign (HRC) to conclude that "lesbian, gay, bisexual, transgender and queer youth *are living in a state of crisis.* Whether it is being bullied in school, poor mental health or substance use, LGBTQ teens experience marginalization from multiple angles."

The consequences of marginalization and minority stress for LGBTQ+ youth are staggering:

- 31% of LGBTQ+ youth, 43% of transgender youth and 40% of questioning youth have been bullied at school, compared to 16% of their non-LGBTQ+ peers.
- 54% of LGBTQ+ youth, 61% of transgender youth and 61% of questioning youth are battling symptoms of depression, compared to 29% of non-LGBTQ+ youth.
- 35% of LGBTQ+ youth, 45% of transgender youth and 40% of questioning youth have seriously considered attempting suicide, compared to 13% of non-LGBTQ+ youth ("LGBT Youth"); suicide is the second leading cause of death among youth ages 10-24, and LGBTQ+ youth are four times as likely to attempt suicide as their peers ("Facts About LGBTQ").

Sadly, family of origin rejection is a primary source of stress for LGBTQ+ people (Meanly 41), and stressors can be even greater for those who identify as bi (2019 Bi+). Youth with rejecting families are frequently forced to leave their homes: In addition to being dramatically overrepresented in the foster care system, they comprise 40% of the 4.2 million homeless youth in the United States, even though they represent closer to 10% of youth overall. A recent study from the University of Chicago concludes that LGBTQ+ youth have a 120% increased risk of experiencing homelessness compared to youth who identify as heterosexual and cisgender (Morton 12).

When I first learned about this crisis, I *hated* the idea that I could even belong to a group that needed to be told, for example, not to reject their child. I did not want my child to face such risks. Although I had every intention of being on affirming parent, the question—like some ambient spore from the culture at large—momentarily crept in, *"Why would she choose to have a harder life?"*[1]

The idea that people choose their gender identity and sexual orientation is, to be sure, the most widely believed and pernicious idea fueling hatred towards LGBTQ+ people around the world. It supports the dangerous ideas that LGBTQ+ people are either unnatural or sinful and that they can be "fixed." From this dehumanizing perspective, they generally do not deserve compassion or autonomy.

Seven years ago, the Supreme Court, in the landmark case, *Obergefell v. Hodges*, ruled that the fundamental right to marry is guaranteed to same-sex couples.[2] In the years following the legalization of marriage, the visibility of LGBTQ+ people (married or not) increased dramatically, in real-life as more people came out of the closet, and in cinema ("Observations"). Another landmark case in 2020, *Bostock v. Clayton*

---

1   Acknowledging this is important, because doing so speaks to the power and presence of such notions, despite their mistakenness.

2   In *Obergefell v. Hodges*, fourteen same-sex couples and two men whose partners were deceased successfully argued that denying them the right to marry was a violation of the Fourteenth Amendment. The Supreme Court held that same-sex marriage is protected despite four dissenting opinions, three by current Justices Clarence Thomas, Samuel Alito and John Roberts. See "Obergefell v. Hodges." *Legal Information Institute*, Cornell Law School, https://www.law.cornell.edu/supremecourt/text/14-556#writing-14-556_OPINION_3

County, held that LGBTQ+ employees are protected against workplace discrimination under Title VII of the Civil Rights Act.[3]

The power of such normalization and protection cannot be overstated.

For people living in some areas of the United States at least, the tensions around LGBTQ+ identity (which peaked during the 1980s AIDS crisis) seemed to have died down. One Article published in *The Atlantic* even declared in June of 2019, "The Struggle for Gay Rights is Over." The author noted, "On television, one cannot change the channel without coming across prominent lesbian and gay characters," reflecting an integration of LGBTQ+ experience into modern life (Kirchick).

The increase in the number of people identifying as LGBTQ+ recently has been a cause of celebration for many. The 2022 Gallup Poll reported that US adults who self-identify as lesbian, gay, bisexual, transgender or something other than heterosexual has reached 7.1%, double the percentage indicated by the 2012 survey, with Gen Z, the youngest group of adults (born between 1997-2003) driving the growth (Jones). The 2021 Census Bureau's Household Pulse Survey puts the figure even higher at 8%, an estimated twenty-million adults (Powell), while the UCLA School of Law's William's Institute estimates that 9.5% of the population of youth ages 13-17 identify as LGBTQ+ (Conron, "Youth"). The CDC's most recent Youth Risk Behavior Survey put this figure at 2.5 million, "with tens of thousands more saying they are questioning their identity" (YRBS). Additionally, the typical age of first coming out

---

3   *Bostock v. Clayton County* asserts that employment discrimination on the basis of an employee's sexual orientation constitutes a form of sex discrimination prohibited by Title VII of the Civil Rights Act. For a detailed description, see "Bostock v. Clayton County." *Legal Information Institute*, Cornell Law School, https://www. law.cornell.edu/supct/cert/17-1618. On June 15, 2022, President Joseph Biden signed the *Executive Order on Advancing Equality for Lesbian, Gay, Bisexual, Transgender, Queer, and Intersex Individuals*, another major initiative to thwart discrimination, with an emphasis on access to health care and strong repudiation of conversion therapy. See "Executive Order on Advancing Equality for Lesbian, Gay, Bisexual, Transgender, Queer, and Intersex Individuals." *The White House*, The United States Government, 15 June 2022, https://www.whitehouse.gov/briefing-room/ presidential-actions/2022/06/15/executive-order-on-advancing-equality-for-lesbian-gay-bisexual-transgender-queer-and-intersex-individuals/

has decreased from about 20 a generation ago to age 16 now, with many children coming out at younger ages.[4]

However, seven years is a relatively short time for legal rights and protections to become deep-rooted. As I write, I have just received the alert that *Roe v. Wade* has been overturned. Already, politicians in some states are making moves to reinstate sodomy laws and to overturn *Obergefell*. America is in the midst of a culture war, and LGBTQ+ people find themselves in the crosshairs.

Despite the fact that the majority of Americans "favor laws that would protect gay, lesbian, bisexual, and transgender people against discrimination in jobs, public accommodations, and housing" (PRRI), conservative lawmakers across the country have launched unprecedented attacks against LGBTQ+ people. In the first four months of 2022, over 300 anti-LGBTQ+ bills were introduced in 36 state legislatures, many of them aimed at trans youth, an especially vulnerable population. Laws that have successfully been enacted so far "range from making it a felony to provide transgender youth with life-saving health care to banning transgender girls from participating in sports to erasing LGBTQ+ people from school curriculum to granting broad licenses to discriminate against LGBTQ+ people" (2021).

Collectively, these efforts work to "normalize antagonism" towards LGBTQ+ people, "creating additional pain and distress for a population that already bears more than its fair share" (Carrasco). The cultural shift that culminated in *Obergefell* helped many LGBTQ+ people to, as poet Robert L. Giron notes, "fully discover and accept ourselves," yet the country appears to be moving backwards, and now, "We are all concerned by the movement to crush the lives of individuals, especially the trans

---

4   While data about children can be harder to track and "coming out" can mean either to oneself, to one person, or to many people, studies over the past decade suggest a general decrease in the age of coming out, with many children coming out between ages 13-16, and a significant number at younger ages. The American Academy of Pediatrics notes that, as society has become more open and accepting of LGBTQ individuals, "young people are beginning to come out at earlier ages than they did a generation ago. Children may first come out to online communities or peers they perceive as safe and accepting before telling their family." For more discussion, see "Coming out: Information for Parents of LGBTQ Teens." *HealthyChildren.org*, American Academy of Pediatrics, 6 Mar. 2021, https://www.healthychildren.org/ English/ages-stages/teen/dating-sex/Pages/Four-Stages-of-Coming-Out.aspx

communities." Author Henry Gass further observes, "Now, legal winds are rising that could uproot the rights that have helped [members of the LGBTQ+ community] feel like safe, valued, and equal members of society."

While much of the existing literature explores risk factors faced by LGBTQ+ youth, now, more than ever, is a moment to emphasize *protective* factors. Numerous studies point to parental support and familial warmth as factors that decrease the impacts of victimization, reducing suicidality and promoting lifelong resilience for LGBTQ+ people. Although it is generally understood that familial acceptance may increase with time (and often begins with mothers), researchers still do not have a good understanding of how to facilitate acceptance.[5]

One thing we know about stereotypes that generate rejection is that they "thrive in isolation but diminish with exposure to members of the outsider group" (Issitt). The anti-LGBTQ+ movement seems to understand this, and many of the proposed and newly established policies are geared towards silencing and erasure, particularly in the school context. This is now happening even in democratic strongholds like Maryland, where the Carroll County School Board just banned the display of rainbow flags as symbols that go against a so-called "neutrality policy" (Goodnight).

---

5   Familial warmth and acceptance make a profound difference in the lives of LGBTQ+ youth. Bittaker emphasizes the high costs of parental rejection, but as narratives included here show, parental warmth can help young people to thrive. While the majority of research has focused on the risk factors faced by LGBTQ+ youth, recent studies call for increased focus on parental acceptance as a protective factor. Sansfacon et al., for example, note that, "Literature regarding parents who support their child in receiving gender-affirming care is scarce," though existing research shows mothers demonstrating a higher level of support and engagement (Sansfacon 1216, 1224). Meanley et al. emphasizes a need for research on how "familial warmth shapes LGBTQ+ adolescents' self-esteem," and posits that "promoting self-esteem has the potential to improve later psychosocial functioning" (Meanley 41). Gorse emphasizes family connectedness as a "protective factor against suicide" (Gorse 17). Newcomb et al., identify a need for research that includes parents and identify this question as a future research opportunity that could lead to innovation: "Why do some initially unsupportive parents become supportive?" (Newcomb). Even with parental warmth, bullying is endemic, and minority stigma too often leads to depression and suicidality for LGBTQ+ youth.

Existing research shows that once parents become "sensitized to the needs and well–being of their LGB children, many family relationships improve" (Ryan).

Parents trying to understand what it means when a child comes out may well feel intimidated by available information and discussions. Connecting with others can be most challenging when one feels vulnerable. Blogs, Facebook chats, tweets and video clips are, by nature, abbreviated.

This book is an attempt to help to advance the dialogue for people who are in the crucial role of parenting LGBTQ+ youth. I understand now that what I most needed as I tested the tightrope I was about to cross were the full, rich, messy, and complex stories of people who had taken the journey before me.

Included here are interviews with 19 people with very different backgrounds and life experiences. All of them have spent some part of their lives in Maryland, but they have hailed from a variety of places, including Ohio, New England, Washington State and Jamaica. They include Gen Z adults and older adults who recall their experiences coming out to their parents, as well as the parents of children who came out—or who began to struggle with their identities—when they were quite young. In some cases, I have been fortunate to capture the perspectives of parents and children in the same families, interviewed separately or together.

These families had different starting points: some had to deal with the dissonance of beliefs and perspectives that too often cause people to reject their children; others, though lacking such baggage, still had to deal with the stigma of homophobia or transphobia and with how that affected their child.

On the one hand, these interviews share how people grew in their understanding of and response to their children and themselves; they remind us that coming out is a lifelong process, and that parents also must come out—sometimes in situations that are very fraught and isolating. A remarkable aspect of parent narratives here is the candor of interview subjects who share the events and turning points that helped them to evolve in their thinking. Another is the degree to which the experiences of their children have led them to different forms of activism and to a greater awareness of and desire to make their communities more inclusive and fairer.

On the other hand, people who describe their childhood and adult experiences attempting to understand and come to terms with difference here exhibit tremendous bravery: the gay man whose mother told him she would "pray for god to kill him;" the lesbian new mother who still weeps over her rejecting father's absence; the young trans person who proudly took on a new name before synagogue and community, and others—all share their intimate narratives in a spirit of generosity and as a form of activism, because they hope that giving readers an opportunity to know them as real people can make a difference.

Altogether, the memories and experiences of these individuals help to undo the harmful notion that gender and sexual orientation are choices and show how the policing and repression of human identity have terrible costs. Proposing connection and visibility as a response to bullying and hatred, they invite readers to dwell for a moment with the courage of LGBTQ+ people and their families, and to admire and celebrate their resilience.

Perhaps even for some readers, coming to better understand, through these voices, "a different corner of human experience than the one you inhabit" will inspire new journeys.

Note:

Participants in this project were given the option to use their real names or use pseudonyms. What follows is a mix of both.

1: TERI AUGUSTINE—
I just knew that I love my son more than anything.

Teri Augustine raised her family in Maryland, and she spent much of her life in what she calls "the evangelical bubble." Her immersion in born-again Christianity strongly influenced her idea of family and her expectations of her children.

Her interview has a special place in this collection because of the unflinching honesty with which she describes her previous attitudes and behaviors as an evangelical Christian responding to her LGBTQ+ son, Peter, whom she realized, from his toddlerhood, might be gay.

Over many years, Teri and Peter both struggled to repress and deny this unyielding reality; now, Teri regrets but is grateful to have learned much from their struggle.

Accepting parents are the single most important protective factor for LGBTQ+ young people, who are in many ways at risk without the shelter and connection of family. Recent major studies thinking about how to support LGBTQ+ youth call for research on how to facilitate acceptance. While time is an important factor, there is still very little understanding of the dynamics that can shift a parent's mind.

Teri's candid narrative is unique in how it details the collisions, side-roads and turns in her journey towards not merely acceptance, but celebration of her gay son and of the LGBTQ+ community.

This journey includes ex-gay therapy, dealing with rejecting church staff… and, finally, deciding to make dinner.

Whatever else was happening, Teri knew one thing very clearly and consistently: that she loved her child. Throughout her story, the reader can hear her affection for Peter, both as a small child wearing his sister's dress-up clothes and as a young adult belting out showtunes in pink party heels.

Here, Teri shares her gradually dawning awareness, once Peter came out, that she did not *know* any LGBTQ+ people. An avid chef, she started hosting a sort of salon at her home welcoming LGBTQ+ people who felt excluded within their religious communities and who might enjoy a home-cooked meal and a safe space to connect.

Hearing the stories of these people rewired Teri's thinking, especially when she came to understand—and to begin to feel outraged by—how many of them had been deeply hurt by their Christian communities. She advises readers, "It's important to sit across the table with someone… and hear their story, and… see them as a person."

She also laughingly recounts finding out, through these gatherings, that "gay people are a lot of fun!"

Since then, Teri and her family have participated in the "I Am Sorry" campaign, holding up signs at the Capital Pride Parade "apologizing on behalf of Christians for the way the church has treated the LGBTQ+ community."

Teri's description of how finally "popping the bubble" has been a liberating experience is compelling. In addition to changing her attitude about LGBTQ+, it inspired her to think about many topics in a new light, including things not previously on her radar, such as the absence of women in evangelical church leadership and white privilege.

Most significantly, her journey has enabled her to take true pleasure in her child and to reach a point where she feels "completely free to see him in all of his beauty and glory and to appreciate him for that."

Teri is also the founder of a support group called Freed Moms which brings together mothers who may have experienced rejection within their religious communities or even lost their families of origin through their acceptance of their LGBTQ+ children.

I grew up in a very traditional Midwestern conservative home, and I was raised Catholic. My mom was a stay-at-home mom, so it was a very stable, happy childhood. And then, when I was in college… my aunt (who was a role model to me, and I was very close to her) got very involved in the born-again Christian movement. She shared that with me, and I was just very drawn to finding out about who Jesus was, and I started [really reading the Bible] for the first time….

At that point, I just started hanging out with nothing but born-again Christians, evangelicals, and you know, I have thought so much about this, because looking back, I'm just like *what the Hell was happening? What was all that about?*

Now I realize that I was in this evangelical bubble for so many years… At the time, this movement was very exciting… there was this whole thing going on in the 80s… it was about Christians becoming political, and there was all this "take back the family" talk, and we just got kind of sucked into all of that.

Fortunately, not as deeply as we could've gone.

When I met Steve, we were going to a Baptist Church, got married in a Baptist Church, and we just really wanted to have this perfect little family unit, and, you know, we were going to do things like, when our girls got older and met boyfriends, they were only going to be allowed to group date. They weren't going to be allowed to wear bikinis!

We were just really trying to do everything the *correct* way. With family values, so that our children would all turn out *perfectly*.

So, we had these two little girls, and from the get-go, our youngest daughter was a little rebel. So, looking back on that experience, I think that was very good for us. I think if we had just stopped with our first child, our oldest daughter, who was always doing everything "the correct way," we would have been like: "Yeah, we have got this down. We are the *perfect* Christian parents." But, thank God, Holly bought us out of that.

So, then, Peter was the youngest. He was the baby, and he was just a very, very sweet, sensitive, artistic, kind little boy. All three of them were. I stayed home... I had a degree in elementary education, but we made just a few sacrifices so that I could stay home, and I really enjoyed those years with the kids.

Peter was, from the age of three, very into everything that the girls did; it is just so interesting now, because I hear from so many other mothers of gay sons [who say that], right around three years old, they went from playing with trucks and trains to dressing up like Cinderella and only wanting to play Barbies with the girls in their neighborhoods.

I started to see, especially as he got older, like around fourth, fifth grade, that boys did not want to come over and play with him. I had this nagging feeling in the back of my brain... All the while, I would try to encourage him to do more boyish, gender-stereotypical activities. He was still drawn to dressing up in pink party dresses and putting his sister's plastic high heels on.

One time, I was baking a cake with him in the kitchen and he was in the pink party dress with the plastic high heels standing on a chair next to me, and he was mixing up a cake. I let him hold the electric mixer, and all the sudden he was on the floor because he slipped on those plastic heels, and the cake batter went *everywhere*, and we laughed and laughed. We had so many great times!

But going back to what I was saying... all the time, I was afraid that he was going to grow up and be gay.

I feel like there was a battle in me of hearing in my conservative community that being gay was "a choice," but yet, I was looking at this little boy and thinking, "You know, one day, I am going to be saying to someone, 'You know, he was *always* like that.'"

And yet, when I would verbalize these fears (because that's what they were at the time), well-meaning friends would say, "Oh no, listen... You and Steve are *not going to raise a gay son*. He is just artistic. And he's just got older sisters. He has just grown up in a home with older sisters, and that's all it is." I calmed myself with that encouragement. Steve and I, we would talk about it from time to time, especially when Peter got to be around 10, 11, 12. And I'd say to Steve, "I don't know... This just worries me." And we would just say, "Ah, *nah*... Christian couples don't have gay kids!"

One of the things that I think was really confusing and really threw us off of a more loving course to take as parents when we were raising Peter was the fact that we would be listening to people like James Dobson. On his radio program, he would have gay guests who were "coming out" of a homosexual lifestyle, and he would interview them. Exodus International, a Christian ministry to help people "exit" homosexuality sprang up. So, in the back of my mind, as I would listen to those stories, I would think, "Well, okay, if this ever happens to Peter, there is a way out. He can always overcome this problem with spirituality. With Jesus. Jesus could help him come out of this."

Peter was always really involved in the churches that we attended. And so, as he was entering adolescence, he had a lot of great older guys who were leading his Bible study groups and the Sunday school types of groups that he went to at church, and so, we just thought, "He is going to be able to be healed." That's not really the right word... "He is going to be able to *overcome* this problem that he has to deal with," just like those guests on "Focus on the Family" did.

There is a way out of this.

It's really interesting, because when Peter was still young, even when he was a baby, we had a really good friend when we lived in Cincinnati, and he got AIDS. He was attacked on a snowmobile... stabbed, [and given] a blood transfusion. He was such an encouragement to all of us in the Bible study group, because as he went through his experience of having AIDS, he spent his days down at the hospital in Cincinnati sitting at the bedsides of a lot of gay men who were dying of AIDS.

We would bake cookies, and he would deliver the cookies to those men, and he would read to them from the Bible, or any other book that they wanted to hear.

At one point he invited those people to his house for a party, and we attended the party; it was the first time that Steve and I had ever knowingly sat down with a gay person and enjoyed their company. It didn't go very deep... We were just playing board games, and we were really having conversations.

Steve's roommate in college was gay, and he did not know it at the time, but he had come out. Those experiences got me reading books, and again, they were only written by Christians, and they reinforced the idea that it was a *choice*.

Then, I read Mel White's book, *Stranger at The Gate: To be Gay and Christian in America*. His whole story was: "This is not a choice, believe me. If this was a choice, I would get rid of this."

I read that book, and that started me thinking, there has got to be something more to this. And I started questioning myself, and that is when I really started coming around to believing that sexuality is not a choice.

But then again, I thought: "If you are a Christian, you can overcome anything with Jesus." And that's what I wanted for Peter when he came out.

Peter and I were very close. He was always so close to me, and such a sweetheart. It's like... I think all of us mothers, when our kids grow up, we just miss those times that we had with them when they were little. It was so precious. He had a harder time connecting with his dad, which we would later find out really fed into that whole lie about how mothers of gay sons are too close to them, and then they are disconnected from their fathers. We saw a little bit of truth in that, that whole Freudian craziness that we would later buy into when we were, so-called, "trying to help our son get out of this."

So, it was *my fault* because we were just very close. But we later learned that Peter was just more comfortable with me. Looking back now, I just really think that he couldn't be, maybe, the son that Steve wanted him to be.

Steve would say, "Hey, let's build a toy airplane." "Let's go out and throw the ball." "Would you like to learn how to work on a car?" But Peter didn't want to do any of those things. He wanted to draw pictures of princesses at the kitchen counter next to me, and I was drawing pictures of princesses, too.

And so, I think he just didn't really feel connected to Steve.

In the back of my mind, I suspected all along. But it was just so subconscious. But then... I learned that a lot of gay boys get bullied in school. Peter's bullying began early, before the fifth grade. By the fifth grade, it was really ramping up.

It was in fifth grade that I went over to the school and said, "There is this boy, and there is this boy, and there is this boy. They are all picking on Peter, and they are calling him 'gay,' and I want this to stop." So, we had a meeting with the teacher and the principal, myself, and the school counselor. And this was right when the county schools were just starting to adopt that "no tolerance for bullying" policy. They assured me they would do what they could do, and after that meeting, the guidance counselor handed me a pamphlet for PFLAG, and my jaw just dropped.

I just couldn't believe it... Now I could see what their perspective was. They were probably like, "Oh, bless her heart, she has a gay son, and she doesn't even know it!" And this bullying is probably going to go on for at least another couple of years. But for me, I was like, "They are *also* saying that my son is gay. *They are telling me without telling me that they think my son is gay.*" I felt like that was extra bullying.

I had left work that day for that meeting, and I came back to work, went into the office, and I put that PFLAG brochure right through the shredder. And I was just like, "Mmm-mmm. It's not happening. No way."

People at school were used to seeing me because I was a volunteer. So, one day, I went out to the playground, and I found this little boy who was one of the biggest offenders. And I want up to him, and I just said, "LISTEN: I want you to knock it off. I want you to stop calling Peter gay." I don't know what else I said, but that poor little boy was frightened of me.

For the next year, every time he saw me coming down the hallway, he'd duck into the janitor's closet. The interesting thing is, now he's gay. He came out as gay!

It's just fascinating. I want to run into him, and I want to apologize for scaring him when he was scared himself. Poor kid.

Then, after fifth grade, when Peter got into middle school, the bullying just really ramped up, and I would go pick him up from school so he wouldn't have to ride the bus home.

In the conversations where Peter and I would talk about the bullying, every once in a while, he would say, "Mom, do you think I really am gay?" And I would say, "Peter, look. What's really happening, is that all of these people are labeling you, and it's getting to you..." I would say to him: "You need to find your identity in Christ."

But what does *that* mean? Now I look back, and I realize he was probably thinking, "Oh, OK... We are Christian, that's what we say. I don't know how to do that or what that means."

We would be driving in the car, and he would just send out these little, I don't know, like, "hooks" for me to bite... I felt like he really wanted to bring up the topic. And I would say, "Well, Peter do you feel like you might have attractions for guys?" And he would say, "No. No, no mom. That's wrong." At some point, I said, "It's okay if you do, and you want to talk about it, because there are lots of Christians who struggle with this."

By... the time he was in high school, I had been doing a lot more reading, and I knew that [gay Christians] were out there, and I heard those testimonies. So, I wanted to let him know, it would be okay.

And then, he picked a very conservative Christian college to go to. That summer, we were on our way to Target to buy things for the dorm room, and he said, "You know, mom, I have been talking to my bible study teacher about my sexual attraction, and I think I'm going to find some counseling next year when I go to college." And I was like, "Oh, okay. That's good."

And that was really the first time that it came out.

That summer, and the summer before, he and I would be at the pool together, and I would see him... His head follow, like, a cute guy walking across the pool area. (Laughter.) I'd see his eyes follow him. And he would say things like, "Wow, look at that guy's muscles—I need to get some muscles." That was something that was disturbing me, and also preparing me. I just kind of thought: "Yeah, this is a thing. This is a thing he is going to have to deal with."

I didn't really pay that much attention to politics around LGBTQ+ at the time. I remember seeing little clips of Pride parades, and just thinking, "Oh my gosh, they are just all out of control and crazy."

Then, right around that time... there was Maryland's marriage equality vote. *And I voted against it.* I'm really sad about that now. But, they did it without me!

Yay!!

During that time of the AIDS crisis, you just thought that, "Well, that's very risky behavior." I remember Matthew Shepard. So yeah, I knew what was going on there. These things should have made me fear for my son. But my biggest fear was the whole spiritual thing.

One thing that's really interesting is that Bethany, our oldest daughter, right around the time that Peter went off to college, she went and talked to him and said, "Listen, Peter, I have a feeling that you are gay. And if you are, you can tell me, because I know it's going to be really difficult for mom and dad, and for you to have that conversation with them. But it's okay if you want to talk to me about it."

And he said, "NO." He got really offended because he was really fighting it at that point, getting ready to go off to this Christian college, with all of his Christian friends. He wanted to find a girl and get married, and Bethany... she... well, she confronted him.

And he came to me and said, "Mom, Bethany just came, and she said this to me!" I got mad at Bethany. I went to Bethany, and I said... I can't remember exactly. But the gist was it is going to be hard for him to be a gay man in this Christian community. So, don't encourage it. (Laughter)

It's so funny when I look back on it now... But I was like, *stop encouraging him. He doesn't want to be gay!*

Peter came home that summer after his first year in college... I think Steve was out of town, and I was sitting on the deck, and he just said, "Mom this is something that I've been really struggling with. I keep going back and forth and back and forth, wondering if I am gay or not, and I'm just going to go with it."

Basically, that was the way he said it. At that point, I knew what a struggle it was for this poor kid, so I was not going to show, really, any emotion in front of him. I understood how painful it was for him, so I tried to be as calm, kind, and cautious with my words as I could be, because I knew they would be words he would always remember. I just assured him that we would help him get through this and that it was okay. I said, "Peter, it is okay. And he said, are you going to accept me? And I said, of course we will accept you."

Then, as soon as that boy turned his back... I got on my computer, and I just started Googling all the ex-gay ministries I could find and watching all the testimonies on-line about how people left homosexuality. I was trying to find a way to fix it.

I was still trying to protect him, in my way. I think that's the struggle that a lot of moms have. Even though your kids may be over 18, you just think that you know best. And that you need to parent. And so, I just got into this "we can fix this" kind of mode.

And I heard him, downstairs talking to friends in his room, saying it out loud... I could hear through the vent from downstairs coming up into the kitchen, and I could hear that he was happy. His friends were congratulating him, and he was laughing.

And you would think, or you would hope, that as his mother, that would bring me joy to know that he was experiencing that acceptance and that love. But, it just really scared the crap out of me. I just sat in my car. I drove to the mall, and just cried all the way. Part of that grief, that initial grief, was just... I felt like on one hand, "God, you knew this was like, my greatest fear about this kid, and I can't believe that, now, you are letting it happen to me." I took it personally.

And then, the second thing that was floating around in my mind was that I just *so did not want those bullies to be right.*

Again, my little group was my Christian, evangelical friends.... I was like, "Oh my God, I really don't want to... share this with my friends. I don't know what they'll say." So, I called one of them up on the phone that I was close to. Her first reaction was so great. She was just like, "Okay Teri, don't think this is something that will sentence him, right off, to Hell. It won't. You can get through this. Peter is such a great kid, and just don't be too worried about it."

That was helpful. But still, I was afraid to go into Christian spaces and be very real about what was going on because I already knew what they would all be thinking. I already knew what they thought about gay people. That you are broken. If they don't all think that it's a sin—because I think that the Christian evangelical community has come a long way since those Anita Bryant, Pat Robertson days—at the very least, if they didn't think it was a sin and that it would make you go to Hell, I thought that they would all say, "He's broken, he needs healing."

And that he needs to be celibate for life.

Because that's the current thinking now in evangelical communities. I think most of them have come around to believing that being gay is not a choice, but that marriage is still between a man and a woman, and if you are going to live that life, then you need to live it *alone.* In celibacy.

As we started having conversations with Peter, and I was talking to that first friend I reached out to, she said, "Oh Teri, you know Carol has a daughter who is a lesbian."

Carol is a woman in our Bible study group. And I was like, "Are you kidding me? She never mentioned it. Why did she never tell us that?"

Well, because Carol never came out of the closet with it herself.

So, I called Carol, and I was so relieved. I wanted so badly to find another Christian mom that I could talk to, so I called her up on the phone, and I was like, "Carol, hi. I hear Jenny is a lesbian! Can we get together for lunch?" And she was like, "Okay Teri: first of all, we do not say 'lesbian.' We say, 'Jenny struggles with same-sex attraction.'"

That was my first indoctrination into the correct language that an evangelical Christian mom with the gay son should use. So, we met for lunch the next day, and she brought me a stack of books, and she said, "These really help me." And they were all reparative therapy books. So, I started just drinking them in. I went through all those books so fast. And she said, "You are in luck because the guy who wrote this book has a practice in in Virginia, and they also have a woman who works with parents."

And so, I went to Peter, and I said, "There is this therapist… he does therapy for guys who want to get out of homosexuality." You know, I was still using those "out of sexuality" terms. And he said, "Mom, I don't want to change. I have come this far."

But being very compliant, and always trying to make me happy, [he] said, "Fine, I'll go." So, Steve and Peter drove to northern Virginia to this guy's house. They sat down for their session and figured out that the therapist had gone to the same college as Peter. So, when they came home and told me that, I was like, see? It is a sign from God. Peter, it is such a sign that you are supposed to be there! That was just the way my brain was working… *This therapist is going to help you be ex-gay, too.*

The therapist said to Peter, "We are going to work on whatever goals you have, so this is not therapy that… is intended to make you straight." But it was. It wasn't like anything you see in the movie *Boy Erased.* It wasn't anything like that. But it was very Freudian, where if you "heal" the things that went wrong in childhood, so you can find your "heterosexual potential."

So, Peter went back to start his next year of college, and he mostly Skyped with that therapist, for about a year. And Steve and I went to this woman therapist, the one who works with families.

She suggested we come together as a family and go to a retreat. It was in Hagerstown. So, we did, and it was weird... We went and stayed in this retreat center out in the country with Peter's therapist and this woman that we saw, and we had all these different group therapy sessions. It was not aimed at trying to get Peter to be straight. They didn't even bring up the word "gay" the whole weekend. It was looking at each of our relationships and bringing up memories of childhood, and of one another. Their point was, I think, they were trying to identify where we went wrong.

It makes me feel really foolish now when I look back.

But Steve and I are both optimists... when we look back at that we... don't blame ourselves too much because we know that we were primed; just being in the evangelical community and going through all of that stuff in the 80s, and listening to the doctor Dobson on the radio, that we were really set up for that. Our whole support system led us to that direction of, if your child comes out as gay, there is healing in Jesus. And you go to the Christian community for that. You don't reach out to anyone else for it.

Looking back, I think that was really sad that we subjected Peter to that. We've apologized to him for that.

We also subjected our girls to it. But being optimistic, I can look at it and say, well there were some nice things that came out of that... I mean, we saw our kids sitting there, in the chairs, facing each other, and they could say things to each other, like, "You know there was a time when I was afraid to come to you and talk..." So, some things did happen that were really nice that typically happen in therapy. That's what I'm trying to say. We just left with that nugget.

...we look back on it, and first of all, I think, thank God it wasn't anything worse. But we just try to forget the bad, and I think about the good that came out of it.

That summer, I had like three weeks where I just grieved. I was sad. It was a really difficult time. I think it was harder than it needed to be because we had a surrogate daughter whom we needed to confront with alcoholism that summer. She wasn't living in our house, and she had two kids (they were like our grandkids), but her brother was homeless, and he was living in our basement. So, I had, an audience to grieve in front of. I spent a lot of time just in my room, with the door closed.

My older daughter, Bethany, she came to me one day and she goes, "Mom, I don't know how long you're going to do this, but you just need to start living. And we need to have a party." It was Fourth of July, so I said, "You're right." I just decided, I was going to snap out of it.

Peter came to the point where he was saying, "I don't want to do counseling anymore. I am gay and that's it."

I just knew that I love my son more than anything. More than the evangelical bubble I was in. And that I was going to have to find a way that I could fully love my son and still serve and honor Jesus.

So, I said to my kids, "You know, I don't have any gay friends. I really don't know any gay people. I jokingly say that I lined them all up and said, "All right: I want all of you go out and find some gay people and invite them to dinner!" I love to cook.

Peter's friends did not want to come into our house; they were afraid to meet us. They were afraid to come around. So, I said, "Peter, go out and invite them to dinner!" I started cooking for them... And we sat down for the first time and asked for their stories. And that made all the difference. One of the first dinners that we had, Bethany, our oldest daughter had a friend who was an older gay man. So, he came for dinner, and he bought his partner, and we sat down.

By this time, a different book got in my path. It was written by a Christian who said, "Hey listen, we have a history of being very harmful to the LGBTQ+ community, and it needs to stop. And we need to hear their stories. And we need to see them for who they are, because if you think that you are going to lead any of these people into church, you are wrong. They want nothing to do with us."

In that book, there are all these different stories of gay Christians who had been hurt by the church. So, while we were having that dinner with Bethany's friend, I just looked at him and I said, "Did you come from a faith community?" And he said, "Oh yeah, I grew up in a Christian church." I asked him, "Were you hurt, after you came out, by your church?" And he said, "Yes" and shared his story.

That's one of those memories that is just like a flashbulb going off in my brain. We had a lovely time that night, because Peter was there, and one guest played the piano and sang. Peter spent all those years in theater, and he is a singer. We all got around the piano… playing showtunes, and Peter was singing.

We shut the door that night and we were left with two impressions. One was, we have got to hear more stories. And the fact that Bethany's friend was hurt by the Christian community is wrong.

And the second was, gay people are a lot of fun!

So that was the start. That was the start of listening to stories and getting to know people and finding that there is this whole community of beautiful people that we were sad for not having gotten to know earlier in our lives.

The following year, Peter told us about something called the Gay Christian Network, which is now called The Christian Fellowship. It was started by a Christian, Justin Lee, who wrote a book and started this organization. It was maybe four or five years old by the time Peter asked us if we like to go to this conference… the three of us got on this plane, and we went to Houston, and we just spent the whole weekend immersed in this community of gay Christians.

There were close to 1500 people that year. They had keynote speakers, and we went to an entire track of parenting breakout sessions led by other parents. The first day that Steve and I attended worship and heard the beautiful singing voices of all these gay Christians surrounding us, we just got chills. We looked at each other that night back in our hotel room, and we said, "You know, we just witnessed the Holy Spirit. And so, if these people, gay Christians, are worshiping and showing signs of the Holy Spirit, then it can't be a sin. So, what's up with this?"

When we got back from that conference, and after having sat down with so many other, not just parents, but gay, and bisexual, and transgender people, and hearing their stories, we said, "Okay, now we have got some work to do. Now we need to go back to our Bibles, open them up, and ask, what have we been taught? What is really there? What is the difference between what we been taught in churches all these years and what's really written in the text?"

I knew that I wanted to be around more gay Christians, and to get to know them, and to not have to wait for an annual conference.

I thought this is the perfect time... I want to start a parent support group at the church, and I want to encourage the pastor to let the young adults start some kind of an LGBTQ+ group for themselves.

They weren't very receptive. I think maybe it was just too early for them... Steve and I actually went and had a meeting with the pastor, and we sensed that we weren't really going to get anywhere. We left and said, "Let's just do this at home. Let's have dinners. Monthly. And invite anybody who wants to come. And that will be way better than just having some little meeting in a room at church. We can have good food, and wine, if guests are old enough."

So, that's what we did! This was about five years ago... It started out very slowly. We would have, like, maybe two or three people... Sometimes, I'd have dinner cooked, and no one would show up. Sometimes just one person would show up, and it was just Steve and me, because Peter was off to college.

But the last time that we had it, a month ago, there were over 20 people. It has been one of the greatest joys of our lives. We have been privileged to hear their stories and just be a part of their lives, and it has just also been such a blast. *So much fun!*

Peter's and my relationship really got so much better... Peter was very patient with me. When I decided that I was just going to accept him, this beautiful gay man... You know, it happened in stages... It just took this weight off of me that was so great. I could just look at him and really enjoy him for who he was.

And he got to be more Peter-ish. He got to be more himself, and that was a joy to watch. In fact, it was funny because right around that time, it was Christmas, I think, and our son-in-law plays the piano. We have a lot of music at our house. Our son-in-law was playing this Christina Aguilera song, "Beautiful," and Peter loves to sing that song. So, we were all standing around having some wine, and they are doing music on the piano, and Peter goes and he gets this pair of pink, sparkly high heels that he bought for himself and puts the high heels on, and he is just singing this song at the top of his lungs. And we were all laughing… And I just thought, that is who he was meant to be. I felt so much joy in letting him be himself.

Years before, I would've been like, "Oh, does this mean he is a cross-dresser? Oh my gosh I hope nobody ever sees." I would've been worried.

But at that point, I was completely free to see him in all of his beauty and glory and to appreciate him for that.

When we started going to the Capital Pride Parades, right around that time, we did this, "I am sorry" campaign… we went down and held signs apologizing on behalf of Christians for the way the church has treated the LGBTQ+ community. That meant a lot to Peter, I think, and really drew us closer.

At one point, he saw me having so much fun and said to me, "You are welcome, mom. I'm glad you and dad are having such a great time!" And I said, "You had better not ever go straight on me! What would we do now? We'd have to go find some other gay people!"

So, yeah… I just couldn't love him more. I'm so proud of who he is… If I had a magic wand that I could wave to make him straight, I would never. I'd never go back to that idea of him being a straight man with a wife and kids, because then he just wouldn't be Peter.

I am so, so thankful for the experience. It was like the bubble popped. The evangelical bubble popped. I was able to look around and see so many things that I never even thought about before. I now notice other marginalized groups that I never noticed before.

So, it's like that little saying, "being woke." This experience has made me a more loving person... I would never go back to the person that I was.

Eventually, we found a church that was inclusive... this wacky little band of very authentic, beautiful, loving people. Very accepting of everyone...

When we saw that they had a woman pastor, that struck me immediately. And I thought, "Now why, in so many conservative Christian churches, can't women be in leadership?" That's just one example of something I'd never thought about before. The whole Black Lives Matter movement was coming into focus for me...

I had never really thought about white privilege before. But, you better believe I started to then. We are now going to a church that talks about those issues.

Peter was willing to come out and try it with us, and he loved it too.

When your child comes out, if you find yourself having lived a life where you don't really know any gay people, it is so important to rethink what maybe seems like a black-and-white issue. Now it's about a person you have loved all their life; it's important to sit across the table with someone, not even just your child, and hear their story, and not see them as an "issue," but see them as a person who probably cried themselves to sleep many, many nights when they were a teenager. Begging God to take this away from them. That's what you need to do.

That's the gift that you need to give yourself. And then see where God takes you on that journey, because there is so much in store for you.

2: STEVE AUGUSTINE—
A lot of the way that people can get to the place where their fundamental beliefs are not challenged is, you've got to really wall yourself off.

Steve's son, Peter, came out as gay the summer of his freshman year of college. Deeply immersed in a fundamentalist worldview, Steve literally did not understand how his Christian family could have produced a gay child.

His narrative outlines how the clash between his religious perspective and his faith in his son's basic goodness created a jarring dissonance—one he worked hard to get through.

A scientist raised by educator-parents, Steve's process was one of analysis and reflection; here, he thinks through the factors that enabled him to reconsider ideas lodged in the very bedrock of his upbringing and beliefs, laying out the events and connections that led him to a "paradigm shift."

These include drawing on his prior knowledge of his son and of time they spent together, as well as a candid look at his relationship with his own father and at his own understanding of the dynamics of father-son relationships. Steve's interview is compelling for how he positions his experience in terms of men's relations, touching on the "mini-me" concept popularized by writer Andrew Solomon and addressing men's needs within family structures.

Evangelical thinking blames the same-sex parent when a child is LGBTQ+, and Steve was plagued by the question, "How did I screw this up?" It took him a long time to really hear Peter's response:

"No. You didn't—this is who I am."

Compassion also played an important role in Steve's change of perspective. Recognizing for how long and how painfully his child had been struggling—including with bullies in elementary and middle school—enabled him finally to see a larger picture.

Existing evidence suggests mothers are typically sooner and more accepting of LGBTQ+ youth, but Steve and his wife worked together to come to a place of understanding. He emphasizes that a child's coming out can be traumatic for a family, and he worries about the fragility of the process, remarking that, in his family, if either parent had taken a hard line, "it would have really torn everything apart."

Steve credits Peter with having a lot of patience and with finding ways to educate his parents, including bringing them to a conference of the Gay Christian Network.

Meeting others who shared his family's experience was powerful and inspirational for Steve. His family subsequently tried—and failed—to increase their church's willingness to embrace the LGBTQ+ community. They eventually found an LGBTQ+ positive church, and they now seek opportunities to "help other people get to this place because we have been through this journey."

Having traveled around the world as part of his profession, Steve appreciates what he sees as a uniquely American opportunity "to be different together." He regrets that too many people (including evangelicals) live in echo chambers where they do not have to hear other opinions or ways of thinking. Having an LGBTQ+ child can "break that isolation."

Although still mildly antagonized when his son does things like mow the lawn while wearing pink, flowery tights (a story that he shared through laughter), Steve expresses his gratitude that, "The world has gotten bigger for me."

I grew up on the East coast, and then lived around Chicago for high school. Both of my folks were educators. My dad was a basketball and baseball coach at a Christian college, and my mom was a teacher in the public school system. Later on, she became an educator in college as well.

So, I grew up in an environment where education was always very important. My grandfather was a pastor; my uncle was a pastor; my other uncle was a teacher at a Christian college. So again, a very strong, fundamental—we call it evangelical now—but it was very much a fundamentalist Christian upbringing.

Both of my parents were very involved with their jobs, so a lot of times, they weren't around, and we were kind of latchkey kids before latchkey was a thing. When I had a family, I really wanted to do whatever we could to be present, and that was important for me.

I went to undergrad at a Christian school and I got the chemistry and math degree, and then I went to graduate school and got my PhD in chemistry. So, I've been involved with doing research in the chemical industry for, gee… thirty-some years.

So, I've got a background where I've got one leg in the fundamentalist, religious background, and another leg in the science community.

A lot of what I've tried to do in my own life is to try to rationalize those two, and to try to get to an understanding that there are people who disagree with you, and that doesn't make them bad or make them wrong. Sometimes, you are the wrong person. It is very valuable to understand other people because there is so much that you can learn from them.

That is kind of what brought me to this place.

For Peter… When he came out, that was not what I had anticipated. To some extent, just to be honest, it was a disappointment. Coming from that religious background, I believed, at the time, that the Bible taught pretty clearly that homosexuality was a sin and that it was a *choice*. A decision that he made.

So, I came back to him and challenged him… In that challenging, I actually learned to challenge myself a little bit. And some of those preconceptions that I had.

When someone is in an academic environment, they are used to the give-and-take of an academic discussion. You really have reasons to believe what you believe. Sometimes, you think them through and understand them pretty well, and sometimes you don't. Sometimes, you believe things just because there has been some experience in your life that maybe you haven't really worked through, but it affected you pretty strongly. Maybe it was some traumatic experience; maybe it was an emotional experience. Things like that change the way we think.

Raising the family, my wife and I worked together to bring our children to a belief that Christ is Lord… So, I challenged him to go back to that foundation that we shared, or that I anticipated that we shared, and asked him to explain to me how he got to where he was.

For me, it was… an intellectual need: "Okay, explain to me how this can work." Because I just didn't understand.

People talk about "the six power passages" in the bible. There are several passages in Leviticus, and then Paul has a passage in Romans, the passage in first Corinthians, a passage in first Timothy. If you read them in a certain way, they speak very strongly against homosexuality. Those are the things I really wanted him to wrestle with, because, again, those would be the things that, if I projected myself on to him, I would be wrestling with. I wanted to hear him as he wrestled with it.

Ironically, he didn't wrestle with it the way that I had. But he actually had been fighting through that for many years, and it was kind of interesting to learn about his journey through that.

My wife and I kind of came through this at the same rate, and it is a blessing to have a spouse that goes through these things with you.... That was really nice.

There is the "mini me" concept, where fathers want their sons to be like them. Growing up, my dad was a coach, but he was always busy with coaching, so he never really tossed the ball in the backyard or taught me how to shoot a basketball.

So, I wanted to do that with Peter, but certainly, Peter didn't have that interest. So, I think that you want to grow with and become close with your son because, as you know, with your kids growing older, they transform, and they become your friends. And because they have had the shared experience, they can be some incredible friends.

It's selfish, I know, to want to make that person more like you so you'll have that close bond.

I think that's strong with men because, well, personally, I believe that—and I tell this to Teri all the time—she has a much easier time making friends. Women, they are more expressive, more talkative, and so, it's easier to form friendships. With men, sometimes, we are just too involved with our work; sometimes, we are just too focused on what we are interested in. So, it's a little more difficult to form those friendships, so you look for those friendships in your kids.

And there is a disconnect.

Obviously, there are things that he's interested in that I don't have any interest in, and I know he doesn't have any interest in things that I find interesting. For me, it was a little different because I never was all that close to my dad. I knew it didn't have to be that way... I love my dad. We have great conversations, but I don't do the things he did, and I don't expect Peter to do the things that I do. It's about embracing differences.

I'm noticing, at least in our society, we don't like to do that. But again, that's what makes life rich. To be with people who challenge you and make you think differently than what you're comfortable with.

In the evangelical bubble (probably like any bubble), there are certain things that are acceptable; there are certain things that are reasonable, and then there are certain things that, according to the paradigms, to the structure that you look at life with, that cannot happen. According to the evangelical structure, you *can't* be gay and be Christian.

Now, with Peter, the blessing is that we have always spent time talking. As he went through middle school and high school, we would just take time out and go out to breakfast, say, one Saturday a month. And just talk about anything. I *knew* him, I knew that he had a strong faith in Jesus. So, those two things told me that, again, with my paradigms, that he couldn't be gay.

So, yeah, you could see it from childhood. He would dress up like Susie Q, and he would dance around. He liked to play with dolls, all that kind of stuff. But, for me, *I* couldn't see that: that was too inconsistent. I just thought it was a phase. Everything is a phase.

What I had always believed, and what I had been taught—and I can tell you that there are still people who are very close to me who still believe this way—was that being gay is *a choice*. It's a decision. Just like, at some point, I decided that I wanted to marry my wife.

Anything that is natural, you really don't think about. Sexual attraction is extremely natural, so I never thought that it was possible to have a sexual attraction for somebody that looked like me. So, somebody who is "making that choice" is willfully making a bad choice. That's what I grew up with. I can't sugarcoat it... That's it.

Peter's first year in college, there were a lot of struggles. He went in to be a math major and a high school teacher. He got in there, and he found out he didn't like math all that much. And I was a math major, so we spent a lot of time talking on the phone... that was a huge struggle.

We were going through that already, and then he comes home, and, again, he's got a lot of friends in the theater—Peter has grown up in the theater, and he's done very well—and he starts talking to them, and he says, "You know, I think I'm gay."

He *knew* he was gay at that point.

I'm sure you've heard it 100 times. For me, the thinking was, "You've got to fix it." … The wires are crossed somewhere. So, we need to fix it.

With Peter being a very flexible and considerate and caring person, he wouldn't just say, "Dad you are full of shit."

We found a counselor, and I have to say, this guy was really quite unique. This counselor had gone to Peter's college… He said he was gay, and then halfway through college, he changed his mind, or whatever. He is not gay anymore, and now he's married with four kids. We figured, yeah, I guess so. We will go talk to him.

The drives to visit the counselor were our best conversations, because here we were, stuck in the car together for 90 minutes, and we're just talking… In the summertime, I think we went down once a week, and then Peter and the counselor carried on with Skype while he was in school.

Processing that whole thing with Peter as he processed it, and then having this guy is a counselor, was really revealing.

It helped me *see* Peter… they say that when a kid finally comes out, he or she comes out after months or years of wrestling with this and working with it. But when they come out, it's like brand new news to their parents. And so, the parents have those years to go, or those months, or whatever it takes, to catch up with their kids. In all those drives, I got to see, and Peter got to tell me about, him going through this…

To hear his struggles through high school, and even in middle school… That helped me kind of to accelerate my own process a little bit.

There's a certain pattern that is taught to evangelicals, and it's very Freudian. To be honest, it's very ironic. But the whole concept of developmental maturation is that your relationship with your same-sex parent and with your opposite sex parent… forms your identity.

The idea is that when people are gay, the relationship with that same-sex parent, somehow it *breaks*. The relationship is rotten, or there's some trauma there in that development stage.

And so, being a more analytical person, I was, like, trying to understand where I screwed up.

I was working through that blame, and there is Peter, saying there was nothing there. There was no trauma. There was no feeling that, you know, that we disappointed him, or that there was a problem in our relationship.

So, part of that was just saying, *"Where did I mess up?* How did I screw this thing up?"

And him saying, *"No. You didn't - this is who I am."*

The structure I grew up with did not fit. When you build your belief system, there are certain things that just can't be compatible: black can't be white, hot can't be cold. When you experience dissonance, you either have to go nuts, you have to ignore it, or you have to rationalize it.

Peter experienced bullying, and we knew about it. That's a challenge as a parent. I would always want to talk with the bully's dad. I thought, "Let me go talk with the dad," and that he would understand where I was coming from, and we would get that cleared up. And Teri would never let me talk to the dad.

Then, in high school, Peter kind of hit his stride... I was trying to get him to play baseball when he would rather be in a play. And so, he quit the baseball stuff, and I backed off, and so he was in theater, and he got in with a good group of kids... So, the bullying kind of went away in high school.

Even before this, when we would go out for breakfast, he would talk about different types of attraction, and why he felt this way when he looked at certain pictures, and I was always like, "That's okay, that's normal. You are going through a phase, we all do that, don't worry about it."

In middle school, he wasn't a happy kid because we were forcing him, and he was forcing himself, into a mold that he did not fit. As he went to high school, he became more himself, and then in college... it all came together.

And so, I was trying to understand that a little better, trying to understand the situation. He went to a conservative Christian school, and some of the teachers were accepting, but some were not. He actually started a Bible study support group for gay kids. So, learning about them, learning about what he was doing in leadership... That was really powerful for me.

The one thing that really turned it around for me is having this relationship with Peter.

Peter forced us to go to this conference of a group called The Gay Christian Network. Again, the whole concept of gay and Christian didn't fit for me. What's really remarkable about that is that they start each meeting with worship. For the first meeting, I couldn't get there right away because I had a conference call, so everybody else went. I finished my conference call and went down late, so I was all by myself, and there were 1500 people, and they were worshiping...

I felt the presence of God, and I knew that these people were gay or loved gay people, and I had been brought up with the understanding that those two things don't go together.

And at that point, I knew that Peter wasn't unique. I mean, *he has always been unique.* But also, that there were other people like him.

Then I had to, kind of, back up and say, "We are not just doing a one off here. Peter is not the only person like this. He's not the only unicorn. There are other unicorns. Therefore, unicorns must exist."

We went as part of the church group... We had to debrief. So, we had a meeting, the pastor was there, the people that we went with were there, and certain other elders in the church were there. We were sitting around and talking about what we felt we could bring back to the community.

The pastor himself was kind of struggling because he had been kind of overwhelmed…

Peter was there. We were all there.

And I said, "Look, this is pretty clear… We are here to reach out to people like Peter and make them understand that they are not bad people. They are good people. God loves them, and they can be part of this community."

The desire was no longer to "fix" people: the desire was, "There are a lot of people out there hurting because of this dissonance that a lot of people have. How can we make them feel, or understand, that God loves them and values them as they are? That they don't have to change to be acceptable to God, because God accepts us as we are?"

We are the ones that put the limitations and barriers in front of people.

With Peter, we saw that there were times that he struggled with what he thought we expected of him. And we did, before we understood everything. It took us a while to get to where he needed us to be.

There are a whole lot of other people out there for whom it's not happening… That's probably why you're working on this book.

That's where we went to the next step. How can we help other people get to this place? Because obviously, things weren't syncing up for us. How can we help other people… Get them synced up?

One area that for me was very emotional was that my college roommate, after he graduated, he told me that he was gay. I did not handle that well at all… I was very judgmental. So, I called him up. I said, "Look… I have to apologize. I was wrong, and I treated you badly, and it took my son to coming out for me to understand that." He was extremely gracious… I'm really glad that I did that. I was essentially going back and trying to repair some relationships, and then also, we started opening our home to other relationships.

A lot of the way that people can get to the place where their fundamental beliefs are not challenged is, you've got to really wall yourself off. If you don't meet anybody that disagrees with you, as long as you stay in a group where everybody has got kind of safe and similar ideas, then it's pretty protective. It feels very comfortable.

When you get beyond that and try to meet people that are different, that's where you really need to go. *That's what we work to do.*

My dad was all-American everything. Growing up, I thought I needed to be a jock. I love sports, but I'm not good at anything. So, I always thought that I was a failure to him because I couldn't be the basketball, baseball player that he was. *Until* I got to college, and I hit my stride, and I figured out I didn't have to be like him because I was a different person.

I didn't have a close relationship with my dad because I couldn't play sports, and I didn't have a close relationship with Peter because he didn't like sports, and so I didn't get that relationship on either side. When I finally admitted that to myself, I was like, "Well... I didn't turn out to be like my dad, and I'm extremely happy because I didn't."

If Peter was going to be like me, he would be unhappy, and he is much happier being like himself. So that's how I kind of got to it. If that makes any sense.

I have got to tell you, there are things that Peter does that just aggravate me (pretty typical). Like, I asked him to mow the lawn, and he did, which is really great, because he is staying with us now.

But when he mowed the lawn, he had these pink tights with flowers on them, and then, over the pink tights, he is wearing purple shorts. And I'm thinking, that is really annoying. But that's Peter! (Laughter.)

I grew up in a very structured system where you respect certain people, and you definitely respect your dad.

And now I see it differently: he responds in a way because that's just the way he is. If it bothers me, I'll tell him it bothers me, but I don't get angry about it. In the past, I did get very angry. I would lose my temper far too often in those situations.

The world has gotten bigger for me. It is a safe thing to have a small world, and to have things where everything is as expected; nothing surprises you. Life comes at you in a way that you can deal with it without a lot of thought. It's kind of like driving a car. You know, there are so many things that we have to think about when driving a car, but we've gotten so used to it, it's so natural.

What Peter did was to blow that open for me and make my world bigger. So, for example, I definitely was in a situation where if you didn't agree with me, I felt that I needed to change your mind. Now, if you don't agree with me I kind of want to understand more why you don't and what is going on and how you got to that place, and then maybe get to a different place myself.

Not necessarily to change my mind but to… get to a better understanding of somebody else.

I am in a situation now with our pastor where I don't agree with her much at all, but I love her because I know that she believes different things, but she's come to those different beliefs sincerely, and I don't have to agree with them…

When Peter came out, I thought it was really important to tell my parents in Florida… I scheduled a weekend and told them I was coming down.

I talked to them, and I said, "I came down here specifically to tell you that Peter is gay, and he just recently came out, and I wanted to talk to you about it in person, so that if you have any questions or concerns, we can talk about it."

They were like, "Yeah, that's really no big deal." Then my dad started telling me stories that he'd never told me before about how, as a college professor, he had kids in his classes… that were gay.

He also was a women's basketball coach, and lesbianism [in basketball] is much more prevalent with women than being gay is with men... My mom told me stories of friends that she had that were gay, and they were both like, "Yeah, this is really no big deal. We still love Peter."

I was a little surprised. I thought it would at least be some kind of going back and forth... "How can he do this and what is he thinking?" And they were like, "No, we understand."

My wife's parents are in a different place, and I have to say, my sister and my brother are in a different place, too. So, some of our family we can be very open with.

My dad asks me now if Peter is dating anybody he's interested in... That's a blessing. *That is a blessing.*

There are certain parts about the way Peter lives, like with any kids, that make me a little nervous... He was down in DC with a couple friends and he got into a fight. And he didn't even know he was in a fight... That's how Peter is.

The guy was pushing Peter, and then he took a swing at one of Peter's friends, was very much reacting against them being very flamboyant... Somebody pushed Peter and said, "I hate this gay shit." He was confronted by Peter's friend and ended up knocking the kids' teeth out. He had to have his jaw wired shut for a while. It was terrible.

So those are the things that you are uncomfortable with.

There are certain things that I wish... I tell Peter, sometimes, "Just tone it down a little bit... *Don't be so Peter.*" But that's who he is. So, there are certain things that bother me, but that's his life.

He has to live his life, do what he loves.

When he first wanted to be a teacher and he was gay, I was worried that he wouldn't get a job. Because I know there are certain parts of the country where that might be true. But certainly, in Maryland, it isn't; it's much better here. But you feel that worry for your kid…

So yeah, there are certain things that I'm uncomfortable with, but because he is open with me, I feel I can be much more open and honest with him, too. That's really nice.

It's a transformation… he is my son, but now he is an adult, so he is my friend as well.

Why is the homeless rate of LGBTQ+ youth so high, except that families throw people out of their house? I mean, that's the only conclusion… How can you treat your children in that way? It just boggles the mind.

You can go up and down the issues… The way we treat immigrants is awful. The way we treat people who disagree with us is awful. That's not what it means to be an American. So, we have kind of gotten away from what's made this a very unique country.

I have been able to travel all over the world, and it's been a great opportunity. I know that really, what we have here is a wonderful country, and it's wonderful because we are so different. The French are all pretty much French. The Japanese, they're pretty much Japanese. But in America, we have the opportunity to be different together, and for some reason, we have not only walked away from it, *we're starting to call it bad.*

And that's wrong. That's what really scares me moving forward.

We have got to just really embrace each other as a community… Maybe that's what we learn from having a child or close family member come out as LGBTQ+. Maybe when we break the isolation, we can get together and start again, talking to each other, not as people with ideologies, but just as people.

When a kid comes out at LGBTQ+, it has the power to tear families apart, and we see it happening.

It could've happened with our family as well. If Teri and I would've disagreed, or if either one of us had said, "This is not acceptable," it would have really torn everything apart.

But once you come through that, you reach a place where everybody is changed. We kind of focused on me in this interview, but Peter is different as well, because of us, as well as are our daughters... We are all closer because of it.

It was rough; it was a challenge at times, and it didn't fit any of our preconceptions. But we are in a lot better place now from that, and I think that can happen with other families.

You can get to a better place, a bigger world where you embrace people and you don't try to separate yourself from people.

3: PETER AUGUSTINE——
After coming out, I was relieved because it gave my differences meaning.

Peter Augustine was born in Ohio and grew up in Maryland along with two older sisters. From a young age, he was resistant to stereotypically male behaviors like playing sports; instead, he preferred his sisters' dress-up clothes.

The first time Peter was called "gay," in fifth grade, he did not know what that word meant; bullying was relentless and intensified through eighth grade. He even avoided taking his public school bus for a time during middle school.

Later, the revelation that his worst tormenter was gay showed Peter that bullies might also be afraid. It would have been nice to know this at age eleven, but the revelation is still important to Peter now, as a young adult.

A child who figured out that he was "different" early on, he tried hard to fit in and attempted to play on various sports teams (which he hated); he dated girls throughout high school and even had a girlfriend. His family, part of a large evangelical community, was non-accepting of LGBTQ+ people, and he wanted to be a good son.

After many years of repression and struggle, Peter finally started coming out as gay in 2013, while he was in college and still entirely dependent on his parents—both an enormous relief to Peter and a huge leap of faith in them. While many LGBTQ+ people in similar situations wait until they reach independence, Peter, never a person to hide his feelings easily, explains that "being in the closet wasn't really a thing for me. Once I knew and wasn't in denial, I came out right away."

Peter's account of how his parents were already dealing with tensions at this time, including a sister's divorce, highlights how the normal challenges of family life can feel amplified when a child comes out... "coming out was just the cherry on top. It made everything even more hectic."

This is truer still when parents must "readjust all of their learning that they had come to know as truth."

Peter had spent a long time already figuring things out before he came out to his parents. He realized previously, for example, that, "I can still have a family, it will just look a little different," something his parents could not see at first.

Peter now describes his relationship with his parents as very healthy. "I could come to them for anything." They have since joined a religious community that is LGBTQ+ positive, and Peter and his parents participate in this community together.

He knows that he is fortunate. Seeing friends who have been rejected by their families over the years is depressing. Peter reflects on how LGBTQ+ people and their parents can both lose out: rejecting parents will miss "everyday milestones: promotions, buying a new house... Just everything that a person goes through."

He loves the fact that his parents "are so excited for when I get married one day, and they will come to my wedding."

Peter recommends patience for parents and especially for kids, "I just wish that I had the same amount of patience for my parents as I wish they had for me... the more patient you are coming out to your parents, the more likely they are to come around."

When people fail to be accepting, "so much gets lost because of anger."

I have two older sisters. One is three years older and one is five years older than I am. So, I definitely had a lot of influences from them. A lot of what they played with,

I wanted to play with. The friends that they had, I wanted to have as well. Lots of playing with girls growing up.

But a time came when I just wanted to play with those things on my own. It's not like I dressed up or played with dolls only when they were around; it started with them introducing that, but then it became something that I was doing because it was fun...

I would take costumes from my sisters' costume box and put on dresses. I was always playing with Barbies... it was really easy for me to have girl friends as a young boy because girls were easy to talk to and hang out with, but boys were definitely harder to befriend. I had some friends that were boys... but I was definitely more excited to spend time with my friends that were girls...

Once I became eight, nine, ten years old, this started to bother me a little bit more because, I think, the other boys could pick up on those differences I had. I was a lot more creative. I wanted to sing. I wanted to draw. I wanted to play with dolls. Even the way that I communicated with my friends was a lot more, I think, mature than most boys my age because I was so used to seeing how girls worked through problems.

The stereotype is that boys are rougher, more into the rough-and-tumble, and girls are more in their feelings; I grew up being more in tune with my feelings, being the youngest and having two older sisters.

Other boys started to notice that I was different in late elementary school and middle school. I would call my guy friends up and ask them to hang out, and they would always have reasons why they couldn't. I picked up on, "Okay, maybe they don't want to play with me."

I started to be bullied in fifth grade. There was a boy that started calling me "gay" at recess. At the time, I didn't even know what that meant. I was very sheltered when I was a kid, growing up in a Christian household. My parents did a really good job of keeping some cultural things away. It was a conservative, evangelical household... I didn't learn a bad word until I heard a friend say it at school.

They did a really good job of sheltering. That's a good thing but can also be a bad thing when kids are really just shocked at school, or don't know how to react to a situation because you just never even heard of these things.

That was the first time I ever heard the word "gay," in fifth grade, and it was just kind of shocking. And then, it all just kind of came together...

Yeah, I'm different. I don't see what's wrong with that.

But then, the aggression built up in middle school. I started going to the counselor in school to talk about it, and I didn't even want to go on the bus because there were boys that were bullies on the bus. There was just a really big buildup of bullying throughout fifth grade through eighth grade.

I think I gained confidence once I got into high school and kind of realized, *this is me*. I found my niche of people in theater and did a lot of that. There are so many gay people in theater... There were a lot more creative, sensitive guys in theater than in the sports that I was forced to do in elementary school. So, I definitely found comfort there.

Most of the bullying had to do with, you know, the fact that bullies are insecure themselves.

I love this story about the first boy that ever really made fun of me for being gay, because now he's gay. He came out!

So, it's kind of like they are making fun of you, bullying you because they are struggling with the same thing usually, and they are insecure. They don't know what to do about it, so they go out and be aggressive about it.

I would be minding my own business, probably being loud and silly with my girl friends, and they would see that I was with a bunch of girls. They were either jealous that I'm with a bunch of girls and they want to be me, or they just don't like the fact that I am comfortable with myself, and they are not comfortable with the same things that they see in me that I'm comfortable with.

Of course, I didn't feel this way at the time. I was only 11, but looking back on it, that's definitely what was happening. It would just be like, "Why do you hang out with all these girls? Are you gay?" Weird stuff like that.

At that point, I did not even know what "gay" was. I think I went home and asked my mom what gay was, and she was like, "Who is calling you that?" My mom actually came and scolded that little boy during recess time. I was cool with that... I wasn't at the age where I was going to be embarrassed by her being there... I felt supported.

I had some really good teachers then. I think they even talked to the principal with that boy at one point. They got down to, "Do not bully. Stop doing all of this." So, I definitely had a lot of adults that were helpful.

I was never, and I still am not, one of those people who can keep secrets. People who are close to me know everything about me. So, at the time, it was my mom and dad who knew everything about me. So, *they knew...* My parents were in the very Christian evangelical box of "gay is not okay." They didn't know any gay people — well, not gay people that were out. I remember my mom getting some flyers from PFLAG and just being mortified at the time, just because that's not something that she was okay with.

At first, I just didn't let being different affect me too much. And then, in middle school, it started to affect me more because that's the age when puberty hits, and you are just realizing all of these different changes. That's when it started to really bother me that the bullying was still happening.

My mom told me that when I was little, I was showing all of the stereotypical tendencies of what the books say a gay person is like when they are growing up (though obviously, those books are not always right). I think my dad kind of put it to bed. He said, "That's not something that can happen to us because we are Christians."

In middle school, I started singing with the church. It was a band, not a choir, so there were times when I could have solos and stuff like that. That's when I started to become more confident, through singing and performing. Also... I started theater. So, I was able to be around a lot of people that were like-minded. I didn't really put two and two together… I wasn't like, "Oh, we are like-minded because we are gay." I was still very stuck in, "I just can't be gay; it's not possible." I definitely believed that for a long time. But being in theater helped me to be okay with gay people because I was around them all the time.

I dated girls all the way through high school, and I even had a girlfriend after high school. I was definitely… I don't know if I want to say "brainwashed." But in a way, I was. I mean twenty-four-seven, I was involved in church, and youth group, and all of that. I had mentors that told me the same things my parents told me: that gay people are *sinners*. That they are not believers; that they are living in a sinful lifestyle. I don't recall anyone saying they were going to Hell, but in that realm, it basically means the same thing. If you are a sinner, that's just implied. So, it was basically all negative.

When I came out of high school, I decided to go to a private, Christian college. That sounded like heaven to me because I was so *in* to this church life. Why not go to a Christian college? For the first year, I was just so stressed about academics because it was so much harder than high school.

I didn't really have any kind of revelation until the summer after freshman year of college, when I was just lying in my bed one night, and I was thinking these thoughts… I always think guys are attractive, but I always say that it's about, you know, I just want to look like them. I called one of my friends who did theater with me growing up and who came out junior year of high school. I kind of just wanted to talk with him about everything.

It was that summer, and when we had our conversation, we just had so many of the same experiences in common, so many similarities. We both grew up really loving to do more girly things, and just things like that. After those talks, I think I was finally just able to be like: "Okay fine. I am gay." And to come to that realization. But it was so hard because of everything I was taught growing up. I kind of just had to take a leap of faith and be like, "Okay if this is real, if this is how I feel, I am just going to stick with it and see what happens." So, I decided to stick with it.

I'm not really someone who keeps things to himself. So, being in the closet wasn't really a thing for me. Once I knew and wasn't in denial, I came out right away.

I wanted to get the hard people out of the way first, so I told my parents.

Well, I told my mom, and my mom told my dad because it was harder for me to come out to him. I always felt like growing up, it wasn't as easy to connect with him.

I knew that whenever I tried to keep the secret inside, it ate me up. I just had to spit it out. The rest of it was up to them to deal with it in the way that they were going to deal with it. But I wasn't expecting it to be so difficult for them. I was just hoping it would be like, "We will just deal with this in our own way. You live your life the best way you can." I figured there'd be understanding eventually.

But it was not easy for them... they had to readjust all of their learning that they had come to know as truth. I went back to college, so I was away from all of it for a while. That summer, I had to live with my friends for a couple of weeks because I just needed to get out of the house... Coming out just kind of blew it all up.

When I told my mom, my mom was like, "Oh, okay, cool." She made a joke to make it seem like it wasn't as big of a deal as she thought it was. But then, as I was coming out to my friends, and I was coming out over and over again, it kind of hit her, and she broke down.

When I told my dad, it just turned into a biblical conversation, "How do you think this is okay?" Inside, I was really angry because the last thing I wanted to talk about was the Bible. Because that was all I was ever taught growing up, and I was trying to get this new perspective that they weren't letting me have... it wasn't good at first.

But it's not like I was kicked out of the house... it could've been worse.

I knew I was loved, but at the time it was just very frustrating because they weren't seeing it the same way I was seeing it... as starting a new adventure.

I wish that at the time, I was more patient with them because I know that, looking back, kids have to be just as patient with their parents as parents have to be with their kids when it comes to this. They're going through the same impact on their lives.

I remember my mom being like, "We are just trying to get over the fact that you are not going to have a family." Because at the time, they didn't think of alternatives… I mean, you know, I can still have a family, it will just look a little different. They just thought everything was just off the table, so that was a lot of what they were going through. And my mom was like, "I have to go through a grieving. This is traumatic."

I just didn't really understand why they were so upset about it. I mean, looking back. I get it, but at the time, I was just frustrated.

At the same time, my sister was going through her divorce… So, it was just a lot that was happening in my family. Coming out was just the cherry on top. It made everything even more hectic. So, it was nice to go back to college and just kind of not be there.

But then again, it was difficult because I had to go back to a conservative college, now with this on my plate…

I stayed there all four years. Looking back, I'm happy that I did. Everything that I'm sad that I missed in the college experience, that can happen in your early 20s as well. So, I don't feel like, oh, because I went to a Christian college, I missed out on my young adulthood. It was actually kind of a great experience because I was able to help a lot of kids come out. We made a group that was a safe haven for LGBTQ+ young adults. It just started with me and the guy that I dated there.

A part of coming out was that my parents wanted me to go to therapy to work on my relationship with my dad because I wasn't close with him. At the time, they thought that part of the reason I was gay was that my relationship with my dad was not good. That's the ex-gay philosophy.

So, I was like, "I'm not doing this therapy to change. I will do it to get closer with my dad." That was a good thing that came out of that because it did force me and my dad to have conversations that we wouldn't have had otherwise. But I stopped doing it after, probably six months, because I kept going back and forth, back and forth. The therapist gave me the choice to work on the things that will "help you to come out of this." But you also have the choice to just talk about, you know, whatever.

There were times when we would talk about all the relationships I had with boys growing up, and how that could have been the steppingstone to becoming gay. That was just annoying. I was like, "I don't want to talk about these boys that were jerks to me when I was growing up."

And I just kept going back and forth.

At one point, I broke up with this boyfriend of mine in college because I was like, "I don't know if I can even date right now because of the therapy." It was getting into my head.

But... we did find another guy, a freshman at the time, who was coming out. So, between the three of us, we started this group. It became a pretty good 20 to 30 people group by the time I was a senior. We were coming together once a week, people were talking about their day and how they are doing, and it was just a really nice thing because a lot of these kids were not out at all.

We could not become a formal college group... We tried for it to become an actual group, but the college wasn't comfortable with it. But we got word out because there were professors there that were LGBTQ+ friendly. They were just in the closet about being LGBTQ+ friendly. I was studying education, and a lot of the education professors were more liberal. You know, they are working with all kinds of people.

That was really helpful, because I found that so many of my professors were willing to talk and just be supporters. So, at one point we were able to get LGBTQ+ friendly faculty to put a little rainbow sticker on their door so that students knew which professors they could talk to. And then those professors would tell them about our group.

There were definitely professors that were *not* friendly—conservative. *The Princeton Review* named that college very unfriendly to LGBTQ+. But there were still a lot of professors there that were cool.

I think I have a lot of talents that could do well in the entertainment industry, but you have to be really driven to be a singer or an actor. So, I was like, "What can I do to put all those things to use?" And I was like, "You can use all of those things in teaching."

Teachers are doing a great thing, shaping the future of the nation by teaching kids… I switched my major to elementary education in college and one of the first things they make you do is intern in a preschool and see if you can handle it.

I loved it! It seems it is more of a liberal work force than most… the school I work at now is in a very liberal area. There are pride flags and Black Lives Matter signs all over the neighborhood. So, I'm not worried about that at all.

After coming out, I was relieved because it gave my differences meaning. It's kind of weird but being creative and more effeminate… saying that I was gay was a good explanation for those things… it just felt like it put a nice little bow on all of that.

But it also gave me relief for all of the weird feelings I had had for men growing up; I would be like, "Oh that makes sense that I had kind of a crush on that person." I would just be obsessed with the boy and just chalk it all up to, "I just really want to be like them."

But, no.

It was nice to have an answer. But it was also really hard to get through.

I think my personality is, once something is bothering me, I have to figure it out before I can move on. So, I honestly don't know how people stay in the closet because that just sounds painful.

The biggest struggle for me was, *can I be Christian, and can I be gay?* Because I didn't think they can both happen…

I hated our old church after I came out… they were just not being accepting. You couldn't lead if you were openly gay. I really wanted to sing for church, and I knew that I couldn't do it there because they wouldn't get past the whole gay thing. I counseled for their vacation Bible school one year. I had to just lie and say I was single because I wanted to get paid… I just didn't think that had anything to do with how I did my job.

The youth pastor stopped talking to me and stopped showing interest in me, and I was like, *this is weird*. So, my parents found a more inclusive church. It's the most chill church… maybe half a year into going I asked to be able to be part of their band. They didn't even have auditions. They were just like, "Sure!" I've been able to sing with them ever since. And they are super gay friendly. They have all of the different pride flags in their windows.

I just don't know why more people don't gravitate towards places like that… When you are different, you should gravitate towards places that are different so that you are celebrated for your differences rather than ostracized.

The years when I came out, 2013 through 2015, were probably the hardest… I went back to a Christian college, so I had to come out to people that I was close with. I had to lose friends because some people weren't cool with it. That was difficult, but it did help me to realize who my real friends were.

They had the same feelings I had before I came out, that you can't be gay and Christian. So, they were not so great with me. They started to act awkward around me. I remember this one girl… she was so confused all of a sudden. "Now you like boys?"

Yeah, sorry.

I also made a lot of new friends. There were a lot of people who were in the closet. There were people that were just super cool with it, and they were like, "Yeah, that's cool." Coming out to them made us closer.

I think just knowing that my family wasn't good yet with all of it, and having to lose friends, all of that worried me.

I also had a roommate that was not so great about it… silence can be worse than other things, sometimes. So, the fact that he didn't acknowledge it at all kinda hurt. I roomed with him for three years… By the second and third year, I hated being his roommate…. It was depressing, but I found ways to not be depressed. I kind of really had to pick and choose people because this was a new part of my life that wasn't going to go away.

If you are not cool with it, I cannot keep you around because you don't accept me for all of me.

I think the way I grew up really helped with all of that, being more in touch with my feelings, and able to just get through it. I was a very sad person that first year going back to college… I had to get over the hump of the newness of everything, like having to do therapy and letting my parents go through the same journey to realize that being gay is not the end of the world.

It's actually pretty great.

I didn't have faith at first that they would get there, but eventually, they did.

The way that that therapy is run, it makes you second-guess everything… I had a couple of times where I was like, "Maybe I should try the straight thing?" But then, I realized how unnatural it felt. And I realized how natural being gay felt, and realized that, I don't think God would make me feel this way for no good reason.

Overall, I didn't spend that much time repressing. The most repressing I did was when I was growing up because I truly thought that being gay was wrong. I went through the motions and did what everyone did. I dated girls… I didn't feel the feelings I feel now.

I'm pretty lucky because Maryland is a blue state for the most part. So, I haven't really felt any kind of setbacks from things happening on the state level. After I graduated from college, I got a job right away. I never had a parent that was like, "You can't teach my son because you are gay." I never had that. I actually have kids who have gay parents.

I'm not someone who can pass straight. It's not like a conversation I have to have with my coworkers; they just know. One of my first coworkers that I became really good friends with… I came out to her, and she was like, "I know." I don't even find that it is necessary anymore to come out to people.

These years after college, most of my worries are adult worries... But it has been really nice to be able to come home, to have a place to come back to and just to have a *base*, because things get crazy out in the real world.

What do I wish I knew at the very beginning...? I just wish that I had the same amount of patience for my parents as I wish they had for me. There is usually a light at the end of the tunnel. It doesn't always happen, but usually there is. It just takes time and patience and understanding from one another. It's not just the parents' job, and it's not just the kids' job... because the more patient you are coming out to your parents, the more likely they are to come around. If you are angry and upset about everything and just giving them the cold shoulder, they are less likely to be understanding and accepting.

I know people whose families aren't as accepting, and it's a really harsh situation that they are in. I know one person who transitioned... I think they identify as male now, and they were a girl. They come from a fundamentalist Baptist background, so it's like the extreme of going through that situation and also coming from that family background; that takes years of patience.

That family is missing out on milestones. I think that when you have just cast away your kids like that, you are missing out on everything that they are going through.

They are so excited for when I get married one day, and they will come to my wedding.

But I don't know about my friend's family. That's a really depressing thing to miss out on.

And rejecting parents will miss out on everyday milestones: promotions, buying a new house... Just everything that a person goes through.

You're missing out, just because of your child's gender preference. You really have to look in a different perspective and look at the bigger picture and see how silly it is to be angry about someone's preference... so much gets lost because of anger.

4: DEE, ALICE & ETHAN—

I feel like people see you, as a mom, supporting us, and they see that is a very helpful thing.

Dee grew up in Montgomery County, Maryland and attended public schools until his high school graduation in 2007. He now works as a mental health professional, often helping to care for young people who have suicidal ideation, many of whom are LGBTQ+.

Dee, who is cisgender and gay, was first outed in middle school when he admitted to another boy that he had a crush; the consequence was ostracization. A kid who always felt different and shy, he experienced social isolation and depression for many years, including during his time attending college in Maryland.

Here, Dee and his parents, Alice and Ethan, reminisce about Dee's ordeals as a young person struggling with identity at a moment when many LGBTQ+ people did not feel safe coming out. A liberal family committed to the inclusive philosophy of Unitarian Universalism, they nonetheless did not have other LGBTQ+ people in their lives, and as parents, Alice and Ethan lacked models for how to raise and support an LGBTQ+ child.

The horrific torture and murder of Matthew Shepard, a young gay man, had led the headlines within recent memory, and—along with the AIDS crisis—was on their minds when their rising 9th grader confided that he was gay.

Not surprisingly, they responded with fear, but Dee explains, now, that the biggest risk he faced did not have to do with violence or sex because "being gay and out in high school at a time when not many other gay boys were out—I mean, it still happens now—it can cause a lot of anxiety and depression."

Even with loving and accepting parents and belonging to an inclusive spiritual community, the pressures of a larger culture that had fixed expectations of masculinity weighed heavily on Dee, and he struggled with embarrassment and shame, preferring video games, where he could create avatars, to everyday life.

Seeing her son suffer, Alice did what many of the parents interviewed here have done: she educated herself and sought resources, an effort that led to significant community activism. After Parents and Friends of Ex-Gays & Gays (PFOX, the philosophical antithesis of PFLAG), used the public school system to distribute anti-gay materials, she worked with other parents to correct this hurtful message (though with unintended consequences for Dee).

Eventually, she worked with her church to establish a local Rainbow Youth Alliance group.

Current guidance on protective factors for LGBT youth in a hostile climate (primarily directed towards therapists and medical practitioners) emphasizes the power that seeing allies overtly support the LGBTQ+ community has for young people, especially where it leads to their own activism (understood, in this context, as a form of self-love).[1]

Intuiting this, Alice helped her child in a dynamic way. In addition to her various activism efforts within the county and the public school system, she created an LGBTQ+ support group that David participated in as an adolescent. When he was older, he became a facilitator and helper for other young people who were struggling—including a friend whose father subjected him to an exorcism.

Dee recalls that "I felt myself smiling" when he told his friends about his mother's activism, which became a sort of bridge to his later career pathway.

---

1   Research has identified how the support of allies can facilitate resilience and even activism on behalf of themselves and others for LGBTQ+ people. See Gonzalez, Kirsten A., et al. "'In the Voices of People Like Me': LGBTQ Coping During Trump's Administration." *The Counseling Psychologist*, vol. 50, no. 2, Feb. 2022, pp. 212–240, doi:10.1177/00110000211057199.

Here, Dee shares a story from his recent professional life which shows how, despite the fact that his workplace serves at risk LGBTQ+ youth, the political climate still requires him to be discreet. Asked not to discuss his "personal life" in front of patients, he signals to them covertly that he is LGBTQ+ positive by sharing his love of a popular animated show that features a lesbian character.

Dee's story emphasizes how young LGBTQ+ people, even in a more liberal area of the United States or belonging to relatively liberal communities, still experience significant stigma. He explains how "it can be very taxing on your mental health to be an outsider in this way."

Ethan continues to be a loving dad, and Alice continues to advocate for the health and well-being of LGBTQ+ people, especially in Maryland.

Dee's older sister came out as LGBTQ+ after Dee, when she was in her twenties.

DEE: I definitely didn't know other kids who are gay. I know that both of my parents had some gay friends... A guy from Las Vegas who came over and you had a dinner with him, or something. And there was a gay friend whom you introduced me to once... You had them over. From work, or some part of academia, or something. I remember it... It made an impression.

When I first came out in middle school, my friends reacted very badly.

I never really talked with my parents about this happening...

After I got a little older and became aware, more consciously, of the sexuality thing, I was in this group of friends. I really struggled to find friends in middle school, especially friends I felt comfortable around. I was in orchestra at that time. And there were a lot of kids of Chinese descent that were in

the orchestra that were like a group of friends... and they liked video games. It was a big deal. I sat at the Chinese table, and people would talk... It was like, "He wants to be Asian." I wanted to be friends with them because of our shared interests, you know? I was already kind of like a weird outsider in this group, and they were my only friends in the school at this point.

Then I developed a crush on one of them, and then, towards the end of eighth grade, I was really nervous, and I was in the computer room by myself, and I was... I think it might've been email, or maybe it was on AOL Instant Messenger. And I confessed that I had a crush on him. I felt so nervous, I felt sick, you know? My heart was beating really fast. He kind of reacted nicely to it once I sent the message that I was interested in him, but he did tell the rest of the group, and they immediately ostracized me.

They made it so I couldn't sit at their table anymore, or I couldn't really talk to them. It was a tough time.

I had a lot of depression and anxiety through middle school, high school, college. I couldn't function at a level where it affected things, but I could still somewhat do what I needed to do, so I never really addressed it in a real therapeutic or psychiatric way, and I feel like you both supported me, but you didn't fully understand it, either, I think.

Maybe you thought I was being lazy, or maybe you thought... Because you were, like, pushing me to do orchestra, and I just wanted to be left alone. You thought that was how to help me, and probably in many ways, it was. I'm sure I'm more well-rounded now for having done those things.

I was also miserable.

In middle school, I started to play this online game. I somehow convinced you guys to get it for me... Something about, you create your own character in a different world; being a different person. Something about that was amazing to me. It was so much better, I felt, escaping myself, because I was just so miserable in middle school that I loved being a different character in a different world.

I would sneak into the computer room at night and stay up all night, and my grades really dropped in school. I wasn't getting enough sleep, and you guys had to cut me off from that game. That was a big fight between us.

ALICE: That was hard.

ETHAN: You were pretty addicted. You are also incredibly ingenious and clever. You found ways... At that time, it was all on cable... You rerouted the cable.

ALICE: Yeah, you rerouted the cable. We didn't even know it.

DEE: I was really focused on trying to feel better. And video games...

ALICE: Can I just add something? You also came out around this time.

There is a summer camp that he went to that was sponsored by our denomination, which is Unitarian Universalist (UU). We call ourselves "the religious left" because it's very liberal, and we've always been very open and affirming to LGBTQ+ people.

ETHAN: Very accepting of people from all different walks of life. Even people who are atheist or agnostic, or pagan, or whatever the heck they are, we like them.

DEE: It's funny, because you just wanted me to have some kind of spiritual upbringing...

ALICE: Yes, and being that Ethan was Jewish and I was Lutheran (I did not want to raise my kids in Lutheranism, either), this was something that we could agree on. Also, we moved around so much, that the minute we moved somewhere, that became our community, when we found a local congregation. That helped a lot.

DEE: Even in middle school, even in elementary school, I found myself socially having a better time with those kids in the weekly Universalist Unitarian gatherings. They had a Sunday school type of thing, and they would teach us about religions across the world, which I enjoyed. It was like a mythology class, kind of. It was really fun. Socially, I did better with those kids than I did with kids in my regular school. It was really helpful. Even though, it was a battle to get me to go… I didn't want to get up on Sunday morning. I wanted to play video games. But you made me go; that is one of the things I'm most grateful for, that you made me do.

ALICE: Really? That's great, because a lot of Unitarian parents want the kids to just want to go; they don't want to go, then that is their choice to just stay home. But I was a very unusual Unitarian parent

ETHAN: There was a time when you would just hide out and nap on the couch instead of participating with the other kids…

DEE: That relates to the summer camp… I went there…That's one of the first places I came out. I think I came out there first. Before the boy I messaged, who was in my school, I had talked to kids at camp. I was very dramatic. I was like, *I had a secret.* We were in the cabin at night, and I made them guess. And someone made a guess that was close enough, and I was like, "You're right." And they were very nice, and we talked about it.

          Even there, I felt socially outcast just a bit because I was awkward, and they were trying to be cool. I was more sensitive and shyer. Somehow I knew, because we had similar values of social acceptance, from UUism, I knew I could come out to them, and talk to them about that.

ALICE: Plus, you knew when we moved down here that you wouldn't see them again for another year…

DEE: I was very scared to tell my parents, even though I knew that you were both, like, gay-accepting at a certain level. Despite that, I sensed that the culture

at large was not gay-accepting, and that there were negative or embarrassing things thought about gay people that I didn't want associated with me.

I remember there were also UU conventions... I think that was the first
time I found an older gay person, a high schooler, maybe a senior, and I was
just in middle school. So, it seemed like a huge difference to me.... I talked
to him about being so scared to tell my parents and stuff. I just didn't want
you all to think of me differently.

ALICE: Was he out?

DEE: Yes, I think so.

ETHAN: How long before you came out had I found you looking at gay porn?

DEE: That time that I printed stuff out of the printer? That happened after I came
out to mom. So maybe you knew before... But we didn't talk about it.

ETHAN: Your mom and I had talked about it before you spoke to her.

ALICE: (To Ethan) well, you had talked about it to me a couple of years before, at
least. Or maybe it was the year before. Because you said, "Dee doesn't seem
to be interested in girls." And I said, "Well, he still young... They just want
to play video games." I kind of just brushed it off at that point. But you did
have an inkling.

DEE: I remember you asked me what girls I had crushes on, and I really hated
the question, and I kind of knew what you were getting at. That was, like,
seventh grade. I still wasn't ready to think about it, or to talk about it.

ETHAN: I don't remember if I was supportive or not; maybe it wasn't clear yet... I just
had inklings.

DEE: I guess I knew because of the UUism that you were gay-accepting people, and it was starting to become more of a conversation, nationally, at the time. Early 2000s.

ALICE: What I thought later was that you knew I was Unitarian, so I kind of had to be accepting. Or I didn't have a leg to stand on. (Laughter.) To have a negative reaction would've betrayed my beliefs and my values.

DEE: It was the summer after my eighth grade year, before entering high school. I had come out that summer, I suppose. At camp. I had come out to some people, and for some reason, I just thought that I had to come out to my parents next.

It wasn't that long before I told you, but for some reason, seventh and eighth grade… They just felt like they went on for a long, long time. So, it *felt* like a long time.

I was thinking about how I needed to tell my parents, and I knew I would start with my mom just because I was more comfortable with that at first. I remember the scene of when it happened very clearly. We were in the car on the way home from the library, and I just kind of said it to you in the car… And you were kind of quiet.

ALICE: Was I?

DEE: That's what I remember.

ALICE: Well, I was driving. Trying not to go off the road…

I remember. You were sitting there, right next to me. We passed by the Safeway. We were almost home, maybe about six blocks from here. You just kind of said, "Mom, I think I'm gay."

And being in a car, you are close to each other. But you are not facing each other. So, I'm sure I said several wrong things, like…

ETHAN: *Are you sure?*

ALICE: *Are you sure? Are you safe?*

I mean, that's the first thing the parent thinks of. I thought he was going to get beat up behind the football stand or something like that at school. He was just a freshman. I think you were in school for like a week before you told me. It was very early on in the semester, and I didn't know that you had told your Asian group of friends the spring before. Bullying was something I definitely worried about.

ETHAN: We knew about Matthew Shepard… It made such an impression. We were really upset about that.

ALICE: It had only been a couple of years before. Yeah, so I said, "Are you okay?… Are you having sex? Is it safe sex?" That's what I thought about. My immediate response was, is he safe? I was just thinking about risk.

DEE: It's funny because there were a lot of things about that incident that were correct in a certain way, just not how you thought of it. Because, I feel like being gay and out in high school at a time when not many other gay boys were out—I mean, it still happens now—it can cause a lot of anxiety and depression.

So, there *was* a risk for me, it was just different than what you were thinking of.

ALICE: Right. Right. And I didn't tell your father. I said, "This is your information. You have to decide when to tell dad."

DEE: You *wanted* me to tell dad right away.

ALICE: The other thing that you said after that, I think it was right then… You said, "Mom, I don't want you to think that I don't like women or girls, or that I hate them because I'm gay." That was very sensitive. That really blew me away. He is worried about my feelings, about how I am going to react, as a woman, to him being gay.

DEE: I also remember you saying you felt sad that I might not have kids, and I don't think I said anything in response, but I felt frustrated.

ALICE: I don't remember saying that, but I probably did.

DEE: I guess I had never really thought of that (having kids) as a hope or an expectation; it's an obvious thing, in hindsight, that a lot of parents want for their kids. But we had never really talked about it before.

ALICE: Well, I knew that you were great with little kids. The first year that you went to that summer camp, you were still in grade school. I picked you up from the camp, and this one set of parents came up to me... All the counselors were volunteer adults. And they had brought their little kid, and they just raved about you because you took care of this little kid when he was upset. They just thought you were fantastic. There were other instances like that, where you were great with little kids, too.

DEE: I don't have any interest in being a parent right now. I feel like if I ever wanted to have kids, I don't feel like there would be a barrier. But I do feel like me and my sister are not really interested in that. I do wonder how that affects my parents because we are kind of like the last of the line in a way.

ETHAN: I have two sisters who, neither of them were married... Both of them are past childbearing age.

ALICE: I have nieces and nephews... Sometimes I think about it.... I probably would miss just having a little grandchild to play with and have fun with, you know. But, I'm happy. I'm happy I have you guys.

I mean, I almost didn't have children. I had a series of miscarriages before I had them, and I was told at one point that I probably wouldn't be able to have children, but then I did, so...

DEE: That's interesting, because statistically, a younger brother is more likely to be gay.

ALICE: I heard that, and I heard a reason why. It has to do with hormones.

DEE: So, if I had older brothers, then it would make sense...

ALICE: I thought about that when I first heard that.

         It was hard to not tell your dad. I kept saying, "Dee, when are you going to tell dad?" That went on, not a real long time, but a couple of months.

DEE: It was a couple months, but it was just funny the way that you (Ethan) found out. During my nights of sneaking at 3 AM, or whatever I could get away with, onto the family computer, for some reason, I decided to print out gay porn. I think I left it in the printer, and I guess I was really tired... I went to bed and fell asleep. That morning, I went downstairs for breakfast, and the door to the family computer was locked. I went to the door and tried to open it... I hadn't really processed it, but I had this feeling that there was something in there that I needed to get. I don't know if I had really remembered what I left there.

         And then it started to dawn on me, what had happened. And I knew that you were in there. And I knew that you were upset. I tried to open the door, and you were like, "Go away!"

         I don't know exactly what you guys said. But I know you guys talked. And you (Alice) made me hug dad before I left for school.

ALICE: I made you hug dad?

DEE: I was so embarrassed and ashamed. I didn't want to hug dad. I didn't want to be near you because I was so embarrassed and ashamed.

ALICE: I may have not said this to you, but I think I said it to dad; I may have said it to one or two other people. That's what really confirmed it for you... That you felt that way about gay porn. I was like, of course. How else would you know? *You know.*

DEE: It's funny. People find out about it all kinds of ways. But it seems like a very logical way to find out...

ETHAN: When I talked with Alice about it, she came out and told me that you had come out. And then we talked about it. I don't think I was upset with you... I was worried...

I feel like you just kind of grew up in a culture that was just naturally very homophobic and gender policing. I am sure, when you were growing up, that people were saying, "That person's a sissy," or whatever they were saying. That would be bad.

DEE: You were kind of a cool, tough kid yourself. You know. It was just part of your culture at that time. So, I think I just kind of got that sense from you as a kid that that was part of who you were. I'm not saying that you are bad or anything, or that you are not liberal, and accepting, and a smart person. I just knew that was part of the whole male deal... That was probably why I didn't want to tell you. Why I wanted to tell mom first, and I didn't want to tell you. I was embarrassed and scared to talk about it with you. You know?

ETHAN: I'm not sure what I said when we talked. But I think I said, "I love you." And, it's not a problem. Just, be careful. Be safe. I hope I was supportive of you. Do you remember?

DEE: I think, Mom made us hug. You said, "Love you," and then I left for school, and I don't think we really much talked about it after that. Really.

ALICE: So, that was the very beginning of his freshman year, and he had a hard time; he was having a hard time.

DEE: I went to high school with no friends.

ALICE: No friends. I don't even know if there was a Gay-Straight Alliance group at your school at that time?

DEE: Not that I was aware of.

ALICE: Dee did have friends at church... So, I went looking for a place for him to find support. I think it was actually the next summer, when we first heard about a PFLAG meeting up in Columbia, and they had a teen group... I drove him up there several times that summer, on a Tuesday night, I remember. And I remember the first time I drove him up there ... I remember waiting in the car for him to come out of the building, and he came out with a group of kids. And they were talking and laughing, and he just seemed so easy with them. So *relaxed* with them. He was enjoying himself, and I'd never seen him be that way with a group of kids before. So, I thought, "Wow, I've got to find something like that closer to us." We tried going up on a Tuesday night when school started. It was just too far... There was homework... It was tough. So, I thought, "Well, I'm part of this Unitarian congregation. Let me just see if I can start a group here."

And so, that's how it started. We didn't even have meetings... It took a while. Because the church had to have meetings about it... They had to invite comments, and I had to tell them exactly what it was, and I had to make sure that it was okay to invite kids to a church meeting without their parents' permission. I really wanted it to be that way because the kids who need it the most were the ones who weren't out to their parents yet. We went through all that, and we had our first meeting in March 2006. So, this year will be the 14th year that we've had meetings.

Dee was part of the first cohort, and we are still in contact with a lot of the people who were in that first cohort.

DEE: I was definitely interested in my mother's idea.

ALICE: Yes... you were immediately happy about it. I did drag you to a lot of things... I always joked, "What other mom *makes* their kids go to the Pride Parade?"

I'm glad you remember that you were... Because you seemed so happy. The first time, I was astonished. Just watching you from the car, talking with those kids. It was like, "He found his people."

ETHAN: I did go to PFLAG meetings, but not right away. Once Alice got more involved, I went to events.

ALICE: When I started work with Rainbow Youth Alliance, I was really busy with that. Then, I was invited to be on the PFLAG board, which I did for some time. They had galas and fundraisers...

DEE: It was a really nice surprise, you know? I kind of thought of you as, like, a more elegant version of that mom from that show, *Queer as Folk.* (Laughter all around.) Someone who was just very fiercely supportive of their kid and had all the buttons that said "Pride" and stuff. I felt very lucky. I also felt, almost, like, very guilty... Like, what did I do to deserve this?

And also, later on, when I had mental health issues, I felt guilty then, because I knew some other kids who were really struggling with really hateful parents, who were keeping it together...

But when I thought about you being an activist, I felt really lucky. And I felt myself smiling when I would tell people, "I have a really liberal mom and she made a support group for LGBTQ+ teens." I felt really happy about it.

ALICE: *Good.*

When I started the group, I was a facilitator, for a little while. Then I realized, I needed somebody who actually knew what they were doing. We hired a part-time person with qualifications, either in psychology or counseling or something, to lead the group. When I was in those meetings, I could see that there were kids who really, really needed it, much more than you did. But you came, and you were helpful to those kids.

DEE: We all were helpful.

ALICE: What we called it from the beginning was "adult-facilitated peer-to-peer support."

Sometimes I run into parents and kids, and they say: "My parents are fine, my school is fine, I have great friends. Even my church is fine. I don't need Rainbow Youth Alliance." And I always tell them, "Well, *maybe there are kids there who need you.*"

So, we welcome those kids who can come and be here support for the other kids.

ETHAN: I wonder if that influenced you, Dee, to get into the helping professions, and to work with kids with mental health issues?

DEE: I definitely like the support group kind of thing. There are a lot of other factors, too. Some teachers were really influential in high school, and that led me to take AP psychology. But that was part of it, that support group. Nothing else was really therapeutic...

There were times when I was really struggling, and there was one time when I had a psychiatric break, and I had to go to a psychiatric unit my senior year of high school. But after that, we had Kaiser Permanente health care, and they were not very helpful at all, I thought.

ALICE: I know, you had therapists that were not really... good.

DEE: I didn't have very good therapists. And also, meetings were very limited, and... very fast.

When I started high school and I had no friends... I just kind of sat in a quiet corner of the school, during lunch, by myself.

ALICE: You also took your lunch to your counselor and sat and had lunch with her.

DEE: Yes, later in the year. She tried to introduce me to other kids. But I was just too shy and uncomfortable. She tried to introduce me to this other boy... He had a friend group, and I just felt totally uncomfortable. He had all these macho friends.

But I was just way too awkward, and they wouldn't accept me... I never experienced direct bullying, really. I felt like people talked about me a bunch...

ALICE: There was a group... "Family Values." That group from Colorado Springs... They targeted Montgomery County for being very liberal. I knew some people that were trying to improve the sex ed curriculum in the schools. It was actually asked for by the teachers, because the teachers were very restricted about what they could talk about as far as sex. And when this group found out about it, they formed a group that was sort of an anti-PFLAG, and it was called PFOX. They advocated for conversion therapy and that kind of stuff.

ETHAN: Ex-gay ideology.

DEE: Yeah...

ALICE: At that time, in Montgomery County, any nonprofit could send home a flyer, to any kid in any school. So, PFOX took advantage of that, and they delivered flyers to all the high schools... Dee showed up in his homeroom one day, and found the PFOX flyer on his desk...

ETHAN: That PFOX flyer, it had been presented in the school like it was an *official document*. Like they were supporting this position.

ALICE: Maryland had a pretty good organization to try to get equal marriage rights in the state. We went to Annapolis once a year and lobbied our state legislators to do this, and it was a big organization. I let my fellow parents know my son had come home with this PFOX flyer... Then we got to work making our own flyer. Every school would give us the number of flyers that they needed for each homeroom. Then, we had to deliver them to each school. There are 21 or 22 high schools in Montgomery County. Some of them are far-flung. It was a big project. It took a while.

I knew what Dee went through when he saw the PFOX flyer, and it wasn't okay. We were all pretty upset about it. It meant that we were, sort of, righting a wrong. We wanted the kids to know that wasn't their only option... PFOX, and conversion therapy, and denying who they were. They could be who they really were. And this flyer let them know, *we hoped*, that there was support out there for them.

DEE: What did the flyer say?

ALICE: It was about PFLAG, and you don't need to be ashamed of yourself. "If you need help, if your parents need help, you can go to a PFLAG meeting." It was very, very positive and affirming.

DEE: At one point, when those were being handed out, I think they were distributed on the desks at homeroom, or whatever class; they (other students) took them off all of the desks and put them all on my desk.

I came in, and all the kids were just silent, staring at me.

ALICE: So, one of the kids did that?

DEE: I don't know who did it...

ALICE: And the teacher didn't say anything?

DEE: Guess not. I just saw it was on my desk didn't want to confront it. So, I just picked them up and put them in the recycling bin and didn't say anything.

There were also times when people made jokes at my expense.

There were times when kids were yelling stuff about "wanting cock" near me, and it wasn't necessarily directed at me, but it was near me, and I felt uncomfortable.

There was nothing really aggressive, but there were times when it was made clear to me that people were talking about me or thinking in certain ways about me, and that definitely contributed to my anxiety.

That was one of the factors that led to my breakdown in my senior year, where paranoia was part of the issue.

I'm working now. I work at an inpatient psychiatric facility for teenagers in a hospital in DC. I really like the job. When I first started that job, on my resume was that I had been a co-facilitator at Rainbow Alliance meetings. So, it showed that I had worked with LGBTQ+ teens before. My boss, when he hired me, said something very vague like, "We accept all kinds of employees here." But he didn't say anything specific. I'm sure that's what he was thinking of when he saw my resume.

There was one time, my first year working there, when I was working with the younger kids, between seven and thirteen; usually those ages come because of some kind of psychiatric crisis. They stay in our unit in the hospital, for safety, for about a week... I was sitting at the table with my other coworkers while the kids were having their breakfast that morning at work, and some of my coworkers were talking about... "Oh, I'm dating this guy." So, they were talking about their personal lives a bit, and my boss heard that conversation and pulled me aside and said to me, "Never talk about your personal life at work."

ALICE: He just pulled you aside or the whole group?

DEE: Just me.

ALICE: *Wow.*

DEE: You know, I got the message that he didn't want me to say anything about queerness or being queer in front of the kids. I'm sure he was just worried about parents and any reaction, but partly because of that, and partly because several of the nurses and people I work with are older, or they come from cultures from other countries where I just don't know how they feel about gay people, I'm not fully out at work.

            If somebody asked, I would tell them, but I just don't ever really talk about it. And I do feel, partially because I'm gay, and partially just because I'm a shy, reserved person, I don't feel very close to my coworkers, and I kind of pull away from them; some of them are very close to each other and have close friendships, you know?

ALICE: You have been there for a long time now...

DEE: I have been there for five years, but I never talk to the kids about anything specific from my life, but I have a lanyard from *Stephen Universe*, a show that is known to have gay characters. It's kind of revolutionary because it's an animated show for teenagers and kids. The artist who created the show grew up in Silver Spring, and she really, really fought to have queer inclusion in the show. It's kind of rare in a national animated show, and it's kind of like become a cultural touchstone for gay people. Adults love it; kids love it.

            I wear the lanyard to show kids that I am queer-accepting and queer-positive, because we do get a lot of LGBTQ+ patients, because it can be very taxing on your mental health to be an outsider in this way.

            So that's one way I signal to the patients I work with without going against what my boss said, to show them that I am LGBTQ+ accepting, and that

I'm someone they can talk to about that stuff. Also, it just kind of humanizes me to the kids that I like to show that they might be into.

They often ask me what characters I like, and I often mention the character who is very clearly in a lesbian relationship, and they are excited about that, and they open up to me.

ALICE: Dee was the president of his GSA for two years. He started the first anime club at the school.

DEE: It wasn't just an anime club, I tried to talk about language and culture and stuff there… It's almost like there is a Cold War of acceptance or nonacceptance going on in the schools where it's never talked about directly in front of the students… It's kind of behind the scenes, like with the papers being handed out back then, and the different opinions on what teachers are allowed to say and not allowed to say. I have a lot of memories of experiences where things were not talked about directly, but I could tell whether someone was supportive or not supportive, and how that affected me.

This similar kind of Cold War type thing is now going on in my workplace, especially with regard to the trans kids.

I remember one teacher specifically, who I guess I felt she did not like me. And I felt that she did not like me because I was the openly gay one, and I felt that she treated me differently, but she never did anything or said anything *explicitly* about gay stuff at all.

And I had a real hard time articulating that I felt she was treating me kind of differently because I was gay. There was one point where I was really upset by this teacher, and I tried to go talk to my counselor about it, and I was feeling kind of emotional about it. I just blurted out this teacher doesn't like me.

That just sounded silly to my counselor. Because it wasn't articulated as, "This teacher might be discriminating against me because I'm gay…" I wasn't able to say that. And once I blurted out my complaint, the counselor was like, "Well, sometimes people like you, and sometimes they don't." I wasn't really able to say, "Well, maybe this teacher is homophobic," because I didn't have the words, or the sense of safety, or the sophistication, to really explain.

On the other hand, there were teachers like the GSA teacher—she was openly lesbian.

ALICE: Yeah, which was not easy at that time.

DEE: And she was very, very supportive and great, and she encouraged the GSA to, like, try to have a video on the morning announcements about joining the GSA, or to like put posters up around the school saying stuff like, "Join the GSA." We made posters that said "10%," because I saw something that said something like 10% of people may be gay. So, we did all this stuff, and I remember the teacher who didn't like me just acting really weird around me, especially once we put up those posters... She asked if we, like, needed *special permission* to put them up.

Having an affirming teacher gave me some hope. It enabled me to be a part of the GSA and to become president of the GSA. I think, especially at that time, my main instinct and drive was to just be left alone. I just felt like I couldn't relate to anybody; I was too *weird* for everybody. I wasn't very good at socializing. And I just wanted to be left alone.

Having the GSA and the teacher that was able to give me a place where I wanted to go and socialize with people and be part of something, and a way to express what was going on... it motivated me.

I think what you as my mom were doing, and that teacher motivated me. When I put things around school, it turned out that there were queer-affirmative people, LGBTQ+ affirming people... It was just such a big deal for me in a lot of ways.

ALICE: She was more than just affirming. As a member of the community, she was a successful person, and she was out. I always thought she was a great role model as well as being affirming. Was that true? That you took some heart in the fact that she was out there, and working, and successful? And helping high schoolers?

DEE: It was really great that she was there. And I was happy to see her being out. But at the time, I wasn't thinking about the future so much as I was just, you know, *getting through it*. Wanting to be done with high school. Feeling very anxious and depressed.

ALICE: I don't know if I could ever be a role model for a gay kid because I'm not of the community. And, it's funny, I just thought of this, like a few years ago, that I'm doing all of this activism for the gay community of which I am not a member. And what made me think of it was my dad. Because my dad was an activist for the African-American community, of which he was not a member. And also, the American Indian movement. But you can only do so much as an ally.

DEE: People are really excited to see you, at pride parades and stuff. Like, people are happy to see a straight mom there. A lot of queer people are really excited to see you.

ALICE: I always say I feel like a rock star for a couple of hours when I go March with the PFLAG group at the pride parade because so many people come up to me, and they thank me, and they say they love me, and I go, "I love you back!"

    You just feel the love!

DEE: You were very helpful to my friend. He lived, like, a town over... His dad is an older man from South America who is very, very conservative, and a Christian, and very unaccepting. And he really struggled. You were there for him a lot of the time, throughout high school, and even after high school.

ALICE: He had a really hard time in high school. Not just with his dad, but with the kids in his neighborhood. They really taunted him and bullied him.

DEE: But that manifested in, like, his father taking him to South America to get exorcised.

ALICE: *Yeah,* there was an exorcism.

DEE: He tried to get him on a hormone treatment, thinking he had too much estrogen and all this stuff. He was really trying to change him. My friend was really confused for a while because that really hurt.

ALICE: Being the mother of an LGBTQ+ child changed me tremendously. I used to be just as shy as Dee says he was. I couldn't talk... I would never have been able to talk to a crowd. Ever. I would have just died!

But I found a passion in this, and I think I have gotten probably more out of it than Dee ever did. I've met the most amazing people... I never would have met them... these moms that I know from this Facebook page could just seriously support their children in the face of all kinds of family and community rejection, and they are there to support each other. Some of their stories are really heartbreaking.

DEE: I feel like people see you, as a mom, supporting us, and they see that is a very helpful thing.

ETHAN: I think it radicalized you and gave you this mission, not only to support your kids, but to encourage other parents. I think you are really moved by the research that showed that parental acceptance has a huge effect on later life... For these kids, parental advocacy has an effect on suicide, mental wellness, the ability to thrive.

ALICE: *...Kids who are supported become successful adults.*

5: HELENE AND SIMON——
The power of out is huge.

Helene and Simon raised their two sons, Ross and Max, in Montgomery County, Maryland. In the late 1990s, when both boys came out as gay, Helene explains, "the word 'gay' was hardly ever used."

The brothers confided in one another first, sharing in a tremendous sense of loss for their parents. They cried "because they knew we would never be grandparents."

Happily, this turned out not to be the case: to walk into Helene and Simon's house, their walls a loving display of family photographs, is to see a journey that includes celebrations, sons-in-law, and two beautiful grandchildren.

Helene expressed concern recently that their story might seem anachronistic to readers now. Twenty years ago, there were no LGBTQ+ characters on television or in cinema, *Obergefell* was still years from being won, and the need to blame someone or something fell on parents: authoritarian mothers and weak fathers were suspect, and Helene and Simon even participated in an NIH study seeking a "gay gene."

Although they did not have some of the ideological baggage carried by other participants in this book, they found themselves isolated and on unfamiliar ground. Helene vividly recalls, after Ross came out, weeping for three days before finally coming to the realization, *"this is not about me."*

Perhaps most moving here is the image she shares of her children, alone and unable to ask for help. She was shocked to learn that both had known they were gay from age ten but "couldn't tell us, or share it with us... So many years of suffering in silence."

Eventually coming out to their synagogue as the parents of two gay sons, they expressed solidarity in a way that was transformative for their family and for their community. They created a space for others to acknowledge their gay loved ones, and eventually, for LGBTQ+ people to participate openly in their community—important at a moment when most synagogues were not yet welcoming.

In short, "The power of out is huge."

At one point, Helene and Simon's rabbi shared a complaint from another member arguing that "these people" should not be welcomed because "they are going to harm our children." To which Helene replied, "These people *are* our children."

Although having a second child come out as LGBTQ+ at first seemed almost unbelievable to Helene and Simon, the reader can see that this is the experience of many of the families interviewed here. Their narrative offers insight into how individual LGBTQ+ people might view the experience of coming to terms with their identity very differently, as well as into the importance of family warmth and support.

The message of parental compassion and advocacy that Helene and Simon convey here is both timely and needed. As the country experiences a tremendous push to undo LGBTQ+ rights and protections garnered over the past twenty years, Simon's notion of what it means to be a parent, and a human being, is resonant: "The world is a complex place. Our job is to help make a complex place *as loving as it can be* for as many people as we can."

HELENE: At the time our younger son, Ross, came out to us, no one I knew was out. The word "gay" was hardly ever used, and there were no gay characters on television. I never suspected that either of my kids were gay. I used to tell them, "Someday you will bring home a nice Jewish girl."

Ross dated a gorgeous girl in high school. I thought he was going to be a womanizer. But he realized he was gay. He said that when he kissed her, he felt nothing. He was attracted to a boy in his class, and he told a friend, and the friend told Max, our older son.

After school one day, Max asked Ross, "Are you gay? Ross thought that Max was going to make fun of him or mock him. But then Max said, "So am I."

They just hugged and cried in each other's arms. They told us later that they were crying because they knew we would never be grandparents. They realized that they could not tell us at the same time that both of them were gay. They decided Ross would come out to us first.

Ross needed to come out. He needed to unburden himself and be himself, fully himself.

And I just couldn't believe it. I was flabbergasted. I thought it was just hormones. That maybe it was just a stage. I said to my husband, Simon, "We will find a therapist. This can't be happening." We did not know anybody whose kid was gay.

So, we sent Ross to a therapist. And the therapist said, "Oh, he is gay. No doubt about it."

I cried for, I think, three days, I was in bed. I was just a mess, hysterical. I was thinking, "What are my friends going to say? What is my family going to say?"

Everything is relative... Simon has one sibling, a younger brother, who is severely developmentally disabled. He has no speech. Simon's father had passed away a few years earlier, but his mom lived nearby. When Simon told her, she said, "So...? At least Ross can talk to you."

That helped me to step back a little bit... Everything is relative.

My sister helped me. She started sending me books, and I started reading. Suddenly I realized what my son had gone through. I hadn't been looking at it from his perspective. I didn't realize that for years he had suffered in silence. That when he went to sleep at night, this was what he thought about... how was he going to live his life?

Suddenly, my maternal instinct kicked in. And it wasn't so much about me. It was about the child whose forehead I would put a cold compress on when he had a fever. This was the kid that I would sit up with all night with when he had a cough. This was a kid of mine who was hurting.

And I wasn't there for him.

I later learned that both Ross and Max *knew* when they each were ten years old. That was something that shocked me. That both of my kids had suffered for so long alone. They didn't tell us, couldn't tell us, or share it with us. Or feel that they could. So many years of suffering in silence.

And thinking about the pain Ross felt, oh my God, *that* took over. I realized *this is not about me.* This is about him, and his life, and his feelings. And how he has suffered.

How can you have a child who is suffering and not be there for him?

Ross gave us the PFLAG number. I didn't know PFLAG from anything.

SIMON: Ross was very sensitive to the fact that we weren't the enemy. He knew that we loved him, and it was just a matter of us being able to catch up. He had a very, very healthy attitude. He tried to connect us.

HELENE: There was a PFLAG group that was meeting at a local church, so we decided to go. I didn't know what kind of people these were going to be... we went to this meeting and walked into the church.

And there is this big long table with literature. I'm looking at this literature, and it's all about dying. This was 1997, during the AIDS epidemic, which was another reason that I was devastated when Ross came out. So, we are looking at this death and dying literature, and someone came out and asked, "Are you here for this meeting?" We said, "Yes, we are here for PFLAG." And they said, "PFLAG is down that hall. This is *The Hemlock Society.*"

That was our first experience going to PFLAG! Needless to say, we were a little relieved. Things looked up from there.

We went to this meeting, and everybody there was just like us. There were no surprises... just loving parents. We sat around in a circle, and everybody talked about their kids.

After the meeting, they said, "We are going downstairs for our advocacy group, if anyone is interested." And I thought, "*advocacy?*"

We went home. Things calmed down, and Ross seemed to be doing okay. He had a lot of supportive friends. At one point I remember saying to Max, "If you are gay, too, you have to tell me now. I have to get it over with. Just tell me."

SIMON: Max said, "Don't worry about me, I'm fine."

HELENE: He knew that he couldn't tell us yet. And so, we got used to Ross...

This was the end of Max's senior year in high school. And then he went off to college. At one point, there was a young girl that he was friendly with and I thought *this is it.* We kept looking up her picture.

SIMON: The summer after his sophomore year, Max was working downtown, and I would drop him off on my way to work. We'd see all of these beautiful young women in their summer dresses...he never seemed to turn his head to notice, and that seemed odd to me. We were getting a little concerned about how he was doing socially.

HELENE: He finally told us… we said something about being gay, and that's when he told us.

By the time he came out, my attitude had changed. I was determined to be the most supportive parent ever. And I told him, "It's fine. You are okay." I figured I had learned enough that I am not going to make the same mistake twice.

Max had never considered coming out. He had internalized his being gay in a very negative way. He always imagined he would be in the closet and be an uncle to Ross's children (without knowing that Ross was gay). He figured he'd be in the closet, and this was going to be his life; he was never going to come out to anybody.

SIMON: He really did not want to be gay.

HELENE: He repressed it. Repressed it, repressed it, repressed it. It affected him. He was angry.

SIMON: It must have affected him because there would be times, never around anybody but us, when he would have temper and conflicts. Anger. Behavior we could really never figure out. But this anger disappeared once he came out. It had hurt Max, being gay, psychologically; it affected him much worse than it affected Ross because he was trying to suppress it, repress it.

HELENE: When Max came out, Simon had a harder time than when Ross came out.

SIMON: I did.

HELENE: Max looks like Simon… He acts like Simon. Simon saw himself in Max.

SIMON: As a *new and improved* version of me.

HELENE: When both kids came out, this is when we realized, *this is going to be a big part of our lives.* We realized we needed help. And so, we sought a psychotherapist who was active in PFLAG. Even with Ross already being out, we still didn't have a lot of basic information... the therapist was marvelous. We basically did the talking, and she gave us the tissues.

What was a real blessing to us was that she gave us a lot of books to read to help us to better understand what being gay means, how Max differed from Ross (the more "effeminate" child), and she helped us to understand their dynamic as brothers.

We would bring these books home and read them. It really was the best thing for us because not knowing and not understanding is what causes problems.

My own parents never talked to me about sexuality. My mother called menstruation "being unwell." I grew up in a world where there is a husband, and a wife, and kids. My parents said, "You marry somebody who is Jewish." That's it.

I had two perfect children. They were beautiful children, and so bright academically. They were the perfect kids, and we were the perfect family; I just thought everything was perfect.

And then when Ross came out, I thought, *it's not perfect*.

My sister kept saying, "Nobody has the perfect life," but I didn't want that for my child. I couldn't even imagine him loving another man. It's not like today, where you see evidence of this all around you.

Our anxiety about AIDS was a big part of it.

SIMON: We did not have theological baggage.

HELENE: I worried a lot about how my mother would react if she found out. When Max came out, he wanted to tell her who he really was. My sister was caring for my mom and asked me not to tell her, because she would bear the brunt of having to help her through that trauma. I deferred to her, and Max was very upset. She was ill, and when she died, he was very upset that she never knew who he really was.

That was something where, maybe I made the wrong decision. I made the wrong call on that.

SIMON: What's really sad about that is that we will never know how she would have responded.

HELENE: We are talking a different time, so you really have to go back... there was a lot of blame and shaming.

When gay people started coming out of the closet there was this need to know... Everybody wanted to know *why*. Why are people gay?

And there was a lot of discussion as to whether boys are gay because of authoritarian mothers. And so, I did start to look back, because I'm a perfectionist. I like a neat house... was I too controlling? *Did I make them gay?* Then, somebody came out with this thing that there is a "gay gene," and it comes from the mother.

So, we were tested... We went and got DNA tested, we submitted samples. Some NIH study. Either way, I internalized the idea that "it's all mom's fault..."

SIMON: A flipside of those old wives' tales was that it was a weak and distant father that made kids gay. I was the absolute opposite of distant. So, my conclusion was, *all of that is false.*

HELENE: I was always a person who wanted to just blend in, but having gay sons put us in a "different" category. In our synagogue of 500 families, the word "gay" had never been mentioned. We were very active. I was president of the Sisterhood, and Simon was on the Board of Trustees. We were there all the time...

I felt that there was something, not *wrong* exactly, but I didn't know how to feel. So, for the first few years after Ross came out, we never mentioned it to our congregation. Not to any of our close friends. We didn't say anything to anybody.

We dealt with it alone.

After a time, we were approached by a friend who had been active in PFLAG.

SIMON: We hadn't gone back to PFLAG support group meetings because our kids were not having the difficulties, like self-destructive behavior, that other parents were describing, thank God.

But our friend invited us to PFLAG national galas. We began to get more exposure… I remember being taken aback when people were talking about their *two* gay children. We were getting a slow introduction. We were invited to meet with people from the gay and lesbian synagogue downtown, founded for gay and lesbian Jews, whether they were Reform, Conservative, or Orthodox.

HELENE: In those days, synagogues were not…

SIMON: *Welcoming.*

HELENE: This woman knew that we were very active at our Temple and that we had two gay kids. The idea was that we would convey a request to our Temple.

SIMON: A few years earlier, our rabbi had done a baby-naming for a lesbian couple and had gotten a lot of criticism from older members. So, he backed away from the issue.

In terms of background, in the late 1970s, Reform Judaism had taken official positions that were very pro-gay… We didn't know that! Nobody ever talked about it! There were a series of resolutions at the national level, and

Reform Judaism was becoming increasingly progressive. But we didn't have a clue.

Members of the downtown synagogue explained to us that they needed to find a synagogue in the suburbs where, if their members kissed each other Good Shabbos at the end of the service (couples routinely kiss each other at the end of a service), people wouldn't be looking at them going, "*Gasp!* They're gay!"

They didn't really have to convince us.

We went to our rabbi. And this was the first time that we basically came out. We said that both of our kids were gay and asked if we could invite members of the gay & lesbian synagogue to Friday night services.

He said that of course we would be welcoming. And Helene and I ended up being a two-person committee to help the synagogue become affirming. Our first project was to start a library shelf...

HELENE: So, Simon and I went downtown. It was the first time we went to a gay bookstore...

SIMON: That such materials are mainstream now is just another symbol of the progress made where we live.

HELENE: In those days, to go into a gay bookstore, it was like... The two of us walked in there. My God! It was a new experience for us.

We picked out books for kids coming out to their parents, books for parents when their kids come out to them. Lesbian rabbis. Families. All different kinds of families. We filled a whole bookshelf for our synagogue library, so kids and families in our Temple had those resources.

Max once said to me, even if it didn't come from school or anywhere else, that if our synagogue had given him any clue at all, it would have *changed his life...* if they had just mentioned, "There are times when two men or two women can get married," it would have changed the world for him, because, you know, your church, or your synagogue, or your mosque, is where you get your moral compass.

We had people from the gay & lesbian synagogue at a congregational dinner. They spoke at the service, and we spoke at the service about the fact that both of our sons were gay.

Suddenly, *everybody* in our congregation knew. All of our friends came to hug us. It was our coming out. Our family's coming out. We had a family coming out service, if you can imagine this!

SIMON: We had let some people know we were going to do this. A lot of people came to the service, and huge numbers of our friends, because we had been members of the congregation for decades. And I just assumed, *they are coming to support us.* Well, yeah, but then, at the Shabbat reception after the service, everybody was talking about their gay college roommate, their gay cousin, their gay relative.

It was a coming out *for the entire community.*

HELENE: One person in particular told us that she had a lesbian sister. We were close, but she had never mentioned it. I felt like, *gee,* if all of these people had told us, it would have made our journey a lot easier.

SIMON: The power of out is huge.

HELENE: Yes, the power of out is huge!

Then a lesbian couple joined our congregation. And they said, "We should have a presence at Pride."

So, we had a table at the Pride Festival. It was unbelievable. We had kids coming up and hugging us. The stories... Oh, just so many kids who couldn't come out. Or, who had come out, and they were rejected by their parents, or they felt estranged from Judaism. It was just…

In those days, first of all, Conservative and Orthodox synagogues were not accepting at all, and many Reform synagogues were not.

SIMON: They effectively were "don't ask don't tell."

HELENE: One story made an impression on me that I will never forget. There were crowds of people walking up and down at the Festival, and this tall trans woman comes over to me, wearing a big Jewish star, and she is looking at our sign that says, "We are a welcoming and caring community."

She's crying. And she says, "Oh my God, *welcoming?* I was bar mitzvahed at a Temple of the same name in a different city… I have never been back to a synagogue. I never thought I would be accepted at a synagogue, and now I see from your sign that I would be welcomed."

She was just crying her eyes out and hugging me. It was something that just *changed* me.

We had a lot of moving experiences like that.

So, we became the voice and the face of "gaydom" at our synagogue

At one point, the rabbi received a letter from a long-time member (with whom Simon had served on the Board of Trustees years earlier). The rabbi gave it to us in case we wanted to respond. The gist of the letter was, "Why are you welcoming these people to our congregation? They are going to harm our children. We should not be welcoming these kinds of people to our synagogue."

Simon and I, we sat down…

SIMON: You wrote the letter.

HELENE: I wrote the letter. A four-page response, talking about our sons and their whole journey. I ended it by saying, "You said, in your note, that we shouldn't welcome these people because they will harm our children. These people *are* our children."

Nothing more was said, and that was the end of that.

After Max came out, one day we were talking, and he said, "I always knew you and Dad would love me unconditionally. That was never, ever an issue for me; I just didn't want to disappoint you."

I say to my friends now, "I used to say, bring home a nice Jewish girl. Then I would say, bring home a nice Jewish boy. And then I would say, "Bring home *a nice*."

And they did! I have two wonderful sons-in-law whom I absolutely love.

So, life changes you. But my kids never doubted that we loved them. They knew.

SIMON: Another thing about child raising… You do the best you can with your kids. You love them, but then, at some point, you have to trust that you have done everything you can, and that they are going to live their lives. And you have to respect that.

It is very important to say this out loud because, sometimes, when the truth is told—even if you've never really thought about it before—when you hear it, you know it's true.

HELENE: Max graduated with honors and became an educator. He became the first teacher in his school to come out. That was really big. He said he wanted to be a role model for other kids like him, to show you can be happy and be out. He has been teaching for twenty years, and he has helped numerous LGBTQ+ students and their parents.

Both of our sons got married a few years ago. Max and his husband both wanted to start a family. But Max's husband came from a family that was not accepting until several years later. So, they struggled with that as a couple for a while.

I had resigned myself that I would not be a grandparent. It was hard. I thought that I would just love other people's grandchildren, and I never thought that I would ever be a grandparent.

SIMON: That's one reason that I probably took Max's coming out harder... if you have one gay son, the other one will probably provide grandchildren, and then fine.

But Max had always told me that he wanted to be a father. I knew that he wanted it, and if life developed in that way...

And in time, it did.

I will take yes for an answer!

HELENE: You know, I have learned a lot of lessons. Most of all, I have learned that you don't know what path life is going to take... You cannot predict how things are going to work out.

SIMON: When Max and his husband planned to adopt their first child, the idea that I might not have biological descendants was disappointing for a moment, but I got over that *very* quickly and developed a different perspective. To the extent that we survive beyond our deaths, it is not through our DNA. It is through relationships and memory. We can do something to help other people, or to help change society for the better. *That's* how you live on.

Our relationship with our grandchildren has surely confirmed for me that love makes a family.

HELENE: After Max's daughter was born, we were watching her at our house. She was napping upstairs in Max's old room when he came to pick her up. I was behind him on the stairs. He was standing in the doorway of his old bedroom and he was looking at his daughter, sleeping. Max, who is rarely emotional, started to cry. The tears were rolling down his face, and he said, "So many nights, I stayed in bed crying, never thinking that I would ever have a family. And there is my daughter, sleeping in my room."

He was just looking at her, and just remembering all those years thinking that he would never have a family of his own, when that was what he really wanted.

It's an enormously strong person who can get through that. I think, how would I have been if I had realized I was attracted to women? I don't know how I would've managed. I don't think I'm that strong. That takes a lot of courage and bravery... All those years, that my sons did that alone.

You know, I don't understand people who want to discriminate against people who are different than themselves. I mean, it is really a tough road for these kids. Or adults. Especially for those who are transgender.

And yet when you hear the language of our politics... It is so hurtful.

Max is the most wonderful father with his two kids now, and it's just the role he was meant to have.

Every time we go to pick up our grandson up from pre-school, the teachers say Max and his husband are the most loving, the most caring, the most giving parents.

And Ross is also doing well in his life. He also is married. He is a writer. Through his work, he is trying to make change.

I would have never been the person I am if my children had not come out. I've met so many people I would never have met, and we've had so many positive experiences. These experiences have opened doors and let me walk in places I would never have gone.

SIMON: There is one phrase that's very important for parents: We have to remember that children are ends in and of themselves, not the means to an end. I think a lot of people, when they go to have children, they think "I'm going to replicate myself. This is what I want."

But children can never be seen as "means". They always have to be seen as ends in and of themselves.

HELENE: The important thing is for parents of young children to always tell their kids: I may not like your actions, but I will always love you. There may be something that you do that I don't approve of, but I will never stop loving you.

SIMON: But, in the LGBTQ+ area, there's another step. "I may not approve of what you do, but I also may be wrong in not approving of it." Because I think one of the problems that a lot of families have is that they grew up in communities where anything other than being a cisgender heterosexual is just unthinkable because it's against God's word, is "unnatural," or whatever.

That interferes with people really being able to evolve and to always be loving.

My own personal opinion is that any religious community which cannot accept the proposition that they may not know everything sets itself up for unnecessary loss.

The world is a complex place. Our job is to help make a complex place *as loving as it can be* for as many people as we can.

HELENE: Yes, yes.

6:   JENNY GOLDSTEIN—
This is kind of a rebirth story—
a rebirth of the child.

Like many of the parents whose voices are recorded here, Jenny Goldstein became an activist through her experience of raising an LGBTQ+ child. Jenny is a long-time educator who helped create the curriculum of a popular middle-school magnet program in Montgomery County, Maryland. She has been an ally for her child and for students whose parents are not affirming. She has also worked to create safe spaces for LGBTQ+ kids in Montgomery County.

Mordechai, the middle of three children and 24 at the time of our interview, is nonbinary transgender and uses ze/zir pronouns. Although ze did not come out until college, Jenny realized that her child was probably LGBTQ+ in some way from the time ze was in kindergarten. Her experience with LGBTQ+ people at that point had been limited, but attending a Unity Ceremony that took place before the legalization of gay marriage led her to self-examination—an important acknowledgement because it speaks to the power of exposure.

In her interview, Jenny describes witnessing her child's long struggle with self-presentation. While appearing as a tomboy is acceptable for girls up to a certain age, gender begins to be policed by middle school. Mordechai's aversion to feminine clothing gradually became more problematic. In high school, desperate to fit in, ze began to dress as female, but Jenny knew that this new self-presentation rang false and that her child was miserable.

Jenny and her husband nurtured Mordechai through this difficult time. Ze finally came out in college, and when ze elected to have top surgery, Jenny supported zir through that experience.

In this interview, Jenny talks candidly about her experience coping with her child's name change and what it means to have "19 years of memories of the other person."

Yet, with great certainty, Jenny sees Mordechai as true to who ze has always been and celebrates zir self-discovery and courage. The day Mordechai legally changed zir name felt like "a rebirth of this child."

Jenny warns that parents who don't understand and who reject their LGBTQ+ children put their children's lives on the line and asks, "*Do they want to bury their kid?*"

"I would much, much, much rather have a happy Mordechai then the miserable girl that I had."

As a kid, I babysat for one of my younger cousins. When she was in college, she came out as gay, and I was very close to her mom. That was the first close LGBTQ+ person that I knew, but it didn't rattle me as much as it rattled her mom—and rattled my parents. My dad was like, "All those theater people! She's just doing it because she's majoring in theater, and that's just what they do!"

I went out to California for their Unity Ceremony because marriage wasn't legal then. That was 15 years ago. That was the first time I was within the minority in a community, at that wedding. I remember sitting there thinking, "I have to re-examine," because I was a little uncomfortable. I was marveling at how brave these people all were to live their authentic lives.

Mordechai, growing up, was always a tomboy. And I thought I had a gay girl, probably from kindergarten or first grade on. I would make sure when I spoke to the kids to say things like, "If you choose to marry somebody, make sure they treat you well." I wouldn't say "boy", "girl." I would just put it that way, thinking in my head, *one of my kids is gay.*

Mordechai came out during college when ze was 19.

Ze was always a very sensitive kid growing up, as was I. I held zir back from starting kindergarten... ze just cried a lot and was very sensitive as a preschooler, and I just thought, "I've never taught any kid whose parents were upset that they held their kid back."

You could mistake Mordechai for a boy, definitely, from third grade up. In high school there was about a year and a half ze grew zir hair out and started presenting as feminine. My mother-in-law was like, "See, it was just a phase." And I was like, "No. I'm not convinced."

Mordechai had a boyfriend, but ze was miserable. Ze wanted to go to a boarding school and to get out of town. What I didn't know was that Mordechai was being bullied in school, and that's why Mordechai started trying to just blend in and dress more feminine.

Ze had not come out to us at that point. Zir dad and I knew that it was a possibility, and we were okay with it. We had actually talked with our pediatrician years before because I was worried about zir being bullied in middle school. But it was high school where things started to unravel. We were not aware of it, but Mordechai was becoming anorexic. Right under my eyes. I did not see it. My husband and my oldest child are very tall and lanky, and I just thought ze was thinning out. Still, when ze decided to graduate early, we were supportive because I just knew something wasn't right.

Ze chose Macalester College in Minnesota. My husband went with zir to go visit, and he called me and said, "If ze can get in, this is where Mordechai is going to go." He mentioned the nongendered housing and the rainbow flags. It wasn't that Mordechai was out, but we were like, "Okay, this is a safe place if this is who Mordechai is."

And Mordechai was always looking out for other people's rights and things. Ze was always an ally, so it wasn't an unusual choice.

When Mordechai came out, ze called from college and basically said, "I'm gay, or I'm not sure." And I said, "Okay, okay, we are good."

To be honest, I didn't remember that ze came out twice until about three weeks ago. It didn't stick in my mind because it was kind of unremarkable by that point. Some parents are like, "I can tell you what day it was, what time it was."

But I didn't realize there were two coming outs until Mordechai corrected me a couple weeks ago. And I said, "I think I don't remember because it was a good thing, and by that point, we had assumed."

Ze called the second time and said, "I just wanted to let you know, everyone here has been calling me Mordechai." That's the name we would have used had ze been male assigned at birth.

That name is not even close to zir birth name.

And then ze said, "I'm going to be putting it on Facebook in about ten minutes." And I said *okay*, and I was pacing around, and all I could think of was that before we had Mordechai, the dead name was for a favorite aunt of mine, and I had always told my husband that if we had a girl, this was the name I wanted.

So, I was mourning the loss of the name more than that my kid was coming out transgender. Like I said, I love that name. Even before we got married, there were four cousins named after this aunt, but they had it as a middle name, and Mordechai had it as a first name.

I was like, "Okay, I have ten minutes to talk to my parents," who were in their 80s at that time. And my husband's mom. They were all on Facebook, and we wanted them to hear on the phone, from us, before they read about it.

I assured Mordechai we love zir, and asked, "Is there anything else you need?" Ze got off the phone pretty quickly after that.

My husband wasn't home... I called him up, and I said, "Okay, this is happening. You've got to call your mom. I'm going to call my parents."

For him, it was a matter of adjusting, though there was never an issue of accepting. He was mourning the loss of the person who he thought he was going to have as a kid. We talked about it a lot. He's very honest. You know, he just said he was feeling sad about it.

I kept saying that I understood that he felt sad for what would have been, but let's look at how sad and miserable Mordechai was. I would rather have a happier, more grounded Mordechai than the other.

My husband said that it was one of those things where logically he understood that, and he had to work through it.

And now, he's there.

I pretty much had already reconciled myself... When I would go into zir 3rd grade bedroom, I don't know what kind of bomber airplane poster was up there! And if you look at any pictures of Mordechai as a kid, the images look like a little boy named Mordechai.

So, I wasn't mourning because, for the most part, I never had a traditional girl as a middle kid.

It was more the name. The hurdle for me was getting the name correct and getting the pronouns correct. That was the hardest part for me.

What's ironic now is that once ze started to medically transition, there was some solace in that strangers would think that my kid was a boy, and that this meant ze would be safer than they were as a girl.

I have a friend who is a transgender woman who has to *remember* when she sees a car that is broken down: As a guy she wouldn't give it a second thought, and as a woman, she has to keep that threat in the back of her head.

I still worry, yes of course. I'm the neurotic Jewish mother, but I will say that I do worry less because ze presents as male. With the testosterone, and top surgery, Mordechai really passes. So, I'm kind of confident as far as zir safety.

Because of the network of friends that I have met through Mordechai and through volunteer work I've done, I worry more about my non-binary or trans friends who, when they walk in, somebody might give them a second look. I worry for their safety.

So, my parents, when Mordechai came out… neither of them was against it. I don't think they quite understood it. And for sure, my dad really didn't understand it and kept saying, "I love Mordechai, but who is going to love Mordechai? Why would Mordechai want to do that? I don't understand."

Mordechai is non-binary transgender. So just getting the gender identity and sexual identification and all of that right seemed overwhelming to them. And I just said, "You don't have to do anything; you don't have to understand it. Just talk to Mordechai the same way you would before. It is the same kid. It is a happier kid."

My mom, every year, for the kids' birthdays, would get what we called, "the bottomless bag of clothes." She loved to shop, and it was like Mary Poppins's bag. Just when you thought there was no more, more would come out. From the time ze was little, she would buy stuff from the boys' section of Target for Mordechai without blinking. It was just that's who ze was.

My mother-in-law felt it was a phase. She was never supportive when we let Mordechai dress as a boy. One time, we were on a family vacation and there was a formal night. Mordechai, who was thirteen at the time, was wearing black pants and a sweater, which was already out of his comfort zone and something ze had put on for my sake. Debi, my youngest, loves to dress up. My mother-in-law went over to Mordechai and said, "When are you going to dress pretty like your sister?"

Mordechai came over to me with tears in zir eyes and said, *grandma just said this.*

I said, "You look fine. You look appropriate. Grandma was wrong." My husband went and talked to her.

My parents live up here and so would see Mordechai much more often. I think that was part of it. But also, my mother-in-law was definitely southern. I think it was a combination of southern upbringing, but also, how was she going to explain it to her friends, that her granddaughter is her grandson?

Towards the end of her life, one time, she said to me, "I don't think Mordechai should have gone to that Macalester College." And I was like, "Why?" And she was like, "Because I don't think he would be a him." I told her, "I think the writing was kind of on the wall already..."

In our family, everybody got "grandma'ed," so I would point out to Mordechai that Debi was told that she was the pretty one, not the smart one. Everybody got their zing.

When Mordechai got out of Montgomery County after all of the bullying, ze just had a different level of self-acceptance....

For anyone who saw zir growing up, it wasn't a shock when ze transitioned. Mordechai was always Mordechai. The other parents who knew zir weren't surprised.

Some parents *would* say things like, "You are very forward-thinking to let your kid dress the way they want." I always felt that if Mordechai's way of getting dressed up was to wear a sweater and pants when most people were wearing dresses, that's okay.

When Mordechai was in middle school, ze had about an hour-long bus drive. One day ze called me, almost in tears, and said, "The bus aide says I'm not a girl." I said, "Put him on the phone." And I heard zir say, "My mom wants to talk to you." And I heard the person say, "I don't need to talk to your mother. Go sit with all the boys."

I said, "I will be there when the bus pulls up."

I made sure I had my Montgomery County Schools ID on. The door opened, and I stepped on the bus, and I saw the aide. I said, "Excuse me, are you the person who wouldn't talk to me on the phone, to confirm that my daughter, old name, is a girl?" I wasn't yelling, but I was very direct and firm in a way my kids had never heard... I didn't know this at the time, but Mordechai was scared of this side of the mama bear.

Afterwards, the aide apologized to me, and I said, "You need to apologize to my daughter." She did, and Mordechai kind of nodded. Ze was a wreck. The carpool kids got in the car, and they were like, *"That was awesome!"* Mordechai was getting high-fives from the kids on the bus.

Our Jewish community was very accepting. Our cantor at our synagogue suggested (after I had bought Mordechai boots and a skirt), that ze could wear a pants suit for zir bat mitzvah. Because even our Rabbi and Cantor knew... that's just who Mordechai was.

When Mordechai came out, we got nothing but support. As soon as Mordechai put it on Facebook, I also posted, "I am proud to announce that *old name* is from this moment forward Mordechai, and we applaud Mordechai."

I got so many messages of support. If people weren't supportive, they didn't say it to my face.

One thing that was pretty cool is that Mordechai came out to his siblings before ze did to my husband and me. At first, I was a little upset about it, and then I thought, "Wow, if they have that kind of relationship, that's pretty awesome." I needed to let go of my ego on that one.

Mordechai would get upset when I would say the dead name or the wrong pronouns...

I've got memories of 19 years of the other person. I know you are the same person. But when I pull that name out... How many times have I called you kids the wrong names? I even used the dog's name one time... so that happens authentically.

The siblings, the cousins, they all got the name and pronouns without making a mistake, and I had to point out to Mordechai, "It's not that I don't love the name (I was going to name you that anyhow), but I don't know who Mordechai is."

As far as the pronouns, that was something else for me to learn. I was familiar with "they/them," but "ze/zir" was harder. Ironically, the only time I'll mess up Morde-chai's pronouns, even now, is when all three kids are around. Because then, it's three different sets of pronouns. It can be hard to keep track. It's like a punch in the gut to me when I get it wrong because Mordechai goes, "ZE."

But I have learned not to be overly apologetic: you correct, and you move on. But I am so super-sensitive. When I mess up, it's like, *agh*. And then it's like a self-fulfilling prophecy: I'm thinking so hard, "ze/zir." Don't say "she," and then "she" falls out, because I'm just so nervous about it.

When Mordechai was younger, I had asked the pediatrician, "Do I say something to zir?" I didn't want to make an assumption because of how my kid was dressing. I didn't know if I should say, "It's okay if you are gay." And the pediatrician said, "Just keep doing what you are doing. Follow your child's lead."

But once Mordechai was out, we had a lot of what, in education, we call "courageous conversations," some of them because Mordechai felt like we were not quick enough to get the pronouns and the name correct without errors, and we felt that ze was being too harsh on us. So, there were a lot more conversations.

The funny epilogue here is that my husband's side of the family now has five different gay couples. When we have a family gathering, we have "the queer picture." And they all get together. So, Mordechai has an amazing position: everyone else is just gay. It's pretty astoundingly wonderful that they all have this network within the family, which is very meaningful.

Maybe as more and more people come out, maybe more families will see that *you do have people.*

College kids definitely get "chosen families" to replace rejecting or unkind biological families, and if somebody is toxic, then—it's hard to think of—but, you don't need to be around that person because they are not living your life.

I really recommend for parents to get support to understand their kid. Without understanding, there is no acceptance; there is no getting that there is no "gay or trans agenda." I feel like these kids are intelligent, strong, and courageous to live their authentic lives.

If you talk to any mom, every birth story is different. This is kind of a rebirth story— a rebirth of the child. When we came from the steps of Baltimore to get zir name legally changed, I was like, "Wow, that was so much easier than the first time when I walked out with a birth certificate!"

We have a sense of humor about it, but I don't joke about stuff unless Mordechai does.

So, I say, really, just follow your child's lead, and have those conversations, and if you can't navigate those together, get the support of a professional, or even a school counselor. If you don't have insurance and your child is in middle school or high school, really, the counselors are a great resource for helping you and the child navigate your way.

One thing I was worried about was "What's it going to be like when my child is in a relationship?" Mordechai has been in a relationship for about a year, and I absolutely adore the person Mordechai is dating, so it's like, *that was easy.*

What's sad is that zir partner's parents are not supportive. They think that their child is going to Hell and needs to be saved by God. So, it's a very different type of situation. Mordechai's partner is the coolest person ever, and I feel sad about this.

I always pointed out to my dad that some of the hetero-normal relationships we've seen in our family — cousins who ended up in divorce — were tremendously dysfunctional. Relationships with two Jewish, heterosexual people. Just because somebody is not a religion, or not in an orientation that you are familiar with, does not mean that they are inherently bad, or good.

I've always said, I just hope that whoever my kids end up with, that they treat them well and make them happy.

Mordechai eventually moved to Boston, where ze lives now, because a lot of the Massachusetts laws are very LGBTQ+ friendly. Medically, the Boston area is tremendously supportive of the trans-community. So, it's not a matter of finding a doctor that would work with non-binary, trans person, it's which one do you want?

When Mordechai decided to have top surgery, a lot of it was covered by zir insurance there. I came up for the surgery last summer, when ze was 24.

We were waiting to go in for the preop, and my husband and I were on the phone. His voice was all quivery, and I was like, "This is a *happy* surgery."

Mordechai had been binding for about five years, and we had discussed just how uncomfortable, and medically, just how bad that is. Mordechai and I were like, *"This is going to be a party."*

We were so excited… they did it laparoscopically. Ze was small chested, thank goodness… so surgery was way less invasive.

Your kid is your kid… I can't fathom any religion that would put your kid's identity over you loving them. I've talked to a number of kids because I became kind of the teacher that kids knew was an ally. They would come to me, and I'd hear that their parents think they are too young to know, or it's a phase.

That's the hardest part: the ones who are under 18 where parents take the position, "My house, my rules. You will not dress that way; you will not do this."

I have tried to help the kids to understand that, "Things will change when you are 18. In the meantime, take over as much of your narrative now as you can. Tell your parents to reach out for support because if your church doesn't offer support, there are plenty of churches and places that do."

I would much much, much, much rather have a happy Mordechai then the miserable girl that I had. I just don't get it when parents are rejecting. I feel sad for both the kid and the parent. The kid is getting the consequences.

As a kid, you don't choose who your parents are. And parents, they may not understand, but the parent needs to find support so they *can* understand because, in many cases, their kid's life is on the line.

Look at the statistics. Suicide. Chemical dependency. Homelessness. I don't think that's what any parent would want for their child.

So, do they want to bury their kid?

One of the things that I said before Mordechai even came out is that, as a parent, you must surf the waves because you will drown swimming against them. I've got three kids who are very different. They all have their strengths. Their uniquenesses.

As a parent, you follow their lead, you support them, and you help them navigate.

But to tell a kid, "You are too young to know who you are," or, "You are going to go to Hell because of who you are," or, "You are a freak," or just all these awful things that parents say...

For this to come from come from the people who are supposed to accept them and love them no matter what...

When the world comes at them, those are the parents who are going to, I don't want to say *betray them*...

But.

Some parents turn their backs. That's what I've learned.

7: MORDECHAI GOLDSTEIN——
Parents who do not accept their LGBTQ+ children are missing out on having a relationship with the fullest, happiest version of their child.

Mordechai is a twenty-something trans person who identified from an early age as male after being assigned female at birth. Mordechai is nonbinary and uses the gender-neutral pronouns ze/zir, similar in usage to she/her or he/him.

Starting at three or four, ze secretly referred to zirself as "he." Dressing as a tomboy helped to mask zir discomfort with presenting as female, but the process of facing a female puberty was terrifying.

Zir narrative is powerful because it describes, firsthand, what it feels like and what it means to experience gender dysphoria (the sense of unease a person has when their biological sex does not match their gender identity), both internally and in terms of dealing with the external world, including family and peers.

In light of current efforts to regulate athletics in ways that exclude trans people, Mordechai's account of zir involvement in sports up until sixth grade is striking. Though ze was still several years from coming out, participating in girls' teams that did not match zir gender orientation was awkward, and opportunities to join the boy's team, or to participate in karate, a non-gendered sport, took on real significance.

The transition from a diverse, multi-ethnic middle school to a primarily Caucasian, Protestant high school meant that Mordechai, as a Jewish and as a gender-noncon-forming person, experienced intersectional discrimination. At one point, zir peers came up with the insult "dyke-kike," which haunted Mordechai for some time. Zir account highlights how antisemitism and hatred towards LGBTQ+ people thrive in the same environment.

Though many young people come out—at least to themselves—in high school, Mordechai instead worked very hard to "outgrow" boyishness, per expectations, and to lessen zir experience of exclusion and bullying, which had become relentless.

This was a very miserable years-long process, and the effort to conform increased Mordechai's social vulnerability. Seeking belonging, ze entered into an abusive relationship, which exacerbated feelings of despair and hopelessness.

Understanding their child's desperation, Mordechai's parents helped zir to utilize Montgomery College as a pathway to early high school graduation. Attending a four-year liberal arts school, Mordechai began to meet others who shared some of zir experiences. Finally in a safe place, Mordechai came out—surprising zirself, but not the people who knew and loved zir.

Mordechai's Jewish community's embrace of zir is another meaningful part of zir story. Ze describes zir re-naming ceremony, a culturally significant event, and a healing "full-circle" moment. For zir, this powerful gesture of acceptance by zir synagogue and family marked "one of the most significant days of my trans journey."

Mordechai's description of zir LGBTQ+ positive family is heartening, and ze makes a point of emphasizing how meaningful this support has been, especially the responses of zir parents and siblings. Offering insight into continued discrimination faced by LGBTQ+ people in the workplace and in society at large, Mordechai stresses how parental acceptance can literally be a life-and-death matter for young LGBTQ+ people in a world that makes it harder for them to meet their basic needs.

Without support from his family, "I don't want to think about what would've happened."

Zir narrative begins shortly before the start of middle school.

By fourth grade, I was wearing "boys'" clothes full time. My mom let me start venturing into the boys' section of Target. I got my wish!

My grandmother, my mom's mom, every birthday, she would do what we called "the bottomless bag," and she would fill it with clothes and those were your clothes for the year. I think it was my tenth or eleventh birthday that she just got me boys' clothes, *and it wasn't a thing*!

My mom... it was such a non-issue for her, and for that whole family.

I tried a lot of different sports growing up. Soccer, and basketball. But I didn't enjoy being on all-girls' teams. I played on a girls' basketball team for a year, and I got hit in the face every single game.

The next year I played soccer, again, in a girls' team, and I hated it.

After that, I just stopped doing team sports. I loved karate because it wasn't gendered; the uniform was the same thing for female and male, and it was a very gender-neutral experience, and so it didn't matter in that way. That was a big part of 5th grade for me... I got my black belt.

Fifth grade was also when we did our family-life unit, when you learn about sex ed. I remember being absolutely terrified of going through puberty. I was *terrified* of it. I specifically wrote that in my journal at one point. I didn't want to get my period... it was being upheld as the rite of passage for a young woman. I knew, "I don't want that. I don't want a young woman's rite of passage because that means I have to become a young woman."

One of my mom's very good friends from when she was growing up was a swimmer and had a very small chest. You could barely see that she had a chest when she wore a shirt, and my mom has a very big chest. And I remember writing in my journal at one point, "I hope I can have a chest like Joan's, because that's one less thing to worry about."

I have been a writer my whole life. In my internal dialogue/monologue with myself, I was referring to myself with he/him pronouns starting in 3rd or 4th grade. That's what was going on internally, and I remember anytime I made a birthday cake wish or had any kind of wish opportunity, that was what I wanted, "I wish I was a boy, I wish I was a boy."

I pretty much never got a hard time from my peers for the way I looked in my Montgomery County magnet middle school. I'm one of the few people in the world who loved 7th grade. I felt like I belonged… I had a community.

The first day of school was always a thing: "This is the day I have to tell all of my teachers I'm a girl." I liked it when they called me a boy. It was very affirming. But I knew I had to be honest and couldn't maintain that gig all year, so I just addressed it up front.

In 7th grade, a teacher whom I'm still in touch with said, "You've probably heard this before, but [birth name] is a pretty unusual name for a boy." And I said, "Actually, I'm a girl." That's a joke she and I have now. When I put my name change up on Facebook, she wrote, "I always thought your name was a little unusual for you." And so, it was a very, kind of, full-circle, poetic moment.

So, it wasn't a problem, except for the odd substitute teacher, or a security guard thinking I was a boy going into the girls' bathroom—people who did not know me.

My mother took me to the pediatrician, and I just thought, "This is your sixth-grade doctor's appointment." But, I found out later, she had told him, "Something is going on and I'm not equipped to navigate this. What should I do?" And he asked me a lot of questions about gender stuff.

I remember I was hiding something in the answers I was giving him… that I wanted to be a boy. *"He can't find out."*

Apparently the pediatrician went back to my mom and basically said, "She seems happy with who she is, just let her keep doing it." And so, I did.

I remember when I wanted to get my hair cut for the first time… My mom said, "No, you can't because you are going to look like a boy." And that, to me, meant, "OH. I can't do that. I can't *want* to do that. I can't want to look like a boy."

We had a LOT of conversations about this after I came out. And she said, "I was afraid that you were going to get bullied."

Her intentions were good. You can't be perfect.

In Hebrew School, there were more girls than boys. Whenever we did a team thing, they would always divide us up, boys vs girls. And I was always volunteering, "Oh, what a shame, I'll go play on the boy's team to even it out."

And it became a thing: it was always, "Mordechai and the boys against the girls."

Hebrew School was very difficult for me because it was such a gendered experience… dressing up in girl clothing for Schul or for High Holidays was a *very* hard thing for me. I remember feeling, especially during Yom Kippur, really guilty—not in the way you are supposed to feel guilty… This is the day you are supposed to be honest, but I felt as though, "I'm just lying."

But that was my little affirmation… that every couple of weeks, I got to be on the boys' team.

My mom would pick out clothes for me that were kind of like the "tomboy" style of clothes, but from the girls' section. As soon as I knew it was from the girls' section, I didn't want it.

L.L. Bean catalogues fascinated me because they have no gendering of their kids' clothes. And I would go through the catalog and circle the stuff I wanted, even though I knew my family never shopped there. It was a thing: "These are the clothes I am allowed to want without feeling like I am not supposed to."

It wasn't anything about maleness that I coveted; it's just what felt right. It was the clothes that, when I put them on, I was like, "That's me. That's what I look like."

When I started high school, I realized I had been sheltered by exposure... I had come from this diverse middle school. My mom used to joke that my friendship group looked like a public school health textbook.

The things that made me different were what made me cool there.

So, I got to my significantly less diverse high school and was blindsided... I got teased for the way I looked, the way I dressed, for being Jewish. I got teased for being a nerd.

The bullying I experienced was mostly verbal and included a lot of intentional exclusion. People would say things about me behind my back, or pretend to say things behind my back, but in a way so that I could hear it. One girl in the theater club was handing out invitations to her birthday party and made a point to make visible eye contact with me and not give me one. So much little stuff like that.

I remember taking AP government in 10th grade and my teacher saying something that was racist. I raised my hand and said, "I feel like that's maybe not an appropriate way to say that." I was trying to navigate this as a 15-year-old. The kid behind me said, "Oh my God, shut the fuck up."

That kid sat behind me in *three* classes, and the comments, and things like taking my pencils... it was just constant.

My brother got me a hooded sweatshirt that said "University of Maryland" on it, but it was in Hebrew letters. That day in band, a kid said, "Oh, you're a dyke and a kike. You're a dyke-kike." A bunch of the kids laughed, and that "nickname" kind of stuck around for the rest of my time in high school...

And so, I did not wear that hoodie again until the end of my sophomore year in college, not for three-and-a-half years.

By sophomore year, I had one friend. I looked into transferring, but Montgomery County intentionally makes it very hard to transfer to avoid "white flight." My mom made a joke: "They make it hard to avoid white flight, but not the kind you're trying to do." Which was to flee the white people.

There was a dress-up day, and I decided, "Oh, I'm going to dress up for the shock factor." I wore gauchos and a fitted blouse that was halfway buttoned with a camisole under it. So, I was dressed the way a lot of girls dressed just to come to school. And people were *so much nicer* to me that day. The whole day I wanted to crawl out of my skin... this was supposed to be a *gag*; that's how I meant it.

Ironically, or maybe fittingly, the first day that I wore girls' clothes by choice to school was Halloween my sophomore year of high school. Sometimes, poetry just writes itself.

Everybody had always talked about how I was going to outgrow looking like a boy someday. And I figured, "Well, it is time for me to outgrow this." And that's what I did. It *worked*. People started being nicer to me. And I made friends. Or, I was accepted into a friend group.

I still had my hair short. There was this boy I liked whom I was "friends" with... he was the closest thing I had to a best friend there, and he told me, "You would be hot now, if you just didn't have boy hair." He was the person whose opinion I cared about. So, I thought, "Well, I guess I should grow my hair out."

The first time I wore those clothes by choice, my family commented, "Oh, you are dressed nicely today." And I just let it sit at that. My mom was trying to help, and she asked me if I wanted to go to Target with her. "If you want to look at clothes." She wanted to let me try stuff out.

But my dad's side of the family, the side that had always given me a hard time about the way I dressed, commented, "Oh, you look *so much better* now." The backhanded compliment...

My brother's really good friend asked, "Mordechai, when did you start dressing like a girl?" And my brother commented, "Yeah, I was wondering about that, but I didn't want to say anything."

(I always refer to myself as Mordechai when I talk about the past.)

So, I said, "Oh, I just felt like it was time."

My change in appearance *was very much congratulated* by my social environment. Especially at school, including from my teachers, which to this day I find so inappropriate. To comment on a kid's appearance that way. That was 10th grade, and at that point, I was trying to get the Hell out of that school.

I was struggling socially and although I was doing well academically, I was bored out of my mind. My mom came upstairs one night when I was doing my AP government homework, and I was crying. She thought something had happened socially and was surprised when I just ranted to her about how boring school was, how we just read from a textbook and then repeated it back in class.

I was just so infuriated by the school environment. We started thinking about dual enrollment, but then one day my mom asked, "What if you graduated early and just got out?"

Before that, whenever we saw some story in the newspaper about some kid who went to college early, she would always say, "You only get one childhood. You have your whole life to be an adult and to be smart and accomplished and successful, but you only get one childhood."

So that was very ingrained in me; graduating early wasn't even on my radar because you only get one chance to be a kid. So, I said to my mom, "But I don't want to waste my childhood." And she looked at me… and said, "But are you really having a childhood worth having at this point?"

And that, for me, was the moment where I realized, *"Oh, she gets how bad this is."*

I will never forget that moment, and I will never forget that those were the exact words she said because I was just blown away by how perceptive it was.

So, we pulled all this stuff together for me to graduate early... the last year of high school I was taking 11th and 12th grade classes at the same time and taking online classes at Montgomery College.

I was also in a relationship with that guy I liked. I didn't have the words for it at the time or an understanding of what was going on, but I was being sexually and emotionally abused.

And with the combination of stress from school, and from that, and from dysphoria... I developed an eating disorder. I look back on it now, and I know that was super dysphoria-tied, specifically about my having thighs.

So, I graduated early and got to college, and I thought, *"Whew, we are ok..."*

The first year of college, I just kept doing the girl thing because, "I outgrew this." That's what I thought: I outgrew it.

My first year, no one was out and trans. Then sophomore year, I was in an English class with this person, a first-year who was trans. And there were four freshmen who were trans.

One thing I'll never forget is when that change of wardrobe was happening from before, going to donate my old clothes. I put on a black pair of black-and-white cargo shorts that had been mine and looked in the mirror and thought, "I can't wear these anymore."

That's an image I will never forget. *"That's what I look like...* That's not what I'm supposed to look like."

But then I got to hear about other people having this same kind of experience. I would listen to them, and I kept thinking about that image and that moment. That was definitely a feeling of grief when I looked in the mirror... That always stayed with me.

In the spring of my sophomore year, there was a trans history event offered by the women's gender and sexuality studies department. People introduced themselves with their pronouns, which I had done a million times, but for some reason that night, I said "they."

And, as soon as it came out of my mouth, I realized, "There is no going back. We have opened that door. We are acknowledging this publicly."

And it was the first time I acknowledged it *internally*, too.

I don't even remember what was going through my head before I said it. I hadn't thought about it before; it was just like, "This is happening now."

I came back to my dorm, and I was furious with myself. I remember taking a shower and crying in anger.

One of my really good friends had come out as trans when we were in ninth grade. My family had been very supportive of him, which was good because that was my sign, "Okay, my parents are cool with that."

I had known several trans people at this point, and this was not supposed to be my thing. This was April, and I had just started taking medication that January for PTSD. I had just started getting more intensive mental health care for my eating disorder, so I had a lot of other stuff going on at that point, and this was not supposed to be on the list.

But I knew, "I can't go back."

I told my roommates a couple days later… And they just said, "Okay. Do you want us to call you the same name?" Then they asked, "Do you want us to tell other people or to correct other people when they refer to you?"

They handled it just exactly the way you are supposed to. It was exactly what I needed to hear.

Soon after that, I realized, "I just need to tell my parents and get it over with." I knew they were going to be fine with it, but it was just *telling them*. I thought, "The worst that can happen is that they are going to be confused. And we can get through that."

My mom, when I told her, she said, "Do you want me to tell the family or do you want to?" And I said, "If you could tell the family, that would make my life so much easier." *So much easier.*

She said, "I'm going to have to do more research but, cool. I'm happy for you"

My mom has since told me that during those few years when I was trying to be a girl... everybody was saying, "Oh, she finally outgrew it," and she told people, "I don't buy it; I think this is social pressure."

My siblings were both super supportive and lovely.

I sent a text to them a couple days before I told my parents, and my brother replied, "Hey, super cool. Not going to lie, not really surprised. I'm really happy for you... Do you want me to call you my sister, or something else?"

And I remember thinking, "Where did he learn this?"

My sister, who was still in high school, was at the table with my mom and dad and our grandmother—the one who compared us a lot. She saw the text, and out loud went, "Oh cool." My grandmother asked, "What?" She had to totally lie and make something up on the spot to cover my butt. "Old name sent me something."

Originally when I came out, I came out as gender-fluid. And that's a super valid identity. But for me, in retrospect, what was really happening was I was bouncing sort of back-and-forth between, "This is what's comfortable socially, and this is what's comfortable internally," before finding a place where I was happy.

The whole experience was liberatory for me. Especially on the pronoun front and then the name front.

I didn't change my name for another month-and-a-half after I came out to my family. The person I was named for was my mom's aunt who had died of breast cancer... she had basically been my mom's second mother. I had grown up my whole life being told how much I was like her in personality and in appearance, so she was always someone who I felt very close with.

But still, I gradually realized I *needed* to change my name.

That was the hardest part for my family, especially my mom—the name, not my coming out.

There's this really frustrating narrative around parents of trans kids that goes, "Oh, you've lost a daughter," or that sort of thing. My mom's response to that is, "I haven't lost anything; I've got the same kid who is a much happier and healthier and more fulfilled version of themselves."

When I was home at one point, shortly after changing my name, she asked, "So, if I am referring to you before, do I call you Mordechai, or do I call you the old name?" And I said, "You'd call me Mordechai." I could see that was really hard for her.

She has talked with me about that moment, and we both remember it... I was fixing her computer because that's what I do for a job. I've always been very klutzy. I turned to face the computer and I banged my knee on the desk, really loudly, right as she turned and left the room.

And she said that, on hearing me whack my knee and go "OW!," she was like, "That's still my kid. That was all I needed to snap me back into, 'I haven't lost anything.' I have the same kid who bangs into everything all of the time."

When I told my mom that I was going to change my name, one of the first things she said was, "You are going to have to pick a new Hebrew name."

In Orthodox and Conservative Jewish tradition, you can't take away a name; you can only add them. In summer 2015, after my legal name change had gone through, the week before Thanksgiving, my dad asked, "Would you want to get renamed when you come back home?"

And so, he put me in touch with the Rabbi, and we had a naming ceremony. My three month old cousin was there, and everybody was wondering, "What's the baby getting named?"

And then a 20-year-old got up on the bimah...!

The Rabbi found these two prayers that talk about enabling us to embody our many genders, and to find our true form. Two very affirming prayers.

Then I spoke...

My parents have said that was one of the best days of their lives. And that was also true for me. All the complicated feelings around my name, with my family, that was *such healing*...

The traditional aspects of the name I had been given were being maintained but changed, and I was at Schul, *wearing a suit*, and being called by my Hebrew name. It was a very full circle moment.

That is one of the most significant days of my trans journey.

Parents who do not accept their LGBTQ+ children are missing out on having a relationship with the *fullest, happiest version of their child.*

You're missing out on actually getting to know them as the person they are.

Not only are you cutting the kid out of your life, you're missing out on your kid being the best version of themselves.

I've seen that with a lot of friends.

Feeling like you have a family is especially important with all the external challenges. I had a really hard time with job stuff after I came out as trans because, as an educator, I work with kids, and people think that trans people are dangerous for kids.

My primary age group I like to work with is middle school, and that's the age where kids are thinking about stuff like this. They are thinking about gender and sexuality and identity much more. That made my presence that much more important, but it also made it dangerous for me because it was seen as me "converting" or "recruiting," as opposed to people recognizing, "Oh, this is why representation matters in teaching."

If I had had to go through that without the support of my family, I don't know what would've happened. And I don't want to think about what would've happened. That's why there is that high suicide rate. Because it is so hard to just get your basic needs fulfilled...

The homelessness rate for LGBTQ+ people under 25 is about 40%. But if the family is accepting, it's very low, under 5%.

I got fired from a job. I had been "employee of the year" the two summers before. And then I got pushed out. I was fortunate to have my parents to financially support me. But just knowing that I had someone to call and tell what was happening... Even when it was happening, I didn't *realize* that was what was happening. My parents, coworkers and friends were the ones to say, "Mordechai, this is super thinly veiled."

Being connected to history and feeling like you're part of a culture, part of traditions, a story, a lineage is very meaningful. This necklace chain I'm wearing is from my grandmother. After she passed away, my grandfather picked out a couple pieces for me. And this is what makes my heart melt: he picked them out for me, and he asked, "Does this look masculine enough for Mordechai to wear?"

My mom has de facto adopted so many of my friends who don't have supportive families. She's like, "You're mine now." Which is how Jewish mothers are: if you are a friend of their child, you are their child. One of my friends stayed with them for the summer when they didn't have a place to stay.

For people who don't have their family's support, I can't imagine how disorienting that would feel. And how destabilizing that would feel, to not have a place that's home.

One of my friends has their chosen family here, but when we talk about going home, they don't call it that. They call it "going back to Connecticut." Because that's not home. They say, "I can't go back to Connecticut."

I can't imagine what that's like.

Parents need to hear *it's not about you.*

Some argue, "I didn't sign up for this." Yes, you did. *You sure did.* You raised a person. Just like you are not your parents, they are not you. And you are failing to rise to the occasion for something you *did* sign up for.

You want what's best for your kid right?

Well, this is what's best for them. Your not being accepting is what is worst for them.

Note: Resources used by Mordechai's rabbi and the prayers used for zir re-naming ceremony can be found in the Works Cited.

8:   ELIZABETH ROBERTS——
Kids who have been rejected by their families want to know how I came around.

Elizabeth Roberts is the mother of Andy, a trans man who first came out as lesbian at age 14 and then again while in college. Raised in New England in the ultraconservative Presbyterian Church of America, Elizabeth explains that she "bought into the whole thing completely," and this included very limiting ideas about both gender and sexuality that impacted her life and her child's life in profound ways.

As a daughter, wife and then mother, Elizabeth worked to meet the expectations of her culture. This included staying home with her children after earning advanced degrees and accepting her church's conservative rhetoric without question. In her world, AIDS was God's punishment of "the gays," and Coronavirus, God's response to the failure to "uphold marriage between a man and a woman."

Because she understood homosexuality as deviant and sinful, Elizabeth was utterly unsuspecting and unprepared when she discovered six practice suicide notes in her 14-year-old child's bedroom addressed to different members of the family.

The notes explained, "I am gay."

Here, Elizabeth, shares her experience as a parent who ultimately lost both church and family (her parents and siblings) in making the decision to stand by and love her child. It also provides a window into feelings of guilt and blame that parents might feel when their children come out as LGBTQ+.

In fundamentalist thinking, same-sex parents are especially seen as shaping their children, and Elizabeth faced terrific condemnation. In short, her world was telling her, "This is your fault."

Her parents disowned her when she disagreed with their harsh approach to "fixing" Andy, and she finally lost faith in her church (but not in God, she is careful to point out) when her "blinders" began to come off.

Andy's struggles with identity ultimately helped Elizabeth to recognize how she, too, had felt constrained and miserable in trying to live up to the role of "woman" as prescribed by her church. In short, her child's transformation led to her own self-realization and growth.

In her embrace of her trans son, Elizabeth has come a long way. A second child has since come out as lesbian, and Elizabeth is tickled that she took her daughter to the event where she met her wife.

Parental acceptance is the number one protective factor determining the future well-being of LGBTQ+ children throughout their lives. Despite urgent calls for research among the social work and other communities, there is very little understanding about how to alter the attitudes of rejecting parents. Here, Elizabeth offers a valuable window into "turning points" that helped her to accept and celebrate her trans son, a caring and compassionate person whom she admires.

I grew up in New England... I went to the town elementary school, town middle school, town high school. I started kindergarten with the same kids that I graduated with from high school. My mom was the one who upheld the faith church that I grew up in and stayed in until I was 45.

That was the Presbyterian Church of America, which is the ultraconservative branch of Presbyterianism. It was very gender defined. Mom was the one who had a handle on the faith... but she wasn't allowed to be a leader. My dad became a deacon, and later, he became an elder in the church.

In my marriage, I was the one who had been through all of the Bible studies and the youth groups and the camps, and who could quote Scripture. So, when it came to teaching my children, I was the one who bought them up in the faith.

The church was highly restrictive. I was the first born child, and when I got into school and started having school dances, I wasn't allowed to go. We were of that flavor where you don't drink, you don't smoke, you don't dance, you don't swear, all of that. The idea is that God dwells in you, and you need to keep yourself pure... your body, your physical self. God moves through you, so all of those things were considered bad.

I was in second grade and I found out that my Girl Scout leader smoked.... I went home, and I cried. In my world, it was black and white. You were either a good person who was a Christian and followed the faith, or you were... off the track, and *who knows* what other areas you might be off the track in, if you are off the track in this area.

I was *so* sheltered. I was terrified to go into a bar because I had these ideas about people under the influence of alcohol. I was the compliant good girl.... I never rebelled. I bought into the whole thing completely.

We were always taught that no sin was greater than another, but somehow, homosexuality got elevated to be the ultimate sin of all sins. If you follow the church on AIDS, it was, "God is bringing the plague because of the gays." And even this week, Pat Robertson is saying that the Coronavirus was caused because we didn't uphold marriage between a man and a woman.

The church was extremely gendered. This was God's will for my life. This was what he wanted for me... Gloria Steinem was the nightmare. She was an *awful woman...* that was the rhetoric of the time.

I was born in the 60s... there was that free love generation, and the people who were conservative got polarized. You see it all the time, when something is happening in society, conservatives just go extreme. That was the world I was brought up in: *those people over there are horrible, awful, sinful people.*

You know when you go into therapy, and you start having realizations? You are looking back and going, "I should have known this all along." That happened to me when I recognized that I was miserable. When they talk about being Christian, they say you are supposed to be joyful. And if you are not joyful, you are not praying enough, or you are not close enough to God, or there is something wrong with you.

And I was miserable because I don't fit into my gender... When I was married, it was like, "men over here and women over here," and I couldn't connect with the women. We didn't have the same interests.

A lot of times, when people think about oppressed women they think of them as like Cinderellas, being pushed down. But the examples of women in my life all were highly educated, even though they were submissive. Both of my grandmothers had master's degrees. My dad's mom had a master's in physics from RIT. There was this expectation in the family that you would be pretty well educated. I was a people pleaser. That's how I fit so well into the church.

The full expectation from day one was that as soon as I had children, I would be staying home with them... My husband defended his PhD when I was four months pregnant, so when he took his first job, even though I had earned an engineering degree, I never actually had an opportunity to work. I immediately stayed home.

In the church, they act like there is a formula: if you do A, B, and C, then your child is going to turn out right. If you don't do it right, they are going to go astray. There is a lot of literature, seminars, and things like that put out there that amount to serious guilt trips for parents. If you didn't do it *like this*... if your child had to go to the church nursery and they weren't on the right feeding schedule... There was a lot of judgmental stuff.

There wasn't an openness to individuality in the church. You had to think this way, and dress this way, and raise your children this way... There wasn't a handbook. *But you knew.*

My oldest is Andy, my transgender child. He was born as a girl, a very confident little kid. I hardly had any difficulty with him at all. First time parents are always trying to do everything exactly the right way. Andy was very eager to learn, very smart, and when he was four, my mother, who had been a first-grade teacher, and the pediatrician both came to me and said, "this child needs to be in school."

I was never suspicious, ever. For me, LGBTQ+ wasn't a personality thing, it was a sin. It was a *behavior*, and the way that the Christian world looks at sexuality, you can't say that a child is a homosexual because the concept is based on having homosexual sex... it would not have been part of my thought process to imagine that my child was gay.

Gay was not who you were; it was *sexual behavior*.

When my child came out as a lesbian at 14, I heard my child *admitting* to me that they were having homosexual sex in a very promiscuous manner. I couldn't breathe. It was the equivalent to being told by my child, "I am a heroin addict." It was horrific. The way the church has spun sexuality, the sin of all sins... it was unconscionable to me.

We were close. I felt like we had a really good relationship. We didn't have any tensions. Because of the way that my marriage was, my child, Andy, actually stood up for me against my husband. I didn't think twice about that at the time, but when it came out in therapy, the therapist's eyes got really big. I didn't realize what an impactful thing that was for a 10-year-old kid to go up against their father. That's a big deal. He had had enough of my husband berating me; he stood up for me and said, "Dad, why are you treating mom like she is a kid?"

So, he was very protective of me, and we had a mutually supportive relationship. He was my right-hand man. Or woman. Or *whatever*.

He had his princess birthday party when he was a Girl Scout... that's how it goes.

I had two other children, and he was my helper. He was very responsible... the oldest of three girls, just like me. He was always willing to help, and to this day, is very helpful and caring.

I was working at the church at the time when he came out, and my youngest was six. She was home sick from school, so I was home with her from work. I don't know what caused me to do this… if you believe in God, he compelled me. But I went into Andy's room, and I read the last page of his journal. I never, ever had done anything like that before.

The last page of his journal included six suicide notes written to each member of his family and his friends, basically saying, "I have tried to do everything as best I can. I've been the best person I can be. I love God, but I am gay."

I was *terrified*. I called the church counselor, and I said, "What do I do?" He said, "First call the school and make sure that he's there. Don't tell them it's life and death because they will call social services." So, I found out that he was there. I called my husband at work. When Andy got home from school, we confronted him together. He kind of denied it… what he said was that this was the way he was feeling, but he was praying about it and trying to get over it.

I always wanted home to be a refuge, not a stressful, tense place to live. So, I said to him, "I am not going to be in your face about all this stuff, but I want to check in with you once a week. We will set, like, Tuesdays, and on Tuesdays, we will talk." One of the Tuesdays I talked to him, and he said, "I am over it."

That worked in my world because gay isn't an identity, it's a behavior. Like, okay, I am going to quit smoking today. That's exactly the way my interpretation of it was. So, for a long time, we went on that premise: that he was over it.

It became clear at a certain point that he wasn't over it.

He was 14.

This was the worst-case scenario in my life, to have a child come out as gay. In fact, my girlfriend's son was an addict using drugs, and I said to her, "I'd rather my child be using drugs."

If a child gets caught doing drugs in school they will be punished. If a child comes out as gay in school, there is a gay/straight alliance that they are going to join. So, I just felt like... I did not have society, the teachers, the school—anybody except the church and my family—with me on getting my child *fixed*.

So, I sent my child to reparative therapy. Because it's a *behavior*, not an identity.

The whole thing with reparative therapy, one of the many premises, is that it is the fault of the same sex parent, which was me. I don't think you could have crushed me any more in all of this... according to my religious beliefs, it was all my fault.

We found a therapist that would see him, but it took the church counselor three months, and pulling strings, because apparently, my child was the Christian trifecta of risk: a minor who is suicidal and gay. And I mean, being gay was like being an *untouchable*.

The man who ran the practice that this therapist practiced under would not even be in the same room as a gay person because he was just so appalled. Nobody else would see my child, and this therapist ended up being an hour and 15 minutes away.

We went every week; that's how my child learned to drive, going back and forth to therapy. He got all the hours in and more.

It turned out that they hadn't really been doing reparative therapy anyway. Which now, looking back on it, I'm glad about. Because I now realize that it is hurtful. But... that's what I thought my child was getting.

Remember, I had to be in reparative therapy too, so I *was* in reparative therapy and my child wasn't!

And my therapy was basically, "You did this to your child. You need to fix it. Here is the formula for you to fix it." *Another church formula.*

And it was, "You haven't been nurturing to your child," or "There is some trauma in your relationship, and you need to teach your child female to female touch that is not sexualized." So, I was supposed to hug my child. And I was supposed to hug my child's friends. And I was supposed to have heart-to-heart conversations. I had all this homework, and it was supposed to be covert.

I remember my mother very clearly telling me, when Andy was born, "Your goal is to make an independent adult." And of course, I am an overachiever… I was more like "Pull yourself up by your bootstraps" than "Come here and let me take care of you." So, when they said I wasn't nurturing, I thought, *maybe I wasn't?*

For me, there were distinct turning points in my thinking:

The reparative therapy that I was in also was a group therapy, and women with different experiences could kind of talk across to each other. I was the mother of the lesbian who was not affirming of my child, and there was a lesbian in the group whose mother had rejected her. We spent years together once a week in this group. Her tears, her laying her heart bare, and me hearing how it felt from her side of things, to be rejected by her mother whom she loved… I was able to peek into her world.

Also, a little bit of it was time, because by the time my child graduated from reparative therapy, it had been three years. When my child first came out and I would look at him, all I would see was "gay." All I would see was this awful behavior, like "gay" was across his forehead. But as time went by, we shared laughter. We shared meals and holidays, and life.

And those pieces that I cherished about my child were still there. You know? And that allowed me to see my child as a whole…. He was composed of all of these different pieces, and I could see that.

Those two things happened within those three years. My life normalized in a way. The trauma just kind of died down a little bit.

Then, barely a year later, in November of his (college) sophomore year, Andy came out as trans. *Back to the beginning, all over again.*

I still had that message from the reparative therapy, "this is your fault." And now what I was hearing my child tell me was, "You are such a bad example of a woman that I don't want to be one." So not only had I completely failed as a mother, but now, I am such a horrible representative of a woman that my child doesn't even want to be one.

Every aspect of my life—my family, my church, my husband—were all saying to me, "you failed."

My worldview had been gendered: men can do these things, and women can't. All of the sudden, my child was switching teams. *What does this mean?* The framework that I had believed in for all of this time, all my life, all of the sudden wasn't black-and-white anymore. It was... I didn't know what it was.

As I said before, I never fit. I was never a "good woman." Which made me feel like, yes, maybe everything is all my fault.

I started analyzing myself and my life and my role as a woman. The light bulb came on... I was a square peg in a round hole. I didn't fit as a church lady; I could play a church lady, but it never made me happy because it wasn't my gift. It wasn't who I was. And the things that I really wanted to do, I was constantly being pushed down by the church, and hearing, "No you can't do that. No, you can't do that."

On top of that, the church basically took a very hard stance against my child. Of course, "Gay is not okay." And trans is now the new "not okay." This is the front that they are now trying to attack.

My church, instead of embracing this child that they had baptized and called part of God's family, instead of coming alongside them as family, started to talk about whether they were going to kick my child out. *Excommunicate* my child.

My own family, my parents, started taking this position.

I lost faith in the church. Entirely. There are two places in life where love is supposed to be absolute or unconditional: family and the church. Both of them walked away. I was left just standing with my mouth open.

I never lost faith in God because I always believed that God could see inside of my heart; God knows who I am.

Andy was off to college, which made the situation a little bit more tolerable. It gave me breathing room, time to try to figure things out without him seeing me devastated. He had told us because he wanted to start hormones immediately. It turned out that he was in therapy to begin to transition.

To help us understand what was going on, Andy arranged a visit for us to go see that therapist. She wore all men's clothing. And she explained to us about gender, the things that I talk to people about now when I go out and educate them. She said, "I am born a woman and I identify as a woman, but I prefer men's clothing, so I dress in men's clothing. I present as male…"

I was like, *"This person is indoctrinating my child…!"* I hated it. I tried to get him to see somebody else…

Three days after his sister graduated from high school, Andy reconvened the extended family. They sat around my kitchen table, and he told everybody that he was trans.

We hadn't told anybody about the whole gay thing. We didn't tell his sisters. We told nobody, because we were going to fix it, so nobody needed to know. Why ruin the reputation of your child if you do not have to?

So, when Andy came out as trans, I was such a mess that I couldn't support anybody through it. I needed help myself.

My husband and I would get in the car and drive to a local parking lot and make calls to our parents because we couldn't talk privately in the house. So, we were sitting in the CVS parking lot having this conversation with my parents, and my dad wanted to activate some branch of the church to intervene. His plan was to excommunicate Andy as a form of tough love so they could ponder the error of their ways—like solitary confinement without the walls.

But my blinders were coming off. I didn't like the extremity of this idea. I did not trust the church anymore. I didn't see it as loving. For my parents, the only way that they could see to fix this was to cut him off, to make him suffer: stop paying tuition, cut him off financially, kick him out of the house.

Like you hear has happened to so many kids…

I mean, now I have met them. I know them. Kids who have been kicked out, just like that.

And I said to my parents, "I am not doing it." And they said, "If you don't do it, we are disowning you."

And they did.

They stopped talking to me. Both of my sisters cut off communications. They started going on family trips together without us. We'd find out about all of these family events that were happening that we had been left out of. We weren't invited.

My world had been my family and my church. Both of those just shut me out.

After Andy came out, my parents disowned me, and the therapist that I had been seeing said, "I don't know anything about trans; I can't help you."

Within a month, I was hospitalized. I had a suicide attempt. I finally found a wise and compassionate therapist. He saved my life.

I can see a lot of things now that I didn't see before.

The thing I find so great about Andy is that he is so patient and so caring and compassionate for people in his world. I think that is the reason that I was able to get to the place that I am now.

I interact now in a lot of LGBTQ+ circles. And a lot of the kids there have been rejected by their families. They want to know how I came around... *They want their parents to come around.*

And I tell them.... love your parents. You have been wrestling with this internal turmoil for probably years before you came out. The day you came out (at least for me) was day one for them. So, be patient with your parents.

When Andy came out as trans, we were the two oldest child daughters. When psychologists talk about your "mini-me," he was my mini me. He had the same sense of responsibility, self-reliance, and all of that.

When he came out as trans, all of the sudden, he stopped calling me for advice or to ask a question. All of these phone calls now swung to my husband. He wanted my husband's approval. That was a complete blow to me.

Eventually, I started going to the Gay Christian Network Conference, now called Q-Christian. It's a group of people, gay Christians, who have basically been told, "You can't be gay and Christian. It's an oxymoron."

And yet here were these 1400 people who knew that they loved God and that they were gay.... They were people I could relate to. I sat and talked with these people for hours and shared their journeys, and they shared their experiences of being rejected by their families. Many of them had been kicked out of their homes.

In Christianity, when somebody goes through trials and comes out on the other side, the idea is that it strengthens your faith. And these people were so strong. Their faith was so much stronger than mine was.... I was not able to deny the fact that they were Christians. Just being among them was so liberating for me.

I have taken all of my children to the conference. A lot of kids go, and they desperately want their parents to come and see... In fact, my middle, who is now out as a lesbian, met her wife at the conference I took her to! They just got married last month. And it's her wife who brought her back to church.

I was also doing a lot of reading, and one book in particular helped me: *Far From the Tree* by Andrew Solomon... that first chapter caught me and named my fear. What was I afraid of? Why am I responding and reacting this way? It was because my child had deviated from my dream, my path, what I knew to be the safe place. And I was fearful. I didn't yet know this world that my child was going into.

Those were the turning points for me to kind of come around and understand this new world that has become open to me.

Andy calls me every week. We talk for a long time...

9: ANDY ROBERTS—
…Acknowledge *me*.

Andy Roberts is a trans man who easily passes in most parts of his life now as a cisgender male. He grew up in a conservative, middle class, Christian family in Montgomery County, Maryland. He recalls, "We had that almost American dream kind of family. We had both sets of grandparents. Everyone got together for the holidays. Mom, Dad. Dog. The whole nine…" His family was very religious, and he grew up participating in church, Sunday school, Bible study, and youth groups throughout the week; much of his and his family's social live was centered in the church.

Because his church was overtly hostile to LGBT+, his experience of coming out—first to himself, in 9th grade, and then to his family and larger community—was complex. At different times, he has identified as bisexual and as gay, and finally as trans, although he has issues with limits implied by all of those terms.

Andy's middle school friend remembers him crying many nights on the phone, seeking a way to "fix" the problem. Around that time, his mother found "suicide-type" notes where he expressed his certainly that his family would "never accept this."

Andy's self-discovery occurred in a void of information and exposure. Reared in what he calls a "bubble," where exposure to media was limited, he did not experience affirming messages about LGBTQ+ people; the kindest interpretation available at the time was that they were somehow broken or "confused" as the result of abuse or trauma. A self-aware young person who had not experienced these things but did not doubt his self-knowledge, he wondered, *"What happened to me?"*

Andy found connection through the Internet; his account of how it gave him hope to discover others who were both Christian and gay testifies to the importance of such exposure for LGBTQ+ children and hints at the danger of policies that work to erase access to LGBTQ+ topics for school-age young people.

Here, his intimate description of what it meant to him to transition is helpful and powerful.

Like others in this book, Andy was, at an early age, forced to calculate losses and risks in choosing to live authentically. In 9th grade, the freedom of young adult independence that typically comes with college graduation seemed a desperately long way off. Although he knew that his parents loved him, he was not always entirely sure that they would not kick him out.

They never went that route, but along with Andy, they were eventually cut out by much of the extended family once he began to transition—something Andy anticipated in advance and still struggles with. "Concerns" voiced by relatives that he would not be loveable, or employable, or happy read as ironic given that the strongest indicator for the lifelong wellbeing of LGBTQ+ youth is familial acceptance.

Growing up in a community where very few people knew an out LGBTQ+ person, Andy also felt the burden of representation. He describes adjusting his behavior in hopes of forestalling negative attitudes and assumptions—a terrific weight for young shoulders. Now, feeling done with this role—and privy to the unguarded biases of people in his place of employment—Andy chooses not to be out at work.

He knows that his journey has not been as bumpy as some, and he has landed in a safe place: happily married and successful in his professional life, he expresses gratitude that he has always been able to find support and emphasizes the difference a compassionate family member, friend, teacher or mentor can make for LGBTQ+ youth finding their way.

First I came out to myself, then to people around me, and from there it was a slow transition of coming out to my entire community. In late middle school is when I started figuring out my sexuality. Specifically, that I was attracted to girls.

I didn't really recognize that in myself fully until high school. It was a funny thing: a girl that I now realize I had a big crush on... We were passing notes and chatting in English class. She came out to me and said, "Hey, you know, I am bisexual?" And I was like, "Oh, me, too." And then I had a moment of self-reflection and said, *am I?*

I had never acknowledged anything like that, or truly thought it out, or said it to anyone. It just kind of popped out. That was ninth grade. I immediately texted my best friend and said, "I have got to tell you something!" There were a few weeks of talking about it. And I thought to myself, *this isn't good.* I know enough to know this is not how it should be. She told me later—it is a bit of a blur now—but she told me later that I'd be on the phone crying, asking her to pray for me. "Make it go away. Let's reverse this. Let's change it."

I say, "I knew enough" because I grew up in a such a conservative, religious bubble. I didn't listen to secular music until middle school. I didn't watch PG-13 movies until I was probably 14. The Internet was not what it is today. I knew just enough to ask about things like, "What does gay mean?" This was in the news in 2006 and it was very controversial. You didn't have to be extremely conservative at that time to think that being gay was bad.

I remember when Rosie O'Donnell came out... I asked my mom, "What does gay mean?" And she said, "Well, sometimes people have issues growing up or were abused, and they get confused."

That was one of the first definitions that I heard, so I thought, *"What happened to me?"*

But I was also thinking, "Well, I came out initially as bisexual, so great. I'll just keep dating guys, and we will just ignore the other piece, and will be good to go."

I never really changed from that orientation, but I did discover over time that I liked girls a lot more than I thought; more, usually, than guys. I got to a point where I came to terms with it. I felt like I had done anything I could to push it away or to try not to feel that way. At this point, it just was what it was. This was a slow process of coming to terms with everything, but I was getting into that groove about six months later. I had started looking online, on Facebook groups, interacting with people who were Christian and gay.

That gave me a lot of hope.

At one point, I started a little book outline of a kid who is bisexual and Christian... I was trying to make it a thing. And so, that's when I started to balance both of these worlds and realize that they could come together. And that could work.

I was still being very secretive. I wasn't telling a lot of people. It felt like a very big and vulnerable thing to share, but I was still starting to feel out the waters. When I was a sophomore, there was a girl on the volleyball team and there were rumors that she was gay, but no one was truly out and proud.

She and I had a conversation.

You? Me? Yeah, great.

One day, there was a girl that I had a crush on, and my new volleyball friend and I were IMing about it... back then we had a computer room with the one family computer. After I left and closed out of the conversation, she replied, which pops the window back up. So, my dad sits down. He reads through this whole conversation with me talking about this girl that I had a crush on. For better or worse, in the conversation, I was hesitant because I think I didn't know if she was gay or not. But my parents read into the hesitancy as a glimmer of hope. Like I was hesitant about my feelings.

A little bit ironically, that weekend, when my dad saw the exchange, I was away at a church youth group retreat. I came back, and my parents were definitely being a little weird. That night after I returned, my mom came into my room and said, "Hey, your dad saw this conversation. I want to talk about it." And she told me the story of how when she was younger, there were these older girls that she really admired. She said I could be "mixing up my feelings" about someone who is just really cool, or who I looked up to, with romantic feelings. I remember being like, *just let me get through this conversation.* I appeased in whatever way I could.

I said, "Yeah, I think you're right; I think I'm getting confused." But that was certainly for their benefit; I knew how I felt.

That was when I mentally made a plan: If I can get through college... Obviously, in high school, you are dependent in every way. Financially, every way. Then, if I can get through that, which felt like eternity, then I can come out.

I didn't go through reparative therapy, at least not in a normal sense. I was sent to a Christian therapist, and my parents were hoping they would do that, but the therapist ended up being very supportive. My mom, if anyone, was the one who went through much more of a conservative, reparative-type therapy approach.

After that first conversation, about two or three months later, my mom found a suicide-type note; it was letters to people, rather. In the letters, I was basically like, "I am gay. Clearly, you will never accept this. I hope you will be better people."

That's what spurred me starting therapy.

Yes, I was angry. I think I felt a little bit hopeless. I think I had really come to terms with it at that point. I was like *this is me.* This is not something that I can pray away. I have obviously found these other people online who are supportive and who are fitting into both of these worlds. So, if you are not going to let me be that... And I was thinking about the end of college. I was like, that's *eight years* away... *that's crazy.* I can't do that.

My parents never got to that point where they were threatening to throw me out. The discussion was pretty much framed in, "We love you; we want the best for you." But this was a very uncomfortable split: As a teenager, I thought, "Clearly, what you are thinking of as the best for me doesn't acknowledge *me*."

I don't know if there was ever a real threat. I did, at one point, actually practice running away, if you will. I don't remember what I told my parents I was doing, but I walked 2 ½ miles to a friend's house, just to know that I could do if I had to do it. So, it was definitely in my mind…I didn't know if it would ever get to that point.

My self-presentation started creating a lot of family tension. My mom was starting to get questions from friends and family because I was dressing a little different. I had a rainbow belt that I loved to wear, and she was getting a lot of blame from the therapy she was going to and from my grandparents.

And then that came out from my dad towards me… "Look at what you are doing to your mother."

I have two alive and kicking sets of grandparents. … I'm very grateful for that. On my dad's side, their response to me is a shorter story… We weren't super close or personal. We saw them on a regular basis, but it was a little bit, I felt, surface-level. They never asked, and I never said anything. We just kind of did our regular routine, and that was that. They were never as religious. They would go to church sometimes, but it wasn't as big a deal.

My mom's family was the one that definitely "embodied Christ," if you will. Most of the conversations that were had up until I was in college, when I came out the second time, were behind closed doors with my parents. So, I don't have a lot of direct knowledge. But I know there was a lot of my grandparents, particularly my grandmother, who is more outspoken, expressing their "concern" in a way that put blame on my mom.

My aunts tried to, dodge around the reality. I didn't come out to them explicitly until much later, and everyone just got a little bit reserved.

Obviously, I felt rejected. I'm someone who likes people to like me, so I—and I did this in high school as well—I went above and beyond. In my mind, I decided, "I could be that one person. I could be the only gay, queer person these people know. So, if they have a bad experience with me, I've got the weight of that representation on my shoulders." I went above and beyond trying to be the *nicest*, the most helpful person—whatever I could do, that wasn't counteracting who I was—to better those relationships.

At first, as I said, I came out to a very, very small group freshman year; sophomore year is when I started becoming friends with and realizing there were other gay people in school. It was still a little hush-hush… You would hear a rumor. Or, I would come out to someone, and they would be like, "Oh, so-and-so is also gay, but don't tell." It was like this underground railroad. I came out, and everybody opened up. It was amazing and there were so many gay people. But I didn't know that until later, of course.

Sophomore year was a transition: I cut my hair. I started dressing in a way that was more comfortable to me. More masculine. I think in doing some of those physical changes, I just kind of gradually came out. I started telling a few people, and then a few more people. Then I was like, "Yeah, I don't care if you tell that person." By junior year, it was common knowledge.

The general response was pretty positive in school. There were definitely people that were a little weird about it. Or I would hear about rumors of me making out with some girl. People were just talking about me more. I was able to laugh it off because I had enough close friends. I was always very positive and nice and friendly to people, so I think I had enough good reputation that, even if someone was a little weird about it, they just let it go.

Over the course of high school, when I was starting to look at colleges, I was simulta-neously becoming much more gay in my life, and I realized that I would really love to continue being as out as I am, if not more so. I would love to be able to date anyone. I knew if I went to a school like that, I could be myself. There were other colleges that I was really interested in, more in southern states. I actually tried to look up if they had an LGBTQ+ student group. If they did, I would email whatever contact I could get and ask them about their experience being queer on campus. I will never forget my encounter with one of the schools; it was one of my top three. I talked to this student, and they said "Yeah, it's pretty good. Most people let you do your thing, leave you alone. I've only gotten beaten up once." And I was like, *that is one too many times for me, and I am not going there.*

I wasn't surprised. I knew that my experience thus far had been, at least in school and with peers, very lucky. So, I knew that was very common, and, it was unfortunate, but it was also school in the South. So, I was like, *yeah, that's how it goes.*

I don't remember when I transitioned from identifying as bi to gay. I know I never liked the term "lesbian." I never felt like that fit. I remember having conversations with my friends. We honestly preferred the term "dyke," even though it was derogatory. It just felt more appropriate. "Queer" wasn't so commonly used as an identifier, at least then in our area. And so, I went with "gay." I felt like it was very nice and broad. Even in high school, identifying as gay, there were still times when I would talk to guys. I was open to that fluidity. It didn't bother me: I was open to that fluidity of identity.

When I went to college, I started being made aware of different identities, of how big this LGBTQ+ community really is. I took a Sexuality 101-type course, and there was a lot of really great discussion and awareness of the trans community. There was a video we watched of trans-guys talking to butch lesbians. And I was finally understanding the difference.

To me, I felt like there was a scale. All right: you are lesbian, and then you are a butch lesbian, and then you're a trans guy. And I thought to myself, "Well, I am certainly not butch, so I can't be over here..." It didn't make sense to me then. So, with these courses, and being introduced to other people, I began to grasp the possibilities of what my gender and feelings actually meant.

The girl that I dated for most of college... while we were together, one of her exes came out as trans. Seeing him transition, I was like a puppy. Every time we would hang out, I was asking him all of these questions, and I was just so interested in it. Having that experience is what kind of gave me permission to say, *I can still be me and feminine, to a degree, and still actually be a guy.* Before, I felt like that wasn't possible or didn't make sense. I knew something was wrong with how I was trying to identify. So, that's where that came together. I started out kind of easing in. I began thinking, *maybe I'm gender queer, or maybe non-binary?* I started going by "Andy" way before I even really came out. There was probably about a year-long transition of, like, "Hey, I prefer to be called Andy, but nothing else is changed."

Then, I got a binder, and I was like, I just really like how it looks, and I'm going to wear it every day. And it just cycled into the summer before my junior year. I had been spending every day online looking at YouTube videos of guys transitioning, and reading, and just looking into everything, and I knew, "Whether or not I choose to do any of those things, that's me."

My family and I had gotten into a groove of *don't ask don't tell.* I'd been wearing masculine guy clothes for a while, and of course, I had short hair… I could tell they didn't love it if we went to church and I wasn't wearing a dress, but we moved past it. So, when I hit that point in college where I said, "No, I am trans," it was like, "Oh my gosh, here we go again. We have got to do this whole thing over again."

This time, it was worse. They would have to actually do something, you know, like change pronouns. It definitely was worse. I came out to my parents, and they *panicked.* They reached out to my old therapist who had since retired, and she was like, "Sorry." They found another therapist. They didn't want me to tell anyone in my family. They didn't want me to tell my sisters, which was already a little bit the case. They had not wanted me to come out to my youngest sister as gay so, she was really in the dark, still.

I don't know how to describe it. They didn't know what to do about it. A few weeks after my second coming out, we went on a family cruise with my extended family: grandparents, aunts, cousins, and every time we were alone, my parents were trying to corner me and question me. They were like, "Well, you like chick flicks, right?" *Yeah.* They were almost trying to convince me out of it. "I thought you were gay." They didn't understand that the two weren't conflicting identities.

Then it almost became a different kind of panic when I finally said, "I am going to transition. I'm going to take testosterone, and I'm going to do this." They went from, "Don't tell anyone, don't tell anyone," to "You need to come out to all of them the entire family right now." I guess they thought that I was going to change my mind about starting T.

When I did come out to the rest of my family, I sat down with them in person, and my mom did not take the lead. She was like, "This is your thing. We love you, but we are not backing you up on this one." So, I told them, and they also responded with, "I thought you were a lesbian? That doesn't make any sense. Which one is it?" And I explained, "I can still like girls and be trans." I didn't understand why they were confused about that. My grandparents expressed "concern" that my current girlfriend would leave me, and if she did leave me, how would I ever find someone else that would date me? That I was in a "liberal brainwashing bubble" at college, and once I left, I would never be able to find friends.

I was on course to be a teacher. That's what I was studying to be at the time. And they were, again, I'll say "concerned" (I don't know if it was genuine concern), that I would never be able to be a teacher. That no one would ever hire me. I wouldn't be successful. I wouldn't be accepted by students or parents in that profession, or really, in any profession. I think they thought I was choosing to be a social outcast.

My aunt at that time also said, "I don't think this is something I want my kids exposed to, so I would rather you not tell them." And then it became, "I would rather you not interact with them." That eventually became permanent. I don't think they realized how visible the change would be. By the next Christmas, I was six months on testosterone and starting to pass as male in public. It wasn't like coming out as gay, where you can just not talk about it. That was when it turned into, "I am not bringing my kids around."

Those were my only cousins; those were the only of my parents' siblings with any kids. That was tough. I think I expected a lot of this reaction... I had really come to terms with that as a possibility. I remember when we went on that cruise that Christmas the year prior. I thought to myself, "Soak this in, because this is the last time." And it really was.

After seeing what happened the first time, none of that shocked me. Not to say that it didn't bother me. It certainly did, but I think I felt more guilt. That meant that now my younger sisters were more or less cut off from my cousins. It eventually became a feud. My mom and that aunt no longer speak. That was because two years in, when my mom finally started becoming supportive, it became a mama bear versus mama bear thing. "Don't you come after my kid." They just butted heads and haven't talked in, I don't know, maybe five years.

If I could have transitioned and not told them, I probably would have, to be really honest. I chose to transition because I just felt like there wasn't *any other option*. I couldn't see myself continuing to live in any other way. My body at that time felt like… It just felt wrong.

I have chronic back pain, and I remember talking with my therapist that I started seeing when I was really figuring out my gender identity. I went in one session when I was still deciding if I wanted to medically transition, and I said, "I had a thought the other day that if I had to choose between eliminating that pain forever or being able to transition, I would still choose to transition." I think that was really a mental switch for me. I realized, "This is equivalent to this chronic pain, it's just not in a physical form."

I have been very lucky. Again, I am very lucky that my parents didn't cut me off financially. I made plans for how I would finish my degree and how I would live if they did. I was very prepared for the worst case, and I am glad that they didn't. I am lucky that it only took them, maybe a year or two, to—I don't want to say get on board, because that took a lot longer—but to be respectful of my transition. A year or two is not long compared to what some other people have experienced.

I did experience some panic in my first teaching job after word got around that I was trans. But it never came to any issues or conflicts. The biggest difference, just in my personal life, is that I am now no longer seen as "queer." Before, when I was queer, it was just apparent. And now I live very stealth, which gives me a little bit of internal conflict. I think one of your questions was about the political stuff going on right now, and I am always very torn. I love to help in whatever way I can.

Like, even being part of this book, you know, that gives me a lot of pride, to make a difference, hopefully. But then I also… I don't know why now, of all the times, I'm getting emotional about it… But, I also feel guilt not doing more, out of fear of ruining what I've built.

In my social life and with my wife's parents and her brother, I am out. Most of our close friends are queer or on some part of the LGBTQ+ spectrum. And that's very much still who I feel the most comfortable around. As far as more extended family and work, I'm not open about being trans, or even about having dated people of every gender. It's complicated because there is a really strong and recognized group at the company that I work for of LGBTQ+ people, and, rationally, I know in my head that I could be part of that openly. When there is Trans Day of Awareness, there is a woman, very high in the marketing team, who talks about her experience. *And* she transitioned in the workplace. I am sure it would be fine, but there is still part of me that's like, even if it is fine, are people that I work with going to view me differently? Is it going to become something that people talk about quietly and that alters the relationships that I have or my ability to work my way up the corporate ladder?

I think about that type of thing… being stealth puts me in the situation where I hear people talk about trans people when they don't realize that trans people are listening. It's often out of a place of true, honest ignorance, but nonetheless, it's hearing people that I work alongside, people that I *like*, that I'm close work friends with saying things like, "I don't know, that's just weird." "I don't get it." Those types of comments. Or, going into political issues of, "I don't think we should let men in dresses into the restroom," and not understanding how that connects to who I am. That definitely is a big reason that I'm hesitant to be out.

When my wife and I met, I was already out at the place where we both worked then. So that made it easier for me since there was no coming out conversation to be had. She just, kind of knew, or had picked up on it along the way. She is someone who, in a way, also lives stealth because she is a cis woman who doesn't really identify as anything other than queer because she has dated women before, but she never came out to her family, and she appears very feminine. No one would think anything of it.

So, in dating, we have had the great privilege of passing as a regular-old-white-straight couple. My transition was far enough along that when I started meeting her parents and her family that I passed. Nobody asked any questions.

We dated for about three years before we got engaged, four before we got married. Halfway between engagement and marriage, I said, "You know, we really should tell your parents."

Again, always wanting to be the one that's offering the olive branch, I invited my entire family to the wedding... before we even got the actual invites out, my grandparents responded to the "save the date," and said, "Thank you, no thank you. We will not be attending."

That may have been for the best. Probably... A hundred-and-seventy people came, and it was absolutely beautiful. Having them there would have made me anxious. I would be worried they would use the wrong name or pronouns and cause other people to ask questions. That's why it was important to tell my wife's parents because my grandparents' refusal, by itself, raised some questions.

So, we did have that conversation with her parents. Again, I had mapped out, if this goes bad... who can we drive to quickly? Where can we stay, God forbid it just blows up? But they took it really well. Not too long in, her mom said, "You know we really need to decide on the flowers." And I was like, *okay! This wedding is still happening.* So, that was just really quite a blessing.

I understand families having concern. I understand the fear that comes with your kids coming out, and you envisioning what their life might look like because of the bad stereotypes or because of these statistics, or even just that it's different than your vision for their life. But I think parents and families in general need to be very careful and reflective whether their concern is truly a selfless concern, or is it rooted in their own misinformation or fears of what other people will think, or of having to come out themselves and having to tell people about their child?

And then, even if it is a genuine concern, I think they need to consider the words that they use and how they come across.

And then the non-words. How are they expressing that? You might not be saying anything. You might not be verbally expressing your disdain, but I think parents and families need to be aware of those nonverbal messages that still relay negative feelings.

My grandmother spent many, many years totally avoiding me. Greeting everyone else in the room, and it was almost just like I didn't exist. I am a "If you are not laughing, you are crying" kind of person. So, I would be texting my friends, "You won't believe this, ha ha ha. She's being ridiculous." Just really making jokes about it. It's funny because I am the tallest of all of her grandchildren.

I have always felt a lot of guilt. My sisters have both come out as being somewhere along the LGBTQ+ spectrum, but they both had to see my experience; coming out is not even a hypothetical risk for them... They saw what came of it for me. They saw what the result is.

Before they were even able to process for themselves who they were, my grandmother sat down with my middle sister and had a conversation where she said, "If you want to go to a different high school, we can help with that. You don't want to go to the same high school as Andy; people are going to talk about you. People are going to assume things about you. So, we will help send you to a private school." And so, I feel guilty that she had to go through this conversation and make these decisions and build up this worry that obviously never came to fruition. That's a lot to put on someone who was about 12.

I'm super lucky that both of my sisters are very cool. I heard about that conversation because one of them was like, "Guess what ridiculous thing Grandma just said?" The gist was, "That was really stupid, I'm not worried about it, let's laugh about it together."

I always had someone. I always had a friend, or even a teacher, a mentor. Someone who was in my corner.

That helps...

10: CAROL BROWN——
I had to look in the mirror and determine whether or not I was a good person.

Carol Brown grew up "a little badass" who took care of bullies—her own, and other people's. Early hardships schooled her in toughness and independent thinking, both of which she has relied upon as a masculine-presenting, white lesbian woman with a wife and child who are Black.

Here, Carol shares the influences that shaped her perspective and describes what it was like for her to come out at nineteen in 1986, a few weeks before the first National Coming Out Day. As with many of the stories recorded in this book, she describes a mixed response from her parents; her mother "did her best," and her father only gradually softened in his harsh attitudes towards LGBTQ+ people and Black people. In a sense, Carol had to come out to him twice, first as a lesbian and then as a lesbian who intended to marry a Black woman.

Carol, who raised her younger brother, always knew that she wanted children. She had nearly given up hope of becoming a mother when she and her wife, Georgette, successfully adopted Gracen, a beautiful baby girl, shortly before this interview. The circumstances leading to the adoption were extremely fortunate and relied upon personal connections and not on the formal adoption or fostering systems, access to which is currently being elided for LGBTQ+ people in many states.

Although not from a religious background at the time that she came out, Carol did not escape the accusation that she is a "sinner," or talk of damnation, but she has thought seriously about faith and about what it means to be a good person; how she lives and how she treats people are, to her, what matters.

Here, Carol, a cis-gendered female with a masculine appearance, describes being harassed for using women's bathrooms—an ironic comment on the absurdity of legislation aimed at preventing trans individuals from using bathrooms that align with their identities.

Moreover, having worked for many years in the prison system, she shares her particularly nuanced insight into systemic racism.

Carol's accounts of being turned away from restaurants and of her wife, Georgette, being followed in stores illustrate how discrimination can multiply in everyday life for LGBTQ+ people.

As she has gotten older and as anti-LGBTQ+ sentiment has ratcheted up, she realizes that she now feels fearful in a way that she did not used to. She shares, "with what's going on in the world today... I don't want to be in the middle of it because I'm afraid for my physical safety."

At the time of this interview, Carol's family had recently moved to a new community. Though she and her wife always feel some concern about how they will be received in a new area, neighbors seem friendly so far, and no one has commented on the "Love Wins" Pride flag in her yard.

Getting to know people—having real conversations—has become sort of a quiet, daily advocacy for Carol. "I let people get to know me and then it's like, 'Oh, you're gay, and you're not so bad.'"

Convinced that people really all want the same things, especially to be loved, she remarks that, "The hardest thing for LGBT people to come to grips with is the family that turns their back on us."

I grew up in Florida. I'm number four of my mother's four children. Until much later, when my dad had my younger sister, I was the only girl… our life was pretty hectic. Our parents divorced when I was nine years old. The family that we knew blew up.

We got separated, and for all of us, it was very traumatic. One thing that made it real traumatic was that my father was cheating on my mother, and there was a shootout between my mother and the police. It made national news…

I happened to be standing next to my dad when the first two shots were fired. I was there when the cops started responding… It was kind of crazy there for a long time.

I was the first one in my immediate family to graduate from high school. I always liked school growing up. After the shootout happened, school, for me, was my safe place.

I also played sports, so in order to play sports I had to go to school. I played sports year-round, softball and soccer, primarily. But I'd also play pickup games out in the yard, basketball, football, just any sport I could play. It didn't matter, I was just always playing sports.

When I was thirteen, my dad and his new wife had a baby, and the baby became my responsibility.

At sixteen, I decided that I wanted to go to college. Turns out I was the first one in my family, as far back as you can go, to get a bachelor's degree. Then, later on, I went on to get my masters.

Bullying did not happen to me because I was a little badass. I had three older brothers, and they taught me to fight. If somebody started to bully me, I just beat the crap out of them.

But then I learned that it was best for me, instead of beating everybody up, to defend the people that were getting picked on by the bullies. When they were bullying other people, I would step in, and I would put a stop to it. This was early on, age ten, twelve. I remember doing it most of all in middle school... it got to the point where I would purposefully put myself between the bully and the bullied and put a stop to it.

I came out at 19. When I came out, immediately I realized that, well, maybe I'm not going to be a parent because, *how am I going to be a parent?*

Adoption wasn't talked about. IVF wasn't talked about. I was never opposed to dating a woman who had children, but before my wife, I really wasn't in a relationship with a woman who actually wanted children as well.

My brother that's right above me is gay, and I knew that early on. He came out when I was about twelve. I went home from college at one point, and one of my brother's friends said to me, "By the time you are 30, you are going to have a relationship with a woman."

And so, I thought about it. No big deal.

I got back to college, and I met a woman. I had no idea that she was gay. I got sick, and she came over and was staying with me and helping me, and she made a pass at me. And I was like, "Okay, this is really wild."

Not weird, but *wild*. It was October of my 19th year, 1986. I came out in September, and October was the first National Coming Out Day.

The group of women that I met in college lived in the community, and they, I want to say, fell in love with me, and they brought me into their community, and we would have campouts. We would go have dinner at their houses, and they really took me under their wing. I was the youngest one in the group.

So, for my coming out experience, I was around a lot of older women who just really helped me understand what it meant and what my responsibility would be moving forward.

The first person I came out to in my family was my brother. He was like, "I knew it, I knew it all along." The second person I came out to was my mother because she was always very accepting of my brother, and so I knew it would be safe to come out to her.

Her question to me was, "Are you sure?" She understood as best she could, and she was supportive. She was nonjudgmental.

My dad on the other hand... He was mostly paying for my college. When the whole AIDS crisis came out, my dad disowned my brother. I was still in high school, and he forbade me to go see him. So, I would have to sneak to go see my brother. I knew what my father's reaction would be, so I did not come out to him until I was a senior in college. I was at the point where if he stopped paying for college, I could still finish.

Of course, he was irate... None of my friends were allowed to come to his house. When he said that to me, I never stayed another night in his house. Not until two days after he died. Because if he doesn't accept my friends—and I think I have pretty decent friends, and honest friends—then he doesn't accept me.

When I was sixteen, my dad said to me that I had better not ever bring an "N" home. He was derogatory in saying that.

When I met Georgette (who is Black), within two weeks of meeting her, I knew I was going to marry her and spend the rest of my life with her.

So, here I had to come out to my father all over again. I called him, and he was like, "Okay, I don't care." So, he had dramatically changed over time.

For the last four or five years of his life, he loved Georgette. He was very accepting of her and accepting of us.

I was sexually abused [by a man] starting at about ten years old or nine years old. This went on until I was sixteen.

Quite frankly, when I slept with a woman for the first time, I felt safe sexually. Being sexually abused, there was a ton of baggage that I still carried in my body, but unconsciously; I still carry it in my body to this day, and I will for the rest of my life. I had to learn to be aware continually that, okay, this is what's causing this reaction.

I think that, when I was younger, I was fearless, and I really didn't give a shit what people thought because I had already been through so much.

Then, I had a major surgery, and I lost over 160 pounds. So now, I am of smaller stature. I am not as physically strong as I used to be. I am mentally stronger than I ever was, but physically, I'm not as strong as I used to be, so for the first time in my life… I actually realized that I was fearful for my safety.

I have not been violently attacked or verbally attacked… and I think a lot of it has to do with the way I carry myself. I think a lot of it also has to do with the way that I keep to myself. I don't draw a lot of attention to myself.

From the way I look, most people assume I'm a man. I have the body structure of a man, so most people think I'm a man anyway. When they are confused as to whether or not I am a man or woman, they tend to be quiet.

The worst thing that happens to me is when I go into a public restroom. I go into women's restrooms because I am a female, and I get questioned and stopped and stared at all the time. It's a running joke now… I had one woman that came out of the stall. I went into the stall she vacated, and she actually stayed in the bathroom until I came out so that she could say something to me. She thought I was a man.

That's where the transgender issues with bathrooms come into play. People are so worried that a man is going to do something. Because I look like a man, I quite often go into men's restrooms because there is no line. Nobody says anything to me. As long as there is a stall. The embarrassing part for me is to come out and a man is standing at a urinal. But I'm not looking at them… and I don't care. I just need to go pee.

I was raised Presbyterian. I used to go to church and Sunday school every week until the family separated. After that, I didn't go to church unless it was some special occasion. My dad's new wife was Catholic, so I would get taken to Catholic Church occasionally on special occasions. But church was not a big part of the second part of my youth. When I went to college, church wasn't a part of it.

But when I came out, everybody, even my dad, said, "It's against the Bible, against the religion and God," and all of that. "You're going to go to Hell," and "You're sinning."

It got me to thinking… I'm a pretty good person. I love people. I take care of people. I fight for the underdog. I pay my bills. I have a house. I take care of animals. I am a loving, kind, generous person. To a fault, sometimes.

Being gay must be okay because I'm an okay person.

I finally just understood that God is a loving God, and if God loves everybody, he loves me, too. I don't care what these other people think. I don't care what they *say* the Bible says… there is nothing in the Bible that says it's wrong to be gay and to be a lesbian. I chose to believe that, and I've always had faith.

Right now, my protector aspect is playing out with my family. Georgette, my daughter, and my close friends. When we are out in public, you know, I'm law enforcement. I'm second-generation law enforcement. I learned how to be a protector early on.

When I'm out, if I see something, I say something. I was in Tennessee once, driving somewhere… There was a man beating a woman. I jumped in there and put a stop to it. Scared the bejesus out of me, but I did that.

I'm not one that's real political, and with what's going on in the world today, I just want to stay at home. I don't want to be in the middle of it because I'm afraid for my physical safety. At the same time, I'm also consuming information and reading books and having discussions.

I am not as involved as I'd like to be as far as going out in public and being politically active because that just is not my comfort zone. I'm more a one-on-one person, just like with being gay and meeting people... I let people get to know me and then it's like, *"Oh, you're gay, and you're not so bad."*

You're not the devil. You don't have a horn. Or second horn. Or third horn. Or third eye.

Where we live now, people are pretty accepting. We just moved into a new neighborhood, and I've been doing a lot of work on the house. So, people only saw me at first. Then they sort of saw Georgette and the baby, and they realized that Georgette and I are a couple.

Any time we move into a new neighborhood, we are always concerned... This neighborhood is racially diverse, and the neighbors all say hi. Nobody has said anything. They see me outside with our daughter and they wave. We have a "Love Wins" Pride flag that we put up.

I think that the neighbors are happy that we are here taking care of this house because it was in disrepair. They see what we are doing, and they're commenting on how great the house looks so it's not an issue right now.

I got my BA in Criminal Justice, and I immediately went through the police academy at a community college... I had applied to be a campus police officer, but I realized that I really didn't want to be a cop. I did not want to carry a gun 24/7.

Then I was painting houses. And I was painting the house of a woman who worked in promoting affirmative action. I got to talking to her, and I told her about my degree, and she was like "Whoa, you need to come to work in the penitentiary system."

So, she was instrumental in making sure I got an application and making phone calls for me and getting me connected with the right people.

I was the only female in my role, and I moved up in the ranks to manager, and then moved up higher in terms of level of responsibility.

Prison is the ultimate human experiment. You put people in cells, and a lot of them change. A lot of them flip out. There's a lot of them that are pretty decent people; yeah, they commit crimes, but when you are in a prison, it's a dog-eat-dog world. You have got to fight to survive. There's a lot of bad things that happen in prisons.

At the same time, I met a lot of really decent, nice men. They really had a good heart. They got caught up in crime. Whatever the case might've been, I took the attitude early on that the only difference between them and me was the uniforms that we wore.

Blacks in prison are overrepresented. Furthermore, they are overrepresented for crimes where, if a white person had committed the same crime, their sentences were not as long.

In the prison where I worked we got a lot of the guys from the Maryland area and from D.C. They were locking Blacks up for heroin, but not white offenders. For heroin addicts or crack addicts, that was a crime, but when the white guys started getting hooked on methamphetamines and pills, that was an "epidemic" and they needed help.

I feel like I'm in a unique position because my wife is Black, and my child is Black. We lived for a time in Arkansas, and I saw the discriminatory practices that were in place, and are in place, and I saw the KKK marching up and down the road. There were instances when we would go out to restaurants and not get served, or we'd go to stores, and she'd get followed…

That was the first time that it was in my face; racism was in my face. To see it so blatant… *To see it happening to someone I care about…*

People will say, "I'm not a racist…I'm not calling people the N-word or following people around… it's not me, it's not me, it's not me."

Guess what? *It's not about you.* This is about the system, and we usually only hear one side of the story. I wish we would have real conversations. I wish that white folks would have conversations with Black folks, with people of color.

Have a conversation with the LGBTQ+ community, and the transgender community, and especially the Black transgender community. Listen to how they are being systematically suppressed. Listen to them and understand.

If you can do that and understand how the system as a whole is working, then you can understand why people are protesting.

I feel like for a lot of the white men who are having such heartache with understanding, it's their last stand on holding onto dominance. People of color and immigrants are coming in and that's threatening. How many women were voted into Senate and Congress, and the House of Representatives, including minority women? They feel threatened by that.

My dad was a cop in the 70s and 80s. There were a lot of race riots. He worked in the part of town where the Blacks were. So, his vision of Black people was jaded by that. If people would go back and realize that a lot of the crime that's going on in these neighborhoods is because they have no access to jobs and fair housing...

Crime is a *result*.

Georgette grew up middle-class. She wasn't exposed to those types of neighborhoods in this country, but she was exposed to the racism simply because she is Black.

I think at the end of the day, what I learned early on, and what has carried me through, is that I had to look in the mirror and determine whether or not I was a good person.

When I realized that, *yes, I am a good person*, I had to fight tooth and nail within myself to pick myself up by the bootstraps and not allow the naysayers to have space in my head. Because when I believe the negativity that is being spewed at me, I get down.

I'm okay because *my family is right here.* This life is my choice. I choose to surround myself with people that feed my soul. With a God that feeds my soul. With a church community that feeds my soul.

You have to live with integrity and do what's right for you... At the end of the day, when you talk to people, you are going to find that we all want the same things: We all want to be left alone. We want to be loved. We want to have a roof over our heads. We want to have a good job. We want to have friends and family that love us.

The hardest thing for LGBTQ+ people to come to grips with is the family that turns their back on us.

Well, if they are willing to turn their backs, then they really don't love us.

That's a hard lesson to learn... that if somebody is going to spew hate towards us, it's not about us. If we can honestly say that we didn't do anything to cause the hate, then it's about them.

Being a lesbian is not about sex. It's about the companionship. It's about the understanding and the compassion that we have for each other. It's the shared journey of walking through life together and trying to make it the best and the safest and the happiest that we can.

If you turn your back on children that you raised to be good people because they are LGBTQ+, you are going to miss out on the goodness that they bring to the society. You are going to miss out on the family that they have and on seeing who they become.

The incidence of suicide is highest amongst young LGBTQ+ kids that are being turned away and disowned.

So, quite frankly, you could up missing out on having a child that is *living*.

11: GEORGETTE BROWN——
I was slowly making a list of all of the people that I was going to lose if I were to come out.

Georgette Brown is a cisgender lesbian and a new mom in her mid-forties. She and her wife, Carol (who is also interviewed here), live with their beautiful baby girl, Gracen, in a diverse community in Maryland. A social worker by training, she has 23 years of experience working with the Federal Government. Born in Jamaica, which the Rainbow Railroad identifies "one of the most dangerous places in the world to be LGBTQ+," she immigrated to a small town in Connecticut with her evangelical family when she was six. Belonging to the Pentecostal First Assembly of God, her parents were "very rigid and very strict." Fear of losing their love kept Georgette from coming out—even to herself—until she was 29 years old

Her parents preferred that she socialize only within the local Caribbean community, which was small, and sent her to a wealthy, mostly white private school where, as an introverted, middle class Black student, "I just never really fit in."

It took her many years to come to terms with the fact her otherness was not just about race, religion, and class; her story offers a first-hand, intimate account of intersectionality, the experience of being "other" within multiple frameworks of discrimination.

Now happily married to Carol, her partner of 16 years, Georgette wept openly describing what it cost, even as a young adult no longer dependent on her parents, to live her truth and, after a great deal of struggle, to come out to her family.

Yet her narrative is also beautiful and full of hope. Initially fearing that she would lose both of her parents, Georgette has seen her mother soften and become a loving grandmother and mother-in-law.

Before finally coming to terms with her identity and sharing it with her family, Georgette tallied all of the love and family she would lose. Sadly, this kind of calculation is not unusual for LGBTQ+ people; there are no statistics for how many people, facing such loss, have stayed closeted.

How many parents have caused their children to risk so much loss? What happens to children, still years from independence, whose parents are not accepting and expect to exercise power and control over them? The statistics that answer this question are dire.

Moreover, what happens to these parents? As Georgette's story shows, there is much for them to lose as well.

Although her mother is now involved in her life, her father cut her out of his. He has missed the opportunity to know an adult child with an impressive career that involves working to promote fairness around gender, race, disability, and veteran status. He has missed the opportunity to see his child blossom in a mutually loving relationship, and perhaps most significantly, he has missed the opportunity to be a grandfather.

Existing research shows that many rejecting families of LGBTQ+ people do soften over time, and that mothers are more likely, eventually, to become accepting than fathers.

For Georgette, this pattern has held true, but younger people who have not yet established independence—or who are not lucky enough to find a life-partner—are in a much more dire position while they wait for parents.

I am an immigrant. I was born in Jamaica, and we lived there until I was six. We moved to the states and I spent the rest of my childhood in Connecticut. My parents were very religious, strict, and rigid Evangelical, Pentecostal, First Assembly of God.

I felt very different all of the time and was dealing with very strict parents.

As a young person, I felt like the odd man out racially and culturally. And with my parents being as strict as they were, I was not allowed to do a lot of the same things that my school peers did. My best friend and I, we used to laugh, because in our class, there were three black girls and one black guy, and so even if my parents had let me date, having a romantic relationship during that time was a nonstarter. I was the geeky, odd kid. I looked odd... It was not a pretty story. I just didn't get along well, like, romantically.

We used to joke that if we stayed at the school, by the time we got ready for prom, we have to flip a coin to see who would go with the one black guy in our class.

I always had crushes on girls, but in college, I dated boys. I went through my early adult life thinking, "This is what I'm supposed to do: I'm supposed to date guys, and this is it."

I remember my first celebrity crush was Tracy Chapman, and I used to sit and listen to her record over and over again. Even at twelve, I was just so in love with her, but I never related it to being gay. I always just thought, "Oh, I'm just open-minded. I just appreciate beauty in everyone." Even looking back now, I see I used to get really jealous of my best friend when she had boyfriends. At the time, I thought it was because I wanted a boyfriend. Now I think it's because I wanted to be her girlfriend

As time went on, I continued to date men and have crushes on girls. At one point, I was engaged to a man. Then, I met the woman that I am now best friends with (not my wife) who was an out proud Black woman. Spending time with her allowed me to dispel my previous misconceptions of what it meant to look like and be gay. She helped me feel more comfortable about being me. I realized I didn't have to look a certain way to identify as lesbian or to like women.

That was when I fell in love with one of my coworkers. It didn't end very well... but the experience allowed me to be myself and live my truth. It wasn't until I was 29.

Growing up, I was the kid who wanted to please my parents. Even at that age, I was deathly afraid of losing their love. Which happened anyway, with my father.

I just was always afraid of losing that, so, it was really hard to reconcile my feelings of attraction toward women. I compromised by telling myself that it was, "OK, to feel this attraction, but I couldn't actually act on it long term. I can feel this and do this right now, but in the end, I'm going to marry a man because… you know… I can't bring a woman home."

So, it took a while for me to accept myself and even longer to feel comfortable saying out loud, "I am a gay woman."

I had a very difficult internal battle. The struggle was largely due to the dread that overcame me when I thought about losing the life I had known up to that point and the people who were important to me. During this time, I was slowly making a list of all the people I was going to lose if I were to come out. It was painful. On one hand I argued, "You are an adult, you should act like an adult. You get to make choices as an adult." But on the other hand, I thought, "Yeah, but your parents won't talk to you anymore. And your friends won't talk to you anymore."

One of those people was my mother's oldest brother. I was very close to my uncle. Because he was so much older than my mother, he was very much like a grandfather to me. When I thought about telling him, I cried so hard, my whole body literally shook. I thought to myself, "Well, that's gone. He is just not going to… *No.*"

It took me a while to even say it to my sister. Which is very strange in retrospect because she makes me look conservative. My sister is not a judgmental person, so there was never a fear that I would lose her love. I was mainly afraid that if my parents shut me out, which I was positive they would, I would be banned from the big moments in her life. I was afraid my parents would force her to choose whether to have me there or have them there.

She called me one day, because, coincidentally, she was having a romantic crisis. As it turns out, she was dating someone that she didn't think our parents would like. She was telling me about it, and I saw my window of opportunity. Partly as a joke and partly as an admission, I said, "Okay, here is what we are going to do: You are going to tell them about your boyfriend, and right after, I will tell them that I am dating a white woman, and believe me, he is going to be a nonissue."

So, that's how I came out to my sister.

She started laughing, and she said, "Did you just say... *What??*" She was, and still is, the most supportive person in my family. She told me, "I'm going to go get a T-shirt that says, 'I'm an ally.'" In that moment, she confirmed that she was the person I thought she was.

My parents had gotten divorced when I was 19, and I was always more "mommy's girl" than "daddy's girl," so I came out to my mother first. Carol and I had just started dating, and my sister and I decided to surprise my mom for her birthday. While we were visiting her, I kept pumping myself up to tell her, but I ultimately froze when it came to saying the words. I dropped hints...lots of hints. For example, we went to have coffee at a local bookstore. I was looking at all the lesbian magazines they had... the ones that don't exist anymore. That went right over her head. She even asked, "Why would they have a magazine just for women?" She just was not getting it.

On the very last day, I decided I had to do it. I couldn't go back home without telling her. I had an early morning flight, and she took me to the airport as she normally did. I told myself the night before: "You are going to do it, you're going to do it, you are not going to chicken out. You found this really great person, and this is where you think you are going to be, so you need to figure it out."

This was my pep talk to myself.

It was about a 30-minute drive to the airport. I was making a calculation, "*How far do I think I can walk by myself?*" That was going to dictate at what point I was going to tell her. I just told myself, "If she kicks me out of the car, I can walk the rest of the way and be OK."

What's funny is that she brought it up, and I don't even think she realized what she was doing. She was talking about my cousin, who is also gay. She went on and on about how her sister was going on a cruise with all her children, including my cousin and his partner at the time. She kept saying how she could *never* condone that.

That's how the conversation was going.

I was thinking, "Well, she has unwittingly opened the door, so I will walk on through." So, when we got to the place where I thought I could walk, the last toll road, I said, "Mom, I am dating a woman., and I really wanted to tell you this because I want you to be a part of my life, and I want to continue to be able to talk to you." She paused for a minute and then she said, "You know it's wrong," and I said, "Well, I know that you *think* it's wrong. But I also know that you can love someone, and it doesn't matter what their gender is."

She said it again: "You *know* Georgette, you know it's wrong."

We rode the rest of the way in silence. The sound of that silence was deafening.

She called me the next day and said she still loved me. So, that was nice, but we did not talk about it again until I sent her our wedding invitation.

I told her, "We are having a commitment ceremony, and I want you to come." To which she responded, "I'm not really sure... I might have something else going on that weekend."

I cried a little bit and I said, "OK, well, if you can, you can. I would really love for you to be there." She called me back two weeks later and said, "I can come, but I won't give you away."

She came. She was visibly uncomfortable the whole time, but she did come. And she even dedicated a song to me. She tried. And she really has been trying ever since.

Now, I think she actually loves Carol more. I mean, she calls Carol more than she calls me. So, I think she has gotten to a point where she is OK.

But my father did not surprise me. He turned out to be exactly the person I thought he was. His thought patterns are very draconian. He is still very stuck in the belief that, "This is what a man does; this is what a woman does." I really waited and tried to avoid dealing with him. I held off having that conversation for as long as I could. When I finally told him, he essentially told me that I was going to Hell. That was the end of that conversation.

We didn't talk for a while. When I say we didn't talk, I mean that he would call, tell me I was an awful daughter and that I was going to Hell.

That just got to be old.

I finally reached a point where I said, "I can't do this anymore. I can't keep having this same conversation. Either you love me as your daughter, and that's enough, or you don't love me, and I will never be enough. And if I am never going to be enough, there is no need for me to continue to engage. This is too hurtful."

And I just stopped talking to him.

Sometime later, Carol and I found a church we liked, and I was just starting to feel good again, you know, about who I am. So, I thought, "I'll reach out. I'll be the bigger person." I called him and the number wasn't right. I got that recording, "The number you have dialed…"

I called the forwarding number, and my father said, "I sold the house."

I asked, "Were you going to tell me…? Where are you living…?"

He said, "I'll call you back." But he didn't.

That was 2009, and I have never, to this day, spoken with my father. I don't know where he lives, I don't know what his address is, and I don't want to know.

I have had to just bury him in my mind. I just tell myself, "I used to have a dad, but I don't have one anymore."

And I am going to be OK. I am going to heal.

I have my own beautiful family now. I am a parent. My wife loves children, and to have a child was what she always wanted. I love children too, but I was worried that I would be a bad mother. For a time, I just didn't feel good about myself, and I didn't want to replicate those genes.

Turns out that replicating my genes was not going to be a problem. Because of other health issues, I had to have a hysterectomy. But that wasn't the only barrier to achieving the family we wanted. Carol tried to get pregnant three times. We lived in Arkansas, and at the time, they didn't even let gay people adopt children. There was only one doctor that we knew of who would work with same-sex couples. Each time Carol was ovulating, we would make the two-hour drive from our home to the doctor's office to get inseminated. But after the third failed attempt, we decided to give up...

I thought, "Well, that's just God telling me were not supposed to be parents.

As time went on, we slowly let go of the dream of having a baby. Carol's brother and his wife had two children, and my sister and her husband went on to have five children. Every time my sister was pregnant, I had this tornado of feelings. I was very happy for her and her husband, but a part of me was sad for Carol and me. I told myself, "I will never have a child, and that is going to have to be ok."

Eventually we settled in the DC area. We found a church we liked and quickly became part of the community. By sheer happenstance, we met another interracial couple who had also experienced difficulty getting pregnant. They were a heterosexual couple who, during the IVF process, had five fertilized embryos. They were able to get pregnant using the first embryo, so they had four embryos left over that they couldn't use. They hadn't planned to have more than one child. So, they offered us the opportunity to adopt their embryos. Since I had had a hysterectomy and Carol was over 36, we were cautiously optimistic. In order to use the embryos, we would still need a surrogate. Initially my sister offered to carry the embryos, but then she found out she was pregnant with her sixth child. Disheartened, we were back at square one. Then another miracle: a very good friend offered to carry the baby for us. We were over the moon, but again cautiously optimistic. In the end, the fertility clinic turned her down as a viable surrogate. We were back to square one, again!

We cried. We cried a lot. We prayed some, and we decided to accept what was. We decided our role in life was to be those awesome aunts who spoil our siblings' children.

Fast forward to the afternoon of February 24, 2019. My best friend knew that we had been trying to have a baby. We were sitting around talking about the ups and downs of life and she asked, "Are you guys still trying to do the baby thing?" We explained how crestfallen we had been with all the failed attempts, how expensive it was to hire a surrogate, and that we couldn't bear to subject ourselves to more false hopes, and so had resigned ourselves to being aunts.

Carol jokingly said, "But if somebody was to just drop a baby in our laps, we wouldn't say no." We laughed about that and went on with the day. Eventually we said goodbye and put the conversation and thoughts of motherhood to bed.

That evening, Carol and I were just hanging around the house. I was watching TV and she was packing for a work trip she was scheduled to take the following day. Then my sister called. I answered and asked her what was up. She said, "I didn't want to get your hopes up, and I didn't want to say anything because we weren't really sure, but my friend's daughter is pregnant... She wants to give the baby up for adoption, and she might be amenable to letting you guys raise her baby."

WHAT?!?!!?

So literally six hours after professing that we would only have a baby if someone dropped one in our laps, there was a possibility that *somebody was dropping one in our laps*.

But, like all the times before, we rode the emotional rollercoaster and played the waiting game. I won't lie, it was hard. I think it was harder than any other time we had been on the precipice of being mothers because this was the closest we had ever gotten.

We decided that we were going to leave it up to my sister's friend's daughter. My sister gave her our information and we waited for her to call us.

Silence.

We finally decided to call. When we did talk to her, she seemed sympathetic but asked to meet us, which we completely understood. We agreed immediately.

The following Thursday, Carol met with the young lady and her father over lunch. At the end of lunch, she said, *"I would love for you guys to raise my child."* She even gave me pictures from her latest ultrasound.

By this time, it was March 17th, 2019 and her baby was due June 3, 2019. It was a whirlwind of attorneys, hers and ours, social workers, hers and ours, the adoption agency, background checks, home inspections, and the like.

We flew to Detroit for the birth because the biological mom had asked us to be in the room with her, but after we arrived, she asked us to leave.

So, we waited, AGAIN! She had gone into labor on Thursday but didn't give birth until Saturday. We were very concerned that that she was going to change her mind, and we knew she was well within her rights to do so. We drove around in circles asking, *what are we going to do?* We wanted to be respectful of her wishes, but with each minute that went by, our anxiety and dread (more mine than Carol's because I tend to awfulize), amped up that much more.

Then, Gracen, *our little miracle.*

We started getting text messages, "She has had the baby," and, "Come meet your daughter."

And she has been with us ever since.

Gracen is such an amazing kid. She is so smart, empathetic, and clever, and she makes *these faces!* She is just a little ball of personality.

I don't know if my father even knows that my daughter exists. He is missing everything. He's missing this wonderful little girl that is his granddaughter. That's just the saddest part of it.

He is missing out on getting to know me as an adult, as a parent.

BUT, that was his choice.

Honestly, I would rather him not be in her life then to be subjected to all of the pain that he hurls on me…

My mom is absolutely involved. When the quarantine started, she came and spent a couple of months with us and helped us. It was so good to have her there with me, and it is really nice getting to know my mom now, as a mother myself.

Growing up, my mom and I were really close, and then, when my sister started her family, grandkids became the focus. They would talk about parenting, and I was like, "The weather is good…" It was a little disheartening.

Now, being able to have this mother-to-mother talk is really good. She is intrusive, like any Jamaican mother would be. We do a lot of drawing lines.

And watching her walk right up to the line, step on it, move it, and *mash* it! (Laughter).

A while ago, a little after Carol and I got married, she wrote me this really wonderful letter about how she loved me, saying that no matter what, she would always love me. I think that might've been cathartic for her just to write that down. She knows the kind of person my dad is and that if she were to cut me off, I would have no parent. She did not want that.

Coming around was a journey for her, and she had some good friends who helped her with that. I just didn't give up…

One Christmas after we were married, Carol and I were planning a visit, and she offered to let us stay in her house. You could have knocked me over with a feather.

We have been staying with her ever since. And she has stayed here in our home. That was another big deal.

Not only did this journey bring her to a place where she is part of my life, she's an active part of my life. That's so great to have.

Carol's parents passed away a few years ago, so my child has one grandmother.

If I had come out as a teenager, my parents would certainly have disowned me. I have no doubt, I would have been homeless or relegated to living in a home where no one talked to me except to condemn me to Hell. Repressing that was self-preservation because I knew I wanted to go to college, and I knew that they were the ones who would pay for that. I would have been giving up on a lot if I said who I was. My parents' philosophy was, "We make the rules, you follow the rules." I always felt fear that something was going to happen to make them stop loving me.

But you know, I think my parents knew... They never talked about me in the future tense in a romantic situation. Never. I used to think it was because I was ugly, and they didn't think anyone would ever want to be with me. I think about it now, and I am like, *did you know?*

The one time my father talked about me having a husband, it was to say that he would leave me because I wasn't a good housekeeper. (Yeah, he's a keeper!)

When I was maybe five and we were still living in Jamaica, my father's friend brought their daughter for a visit. We were playing around, playing house, and we were exploring our bodies as young kids do. Not in a sexual way. Just in a "You see mine, I see yours" kind of way.

I was five, right?

My father caught us, and he beat me. He kept repeating, *"You are disgusting."* I remember my cousin coming into my room after that and just being so sweet and tender. She told me, "You are *not* disgusting. There is nothing bad about you."

Funny enough, it turns out that she is gay, too!

But now, I have a wonderful family. Great nieces and nephews. And just a great life.

Sometimes, it doesn't feel real. Carol and I have been married sixteen years. Every anniversary, I'm like, wow, how many years is this? And to have this wonderful, wonderful child. At the end of the day, when Carol and I are putting her to bed, we are like, *how did we get so lucky?*

I just feel blessed. I feel lucky. I feel like all of that other stuff was what got me to this stuff.

I played the "what if" game a lot: what if my parents had never moved to the states? I would not have been able to come out at all. Jamaica is incredibly homophobic. Beat-you-kill-you homophobic.

I never would have come out. I would have been married to some man, miserable, and just kind of trying to figure it out. Putting on the smiling face.

Maybe I wouldn't have gotten married at all.

It really did kind of all work out. Moving here was the thing that allowed me to be… to be authentic. Because I couldn't have this life anywhere else. I wouldn't have had this life anywhere else.

Now I think about what will happen if we lose our rights. We are so happy to be able to have our rights. Carol's retired, so the fact that we are able to be married means that I can have her on my health insurance. All of those things matter, and it's scary to think about losing that.

More than that, I worry about children who are afraid to come out.

Or who are on the streets doing ungodly things because they have been thrown out.

Or the children of same-sex parents who go to school and have people making fun of them because they have two moms or two dads.

We try to surround our daughter with support. We have good friends. We are members of Rainbow Families. We try to make sure our daughter sees, not just same-sex couples but interracial couples. Couples from different countries. She needs to know: Your reality, this life; this is how *rich* life is. This is the Mosaic.

But I fear that we may go back to black-and-white. It's like, we are living our lives in Technicolor right now, but the politics is threatening to bring us back to black-and-white.

I want to tell other parents that I get it. When you have a child, whether you are adopting a child or giving birth to a child, the first thing you do is count fingers and toes. Ten fingers, and toes! Okay, healthy. Breathing. Okay, whew, now I can breathe!

But in that millisecond that you are counting fingers and toes, you are already making plans and having dreams for your children *beyond*. You see them going down the aisle, all of that stuff is happening in your mind, even as you're getting used to the smell of your baby.

I know that as a parent, now. I understand why it's hard for parents to pivot.

But I want to encourage people: by the time many of us get to the place where we are telling you, we have struggled. *We have struggled.* We have asked ourselves questions. We have bargained.

Some of us have even prayed to God to "un-gay me." So, by the time we have dealt with all of that and gone through all of that, we've experienced a lot of grief. Rejection only compounds the grief.

In the end, you have to love your children compassionately, unconditionally. Not "unconditionally when you do what I like," but *really,* unconditionally. Understand that we are just human. We want the same things. It may not look the same; our families may not look the same, but they are just as valid.

And the pain we feel is just as real.

12: JENNIFER SARTORELLI—
You are perfect the way you are.

Jennifer Sartorelli's child, Luca, who was assigned female at birth, first came out to her as lesbian at age nine; within a year, they came out as trans male and then again, more recently, as gender fluid.

As a gender fluid person, Luca embraces they/them/any pronouns. This heading uses "they, them" to refer to Luca, but the interview itself uses "she, her" and "he, him" to reflect different time periods in Luca's journey.

Jennifer, after experiencing, along with Luca, the devastating impacts of bullying, began advocating for Montgomery County schools to provide LGBTQ+ positive learning materials in the elementary school curriculum, something that she believes would help to foster inclusiveness and acceptance. Her story makes it especially clear why such materials must be introduced early in schools.

Jennifer's parents immigrated from South Korea and settled in California when she was young. Her understanding of what it means to belong to a minority group has informed her response to Luca.

Having faced her own childhood struggles, she never wanted her children to feel bullied or abused; this makes Luca's school experience, and the pain that has caused them, more upsetting.

After Jennifer met and married her husband, completed medical school, and had two children, she thought her family was complete. "And then, many years down the line, after moving away from California, after moving here, to Maryland, I had Luca, my youngest."

Both medical professionals who study the workings of the human body, Jennifer and her husband share a worldview informed by scientific knowledge and understanding as well as by the challenges they have faced. "We have a bicultural family and children, and it's been a wonderful and very difficult, challenging life. Two career family, you know, three kids, four dogs, now, one cat..."

She notes that many of the hurtful ideas about LGBTQ+ people are "medically and scientifically wrong. Those are the biggest insults to me."

That Jennifer would advocate for and support Luca was always a given. This has meant, among other things, confronting parents and teachers when other children have told them that they were going to go to Hell for being gay, or that a broken ankle was "God's punishment."

Luca has been hospitalized for depression and suicidal ideation, and Jennifer has cut people out of her life who represent a threat to them by being non-affirming.

Despite Luca having the total support of their parents, Jennifer emphasizes, "... there is still something that they are challenged with that they still have these struggles, and I believe it has something to do with feeling different and not included... if we were not supportive and affirming, I don't know if I would still have a child."

Luca is doing better now, and Jennifer wants the overwhelming message in their life to be, "Nothing is wrong with you. You are perfect the way you are."

For both Jennifer and her husband, parenting Luca has been an important growth journey that has increased their awareness of the experiences of marginalized groups. She explains that she now has a greater awareness of minority stress and its consequences.

"If I can, I am going to do something about making things more fair."

Luca was our planned-surprise baby. He came along eleven years after his sister. He was assigned female at birth and was probably the most challenging child because he was very hard to soothe. I don't think he slept for the first three years of his life... He just generally required more attention from us compared to his older siblings, who seemed so cooperative.

When Luca was nine years old, he came out to me in the car, saying, "Mom, I am gay." But, we knew it was coming because—I'm going to use "she" pronouns to discuss the past—because when she was six or seven, she had said she liked girls. She would ask things like, "Can a boy marry a boy? Can a girl marry a girl?"

And I said, "Yes!" Because this was after marriage equality had passed.

She didn't make much of it, didn't talk about it a lot, but she just kind of planted a little seed in my mind that, you know *she could be...*

I mentioned it to my older kids and to my husband. They were like, "It's too early to tell." So, we just didn't really think about it.

But in terms of her presentation, she presented as female. She wore clothes like a female, had hair like a female. She wasn't particularly tomboyish... None of that. She did fencing as a sport, but her brother and sister did fencing as a sport.

When she told me at nine that she was gay and that she was attracted to girls, I asked her, "When did you know you were gay?" She said, in hindsight, she knew when she was seven, when she went to a summer fencing camp and she had a crush on a girl. So, she came out as lesbian just before fourth grade started.

I immediately went to the principal and guidance counselor and met with her teacher and said, "This is the situation. My daughter wants to come out as gay, and I need you to look out for her." They were all very supportive. They said, "This is not our first rodeo." They had had a gender expansive child before.

So, I was happy with the response I got from the school.

(One of the people who helped us, by the way, is a gay man who is not out to the school community because I don't think he feels comfortable.)

When Luca told me in the car that she was gay, she was *ready* to come out. I think she was very happy. She was like, "Hey, this is me. This is who I am." It felt like a declaration: "This is *me*: I'm celebrating it. So, watch me celebrate it… I want to share it with you."

My response was: "Go for it, kiddo. Be true to yourself. Be happy. Mom and dad are going to love you *no matter what*. And so are your brother and sister."

Because she was so young at the time, my husband was thinking, "I wonder if this is going to remain true?" But I remember knowing, at that age, that I liked boys. So, I said, "Why is it unreasonable for a child, at that age, to know who they like or are attracted to?"

When I say attraction, I'm not talking about sexual attraction… It's just that intense feeling that you have of liking someone that is special. I remembered having that for boys. So… why not? You can't tell me that gay people just realize it, boom, when they become adults, or when they become pubertal. I don't believe that.

As parents, we certainly didn't know what we were doing because we hadn't had an LGBTQ+ child before. So, I said, "Well, I'm just going to educate myself as much as I can."

Immediately, we went to a PFLAG meeting, which turned out to be a disaster because there was a woman who came with an agenda… We did not get what we needed from that meeting, and my husband never went back.

The summer between fourth and fifth grade (after he had already come out as lesbian), I picked Luca up at day camp, and he handed me a note saying, "I am a boy."

I had met two other moms whose lesbian daughters eventually transitioned. So, I had already thought that might happen.

Luca told me that all through fourth grade, he felt like a boy. He finally mustered up the courage to tell me...

Now, that was a little bit harder to take for my husband. You have to understand... My husband is older. He grew up in a teeny, tiny village in Italy, in an extremely homophobic, pro-Catholic, homogeneous white society. He has accomplished tremendous personal growth through his child. His reaction was, at first, *"Oh no, not this."* But within three weeks, he was using the new pronouns. He made mistakes, but he corrected himself.

Luca just turned eleven. We are only out to my mother right now.

My parents watch Korean soap operas. My mother told me that there was a storyline with a transgender character, and that my father was saying all kinds of bad things about transgender people. What would he do if he knew he had a transgender grandchild?

I think in the interest of protecting my child's trust fund, I'm not going to tell him.

We are going to go visit family soon, and before that, I have to let my brother and sister know. It's a problem because my brother, and particularly my brother-in-law, are deeply religious, in a bad way... ultraconservative, right wing.

My message is going to be very short. I am going to give them email links for literature, so that they can educate themselves. But, it is just going to say:

> We have an update in our family. Your niece is no longer a girl. She
> is now a transgender boy, and his new name is Luca, and he uses
> male pronouns. I have provided some links for you to help you

understand what this process might be like for a child, but we as a family are supporting him.

The ground rule will be: You are not allowed to talk to him or to question him about his gender identity or sexual orientation.

If you find that you cannot use his chosen name and preferred pronouns, you will not have a relationship with us anymore.

It just is what it is.

To me, being truthful is very important because I grew up in a family with a lot of secrets and lies. I want my child, and us as a family, to not have to feel like we have anything to hide because we are not doing anything wrong. We are living our lives.

This has to do with someone's *innate substance*. I really feel like, if you hide that, you are adding stigma. I don't think this is something that should be seen in a negative light... this is way too important to not be out there.

Just be who you are... I want to set that as an example to my child. Do not make compromises by keeping something this important a secret. This is true for anybody. You have to be who you are in your life and find your chosen people. Period.

Parenting a gay, or lesbian, or bisexual, or pan-sexual child is not quite the same as parenting a transgender child. There is more violence towards trans people. As a transgender boy, Luca is probably is going to have less risk than a transgender girl, especially of color. But there is the whole bathroom issue... The locker room issue. All the sleep away stuff through school. It's a little bit more complicated.

And many trans kids want new names. My child wanted a new name, and he was picking outlandish names for our family, like "Jordan." I said "We have an Italian family. Can't you pick an Italian name to fit our family?"

So, he chose Luca.

And then, some scary stuff happened. Luca was hospitalized three times for suicidal ideation and one attempt. He struggles with depression, anxiety, social anxiety, and self-harming.

This tells you something: Even though I believe we have been as supportive and loving as possible, there is still something that he is challenged with that he still has these struggles, and I believe it has something to do with feeling different and not included in his kid world.

It might be genetics because we have depression in our family. He might be disadvantaged because of that. But whatever it is, I know, I can pretty much bet my house that if we were not supportive and affirming, I don't know if I would still have a child.

And that is the stark reality for a lot of these kids. I don't know how LGBTQ+ children who don't have supportive, affirming parents survive to adulthood.

Montgomery County is very diverse, but in our experience, it's actually very homophobic. There was a lot of homophobia in my child's school. A lot of anti-gay slurs from children... Also, there was a lot of social isolation. No invites to parties. No play dates.

Even in school, girls would stay away from my child because they were afraid my child had a "thing" for them, even though my child would say... "I do not like you like that."

No more piggyback rides. No more hugs from girls... Cringing if my child got too near one of her classmates. This one girl, she would scoot away and cringe. It was isolation and exclusion like that, you know...

When I have an opportunity to speak in front of educators, especially in elementary school, I say, "You need to treat the words 'faggot' and 'gay'... like the N-word. It needs to be admonished, and it needs to go away."

My child heard those words a lot.

A contributing factor here is no representation of LGBTQ+ people in the curriculum. In the health education class, it is very heterosexual and binary, and also, in the library, there are no books with representation, and I am trying to influence the lower school/middle school curriculum specialists.

I have tried to persuade MCPS to have more inclusion in the elementary school curriculum. Whenever I have the chance to speak, I say, "By the time you go to middle school and high school, it is too late; these kids come with transphobic, homophobic opinions and attitudes. You need to educate them when they are young, in elementary school."

After these scary times of the hospitalizations during the summer, my husband and I made a decision to take Luca out of public school so he would not have to transition where everybody knew him for years as a girl. The new school did us a huge, huge favor. Enrollment was over, but Luca took a test, and he was in. They knew there was a need.

We thought transferring would help him, but he just decompensated even more. He missed a whole semester of school because of depression, anxiety, self-harming. He would cut himself… we had to hide away all our sharps.

Now, he is doing much better and under the care of a Dialectical Behavioral Therapist and a Gender Wellness Child Psychiatrist who are helping him work through those parts of himself that we don't have the expertise to help him with.

He also has a pediatric endocrinologist on board. Luca is in that pubertal stage where puberty blockers would be appropriate if he wanted them, but he said no. The transgender experience is very individual. Not every child wants to take a puberty blocker. Luca does not seem to have the extreme gender dysphoria and unhappiness with his body that I've read about in other transgender kids and adults.

Legislation is pending in certain states right now to block gender affirming care like puberty blockers. The scientific studies are pretty clear. Young people have a much better outcome in terms of mental health later on when they have access.

That kind of decision should come from the parents and the child, with the help of an affirming provider. People who want to block affirming care don't know the evidence-based, medical recommendations out there. They are driven by fear and intolerance. They have said a lot of trans-phobic stuff. A lot of things that are medically and scientifically wrong.

Those are the biggest insults to me.

We are being advised that we should follow our child's lead. If they want it, they will get it. If not, they won't. We want to keep our child safe and happy. I want the overwhelming message in his daily life to be, "Nothing is wrong with you. You are perfect the way you are."

My husband and I wonder... is he non-binary but wanting to fit into a binary world and so identifying as a transgender boy? Because non-binary is much trickier, to expect people to use "they them" pronouns, and bathrooms, and things like that.

But whatever it is, we are just going to educate ourselves as best we can, but also work with professionals who know what they are doing.

We are lucky because we have the means to provide every type of care he needs. Whether they take our insurance or not, we just take our kids to get care. But I know there are many families who can't do that.

To celebrate Luca's identity, we went to DC Pride and Frederick pride. We had fun. We joined Rainbow Families because I wanted my child to see that there are families with parents of the same gender. They are welcoming of families with all structures, so we do fun activities with them.

I also called the Pride Clinic at Children's National Medical Center, and they plugged me in with SMYAL, which was starting a pilot program for kids ages six through twelve, and Luca is going on his second year with the program.

But it's all only because Luca wants to do it.

My husband recently spoke up at a SMYAL event and said, "You know, when you have a child that is LGBTQ+, you don't know a lot of information. You are very ignorant..." I added that kids are coming out younger and younger, and they need support. They need a community. They need to find each other."

The challenge, for parents who want to learn, is that there is a lot of misinformation about LGBTQ+ individuals. When it comes to your child, it is a unique journey, and you really need to follow your child... filter out all this other stuff, and really pay attention to your child's wants and needs.

My relationship with Luca is extremely close. I'm very protective. I have to learn to pull back. Recently, at the pediatrician's office, a nurse who hadn't seen him before called him by the wrong name. I just looked at her like, "Do you want to try that again?"

He should not have to worry about those things.

He should worry about doing his homework.

I have blocked so many childhood and high school friends on Facebook. When confronted with someone who is not inclusive, the thing that goes through my mind is, "Do I want this person in my life? In my family's life?" Some want to connect with me again, and I hit *delete*. You can't believe those things and be my friend.

We have some very close friends who use Luca's preferred name and pronouns. They think he is in a phase, but because they are affirming, we have a relationship with them. But, if they were to come at my child with, "this is just a phase..." *No.*

It's not a phase.

In my profession, I see horrible diseases every single day. Sometimes, in extremely young people. So, if this is the toughest challenge that life is going to present to me with my kids, I'm fine. I am very grateful. Gratitude goes a long way... You have to be able to adapt... I am trying to pass that on to my kids.

I want to stress the need for greater support and acceptance for LGBTQ+ kids. This means inclusion in the curriculum, and especially health education, when they learn about puberty. If you don't like it, exclude your child. But don't take it away from other people.

I sometimes feel like I am losing that desire to try to build a bridge. More and more, I am just saying, "Get out of my way. I am going to do what I need to do for my kid. If you give me a chance, I will tell you, *if* you want to learn something."

Many states still lack discrimination protections for LGBTQ+ people. My husband and I tell Luca, "There are places you will never be able to live. You will never be able to visit. We care for your safety and happiness, so, you need to stay in areas where you will have a strong community." We are very practical and realistic. We are training Luca to be aware and of the things he needs to look out for.

That is why organizations like SMYAL and HRC are very important. I want my child to know where to go to learn about their rights, about legal recourse, and to know what they are entitled to. I don't want them to be able to feel helpless; I want them to have all the legal resources, all of that. It is important to make them feel like, "Hey, there are people out there looking out for you."

Our kids have to find the safe spaces. And they will. And I think the safe spaces are getting bigger...

I can tell you that this journey has made me much more aware of my own internalized bias. Like, I *see* you now. I see you transgender individuals struggling and being murdered. I see you, gay and bisexual, pansexual people being discriminated against and harassed.

I have a greater awareness of the members of this community and their struggles.

If I can, I am going to do something about making things more fair. Especially for my child. I have become more of an activist. And my husband must have peeled away layers of internalized bias, having grown up in that tiny village.

My growth has led me to see the humanity of all of us... I don't think I would have had so much growth so quickly if I had just had my older kids, who are cis-hetero.

I tell whoever asks:

We have become *better people* because of our child. As a family, we are better off because we have a child who is queer.

13: JOHN KEISTER—
It changes your life and it changes the world to live in authenticity.

John is a musician, an independent business owner, and an out gay man in his 30s who lives in Maryland. He grew up in a fundamentalist Baptist community in Washington State. The church was so conservative, he says, that "they thought the Southern Baptists were liberal."

Growing up in an aggressively anti-LGBTQ+ environment forced John to suppress his identity—or at least to discover it gradually over time in a way that created self-doubt and left him, at times, both isolated and vulnerable.

In particular, his story highlights confusing messages that LGBTQ+ people growing up in fundamentalist communities receive about the idea of being gay as a "behavior" and a "choice," which caused John to struggle with his understanding of himself over many years. Ironically, his mother later told him that she first thought he was gay when he was four years old, an admission that exposes the fallacy of thinking about sexuality in this way.

John was athletic and popular and a successful student, even graduating as valedictorian of his class. While his larger community did not perceive him as gay, his family saw difference in him and treated him with suspicion from an early age, forcing him to live in the garage for a time to limit any potential influence on his siblings. He began ex-gay therapy at 13 or 14 (memorizing scripture was supposed to "fix" him), and his parents forced him to move out during his senior year.

Sharing here how, over time, he confronted and only gradually untangled harmful ideas about himself, John's story touches on many of the key issues for LGBTQ+

youth now: family rejection, the need for inclusive education, representation as a life-line, the impacts of bullying, and the long journey of healing.

Parents may believe that by silencing conversations about sexuality and LGBTQ+ people, they are protecting their children, but John's narrative illustrates the costs of such erasure.

Married to a woman at a young age, John struggled for many years to understand and accept himself—a journey of healing that he is still working on.

One thing he knows for certain: "It changes your life and it changes the world to live in authenticity."

In the Baptist culture that I grew up in, everything gay was buried. We didn't know a gay person. I remember hearing in church that gay people, or homosexuals, should be all put on a barge, or something like that, and *burned*. That's the kind of stuff we heard all the time. I was hearing this stuff since age nine. These people are really, really bad... just terrible. They are out terrorizing the world.

The pastor would talk about how, in the past, there was a homosexual boy at the teenage table who would turn red in the face. I didn't really know what all of that meant at the time, and it didn't make a whole lot of sense to me, him preaching on this constantly. It dominated their psyche in a way.

At that age, I was like, *how many people are gay?*

I would lay in bed at night and just wonder... These people like each other, how are they even having sex? I had to go to the library just to understand what male and female parts were. We just were not taught about this at all.

In seventh and eighth grade, I was sitting there wondering, how do guys like each other? How does that all work? I would go get muscle magazines at the library, and then I would cut out pictures and put them in my bibles… I read Olympic diver Greg Louganis's autobiography, *Breaking the Surface*, because I heard he was gay. I tore out the pictures from the library book and kept them for myself.

Because there was someone out there who was *like me*, finally.

When I was sixteen, a 28-year-old guy asked me for my phone number. He said, "Hey, we could hang out sometime, or go to a movie." He offered to give me a ride home one day, and I foolishly said yes. Which was *dumb, dumb, dumb*. He drove me around, and we drove to this park. He gave me a blow job.

He dropped me off, and then later that night, he sat next to me in church… I felt like, if anyone ever found out about the secret, I was going to be sunk, done for. It was totally confusing, and to not really have anyone to talk with it about…

I never told my parents; that was so far under the rug. They didn't find out about that until within the last five years. I kept that inside of me and carried it alone because I didn't have someone I could trust with that information in my community. There was nobody.

We were taught that being gay was a behavior, like picking up a cup. Like I'm gay now (picking up a cup); now I'm not gay (putting down a cup). Just going back and forth, like that, creates a problem because it's not about the desire set that you have; it's more a behavior thing.

You can control your behavior, but your desire set isn't something you necessarily get to manage. Your body doesn't get a chance to pick.

I was a weird kid. I even dressed up in drag… I took one of my sister's swimming suits and made these huge balloon breasts. And I would use pastel colors on my face and eyes and stuff like that. I didn't necessarily want to be a woman. I don't have the desire for that. I just thought it was fun to do.

I was always finding ways to enhance my body. Once I brought lace and some sexy underwear. I would have to hide it… my grandmother found it and decided to show it to my mom and dad. They took it all away from me, and I was so upset about it.

I remember the first day I wore a tank top outside. I just thought it was so sexy to wear a tank top. To go outside like that without a shirt on was such a big deal. I was definitely experimenting with all of this stuff, but I never really admitted to myself that I was gay.

My parents eventually required me to wear pants at all times… I could not wear shorts unless I was getting in a swimming pool; I had to wear a belt at all times. I literally got my ass spanked if I was not wearing a belt.

My dad basically built a room in the garage for me to live in. It was like I was segregated out of the house in a way. That's how I felt about it. It was super awkward… I had no privacy. My dad had built a wall with a doorway, but a door was never put on… if anyone came out to the garage, there I was.

I was able to push through all this stuff and keep going.

None of this is to throw my parents under the bus; I'm just saying that this way is not right. There is a better way to do it. I love my parents, but there were a lot of mistakes made. I understand it was their first time parenting a gay kid in the middle of a Fundamental Independent Baptist cult movement totally hyper-focused on sexuality…

Ex-gay therapy started when I was 13 or 14. The whole concept was like, "I'm going to memorize all of the scriptures, and then I won't be gay." I don't think they really had the concept yet of conversion therapy; they had this idea that if I memorized scripture, a virgin would magically make a desire-set change.

Craziness.

Nothing was open. I talked to a pastor when I was 14 about the situation. Basically, it was like, "John's doing great. Go memorize scripture, and everything is going to be fine. Let's move on with life." It was always shoved under the rug.

By my senior year of high school, my dad wanted me to move out of the house, so I moved into my friend's house. His mom had a computer downstairs, and I was talking to all of these guys. My brother found the Internet history. He printed out all of this stuff from my talking to this guy, Gareth. So, I came home one day...

He and my friend got a box of HoHos and they wrote "Gareth's Ho" and put it in my bed where I slept. I got back, and I knew that they knew.

Aaron, my friend, just apologized within the past year for his behavior and what happened. I never thought I'd hear that out of his mouth.

In high school, I was the captain of the soccer team. I was on the basketball team. I played the piano. I memorized the most scripture every year at camp and at school. I was like the poster child for church and school... I participated in everything. I was cool. I was never made fun of. And if I was, I didn't care. It never mattered to me.

I did not admit to myself that I was gay until I was 30 years old. I was having "gay behavior" whenever I would pick up being gay, and then the rest of the time, I was, like, "I'm not gay." That led me and my ex-wife into getting married... She was thinking that, and I was thinking that.

But wait... It turns out that just because you get married, that doesn't take the desire set away. It doesn't leave.

I was so broken when I went to college because I was gay. And I was crying. I spent like two years just, like, crying. I mean, I was happy at times, but it was just such a long period of time where I was crying and upset about me being gay. Why wasn't God healing me? Why aren't you healing me?

So, I was praying that God would take this away. I started talking to this guy and we had this really great talk.... I fell in love with this guy. I was like 21. I felt so guilty about it. I thought I was going to get kicked out of my Christian college, so I stopped talking to him. I completely regretted doing that.

I started interacting with other guys, and I was having physical interactions with guys all through the rest of college... I dated a lot of girls so I could go on campus activities.

When my future wife and I started dating, I was still seeing guys. But I grew up in a system of inauthenticity, so authenticity was never practiced.

About a year and a half into our marriage, I was still messing around with other guys... It never stopped; I thought it would, but sex between me and my wife... I was thinking about guys almost every single time. It just never went away. I just thought all of this was going to be magically healed when I got married. I thought, it's going to be so wonderful, and all of this gay stuff is going to fall off on the side, and I'm never going to have to deal with this again. *Magic.*

We moved to Maryland. I worked for a local church, and I was going to all of this ex-gay stuff.

It was unhealthy because I was going out and meeting new guys and never really having a relationship... every time I saw a guy three or four times, I cut them off. They were getting too close to my world, where I had to be hiding. *Inauthenticity.*

When I saw an authentic person, I was like, "Oh my God, I want some of that." In my world, everyone else was faking it.

So, I was going to this ex-gay thing. One night, the leader was like, "Somebody name a sin." And this guy in the back was like, "porn." And I was like, "*Seriously,* you are looking at straight porn, and you think you are having a problem?"

I started going to this counselor, and she said, "John, you are gay, and you are treating your wife like shit. You need to decide whether you are going to be gay, or if you are going to be with your wife." I was so mad.

But then, I realized, *"You have this behavior. And when you participate in this behavior, it comes from the desire set of you wanting that. And that desire? It is called being gay. That's what we call it in the English language. It's called being gay. So, you can bounce around and act like you are not gay all day long, but your behavior and the desire that you are presenting is called being gay, and you need to come to terms with that."*

It was the time in my life to acknowledge this. Two weeks later, I basically came out to myself. It was incredible. It was such a freeing moment.

It was around this time, when I finally admitted to myself that this was going on, that my wife said, "I am moving out." I came home, and she was gone. She was gone on Saturday, and I got fired from the church on Sunday. Soccer, Sunday school, all the choirs I was teaching. Fired.

That was the magic reset button. The H-bomb that comes in and resets all of your made-up bullshit and says, "You get to start over."

I didn't have a church to go to participate in. I didn't have a wife to be there with me in the middle of this, or another person there. I didn't have a job to go to. It was just me and the house that I lived in.

That point in my life was like God's reset button. *Hey, we are starting over.* Authenticity was able to come in; I was able to grow into authenticity, and to be able to say how I feel, and that it's okay to feel this way and have these emotions. "You like guys, so go do that now. You have that opportunity." My life completely changed at that point.

I took the resources that I had, and I figured out how to make it work. I started doing Airbnb in my house. I started selling stuff online. All of that allowed me to be resourceful in a way that I had not been up until that point. I also was scared of getting a job because I was gay and I had been fired from all these church jobs now, and regular jobs, here in Maryland, for being gay. I've been fired four different times in Maryland for being gay...

Then I was hired by an LGBT+ positive church. It was such a healing balm for me because I was out, and people knew who my boyfriend was. I wasn't trying to hide anything. They knew I was gay, and they loved me, and I played all the same songs that I did before. It was fantastic, such a wonderful place, and all the people that I

met in the church are the reason why I was able to build my business. Everything has
been built off of the relationships that I formed there.

One of the major lessons I've learned is understanding the concept of love without
expectations. I feel liberated by taking expectations off of my parents, the idea that
they are supposed to love me in a certain way, or do things in a certain way...

I realize that my parents were acting like that because that's what they've been taught.

I have taken my time and my money, taking time off of my work to fly out to Washington state to visit them every year. I'm coming out to love them, because I am a
lover, and not because they are deserving of love... I come out because I choose to, and
how they treat me; that's up to them.

That changes the power dynamic, and it gives the power back to me instead of letting
them be in control of how I feel about how this day goes, or about how this trip goes.
Now I can go out there and see them because I can love them where they are, even in
their brokenness, and not require something from them.

They are still very negative about this whole gay situation...but sometimes we have
to come from the place of being treated with no love to teach those people about love
and to show them how it works.

I don't think I'm totally healed.... We don't get to practice being healed every moment
of every day, but... I have the power in the situation because I am showing love according to my abundance versus my scarcity.

I think the concept of authenticity really is the most important... It battles all of the
teachings that we were taught and raised with... It changes your life and it changes
the world to live in authenticity.

That's my goal in my life right now: to be able to show people how to live authentically
and to live with love and without expectations. It's a practice, a daily practice. And to
be who you are, without hiding. That's my goal: to share that message.

14: DAVID CLURMAN——
I want them to get the message out that it is okay to be Christian and gay at the same time; it's not mutually exclusive.

David is a cisgender gay man in his mid-forties who, as a young person, experienced the silencing impact of the AIDS crisis, and who still remembers how LGBTQ+ people were primarily represented in a very negative light, when he was growing up, as unstable, promiscuous and immoral.

Although he realized that he was gay when he was in his early teens, he "ignored" this reality for a long time, dating girls and passing easily because he never had what he calls a "stereotypical presentation."

College was liberating for David because it offered a safe space. His peers' willingness to out themselves in a social situation meant that *finally*, "I was not alone."

Additionally, David benefitted from living in a college community where professionals were committed to helping young people with issues of identity.

David echoes other participants in this book where he explains the sense of responsibility he felt, for much of his life, to represent gay people well and to take responsibility for relationships, particularly when people lacked knowledge or understanding. Though his thinking about this has changed somewhat, he is still a bridge-builder.

Not surprisingly, David now works in an educational setting; a post on his office door signals that he is an ally.

Here, David shares his mixed experience, twenty-seven years ago, coming out to his divorced parents who lived, at that time, in Maryland and Florida.

His story is unique in several regards: his father was initially more accepting than his mother—a less common pattern. David's dad intuited that he was gay and initiated discussion in a way that was very loving. Interestingly, David's parents later told him that they had discussed the possibility that he was gay when he was a toddler, something he still finds mysterious.

In addition, David's struggle to reconcile his LGBTQ+ identity with his Christian faith in a non-affirming church offers insight into how generating discussion can be powerful.

Drawn to religion after experiencing a crisis that, he emphasizes, did not have to do with being gay, David makes a compelling case for how faith has helped him. At the same time, he also illuminates struggles faced by Christian LGBTQ+ people in a way that readers who are not part of that faith can understand.

In particular, David explains "Side A" and "Side B" perspectives, which have to do with the debate about whether LGBTQ+ Christians should be celibate. The underlying idea, that sex is for the sole purpose of procreation, underscores the connection between current attacks on abortion rights and threats to LGBTQ+ rights coming from the Christian-based political right.

Initially denied the opportunity to participate in leadership activities at a large, evangelical church in Maryland, David persisted, and he now leads a visible and growing LGBTQ+ support group. Courageously present, he has forced conversations to happen and helped to facilitate much-needed community and visibility for LGBTQ+ Christians.

David is deeply committed to his church and to the idea of not having sex outside of marriage. Weddings usually bring communities together; ironically, if he does decide to marry, his church's philosophy that LGBTQ+ people must remain celibate may force David to leave his.

I grew up in Maryland in Prince George's and Montgomery Counties until I was twelve, and then I moved to Florida. My parents got divorced when I was six. There was some shared custody, so I spent time with both of them until I graduated from high school in 1992.

I'd say that we were middle class, not conservative at all. It wasn't until we moved to Florida that my mom started attending a Presbyterian Church. We went there as a family as well.

Right around twelve, shortly before the move, I started to realize, "Okay, wait a minute. I seem to have an attraction towards other boys instead of girls."

For me, it makes sense looking back, because that's when puberty begins, and that's when attraction starts developing anyway. That's when it first came into my mind.

I didn't do anything about it. I dated girls in high school.

I didn't have anybody in my life that I knew that was gay, so I didn't talk to anybody about it. It just stayed all in my head until college. I didn't give a whole lot of thought to it.

I didn't really feel at risk. I didn't fit a lot of the stereotypes back then, and I still don't. Not as a way of passing… it's just that I tend not to have some of the more stereotypical qualities that may exist with people who are gay.

My parents apparently had a conversation when I was two or three years old about the fact that I might be gay. They cannot tell me any specifics at this point in time as to why they thought that. I don't know what I was doing at two or three years of age. I didn't play with Barbies and things like that. That just didn't happen.

During my first year of college, I got involved in leadership activities, a continuation of the kind of thing I had been doing in high school. At a leadership retreat in February of my first year in college—there were probably about 120 people at this retreat—that was the first time that people I knew identified themselves as gay.

This was at a university in Maryland in the early 90s. We did an activity where someone would make a statement, and if it applied to you, you would stand up and sit back down. They would go through a variety of different descriptors about identity, and one of the last ones was "somebody who is gay, lesbian, or bisexual."

I think there were six people in the room who stood up, and I was not one of them. I was just like, *Oh! Okay.* And it was on the bus ride back to campus that I chose to chat with some of those people, and I remember saying on that bus ride, "I think that I'm gay."

It was the first time that I had said that to anybody else.

I don't think that it was so much surprise as, "Oh, there might be somebody I can talk to."

That's almost 27 years ago.

In the early 90s, it wasn't great to be out—certainly not what it is today. The AIDS crisis was much more in the news, and so there wasn't a positive connotation that went with being gay. I think that's one of the things that kept me, and probably a whole lot of other people, from exploring those thoughts and feelings.

I know that being able to talk to these guys, I was able to be, like, "All right." I had some validation. It was like, "I'm not alone." That was incredibly fulfilling.

Coming out happened pretty quickly. I told my parents in April, just two months later. And then, after that, it went to the rest of my family over a couple of more months.

I know that some of the people that I told in college were some staff members, advisors for student organizations I was a part of... I think it was because these are folks who work in higher education. They tend to be supportive of students and safe to talk to. I knew that they regularly worked with students going through identity issues, and that they were not likely to look down on or cast people aside, because part of their job is to support students.

One of the more interesting parts of my story is that I didn't tell my dad I was gay. He told *me* I was gay. I moved to Florida in middle school. My dad continued to live in Maryland, and when I came back up there for college, I continued to live near his home during that time. I have always been very close to both of my parents. I was raised in a very close family; even though there was a separation with my parents, I was very close with both of them, and I would see him quite regularly.

I was a good student. Growing up, I always did well in school... I did well my first semester, but my second semester, I started goofing off. I did not invest as much time in my studies. I started taking more difficult classes because I had declared a major. I was not doing the amount of work that I should have been doing, and my grades were corresponding to that.

Because I am somebody who has always done well in their classes, and my parents were paying for my school, I recognized it was going to come as a really big shock. I did not want my poor grades to be a surprise, so, I tried to lay the groundwork by saying, "Yeah, the semester is just not going the way I thought it would."

Anyway, at some point, my dad decided to join me for dinner. He came to campus and we had dinner at the dining hall, and I was saying this again. "Yeah, I am just going through some stuff right now, and it's making school more difficult." And he said, "Well, I think I know what that stuff is."

Now that kind of freaked me out a little bit. We kind of put a pause on the conversation and went back up to my room. By that point, my roommate had moved out, so I had a room to myself, which was kind of nice. He sat down in the chair, and I sat down on my bed, and he was like, "I think what you are trying to tell me is that you are gay."

And I was just nodding my head.

And it was just like, *wow*. It was pretty cool. That was a pretty easy way to come out to one's parent. He reaffirmed his love for me and acceptance of me, and he said that this didn't change anything in our relationship. Which was great. I think it was probably about as good as it could have gone.

So, after that leadership conference, I joined the GLBT student organization (I *think* that was the order of the letters—maybe there wasn't even a "T" yet). I did that for about two months before I had this conversation with my dad. So, I got to meet other people who were gay, students, and I became friends with some of these people who were gay.

One of them talked about their own coming out experience and how they were essentially shunned from the family and told, "You need to go figure out things on your own now." And that put some fear into me. I didn't *think* that would happen with my family, but I also recognized that there is the unknown...

That had me hesitate with sharing with my family. I was like, I can't afford to go to school in my own. I was very fortunate that they were able to pay for it. That freaked me out.

So, engaging in that conversation with my dad and hearing all of that... I know that I am much more fortunate than some of my friends that I had at the time. It was an incredible sense of relief. Part of that was the fact that nothing is going to change, at least not in the relationship between my father and me. We always had been close, and we grew closer through my college years, and this is part of the reason for that.

Being that I was in Maryland and my mom still lived in Florida, our communication was via the phone instead of in person. She and my dad talked that weekend, and they had a conversation about me being gay. And after that, my mom and I got on the phone and we talked.

It's weird because I remember she was watching *Last of the Mohicans* (a story about American identity and othering). It was in the background where she was. It's just one of those weird things that sticks out in your mind.

I told her I was gay, and she had concerns. Part of this was the religious aspect. Part of this was, "Why would you choose this? Life can be so hard for you." She had a concern about AIDS… I was like, "Yeah mom, that's a concern. I'm not going to be going out and doing things that make me unsafe." So, there was a little bit of me needing to push back on these concerns. But I certainly shared some of those.

I think it was even in this first conversation, or it could have been one we had very close to this, where she said, "Well, now I am not going to have grandchildren." There was a sadness or mourning that she had. I was like, "I have a sister!" She ended up being bisexual anyway and has ended up getting married to a female, so, yeah, there are no grandchildren coming. But we didn't know that back then.

My mom's reaction was not so supportive; however, it was not shunning or hate-filled or anything like that. As I said, I grew up very close with both of my parents, and that was evident through this experience as well… I think I was on the defensive a little bit because I had to say, "You know what mom, I didn't choose to do this. Why would anyone choose to do this? I didn't choose. This is just who I am."

Then, the letter from my mom came… a handwritten note, quoting a lot of scripture, that essentially said I was going to Hell.

It was hurtful… It caused me to not talk to her for six weeks, which is the longest I've ever gone without talking to either parent. Eventually, we started talking again, and we got to a point where we were agreeing to disagree. Any time she would broach the subject, I would be like, "Mom, this isn't going to get us anywhere."

Perspective allows me to know that she bought it up because she loved me. That has never been in question… I have talked with her about how that letter was hurtful, that she did not handle it the best way that she could have. She was doing it the way that she thought she was supposed to, but she recognizes that was not ideal.

After that, I constantly had to come out. It was a constant coming out process, and I had to be very intentional and very thoughtful about it.

I did have some jobs during this time. I worked at the dining hall on campus. I ended up later on getting a job at a restaurant. I had to choose how I was going to come out and who I was going to come out to. I was a resident assistant for three years, and I had to be thoughtful about how I came out there, as well.

I wasn't somebody who was "out and proud" with the rainbow flag hanging outside my room. It was part of my identity, but I didn't make it my sole identity. I think that made things easier for me. When I saw that with some other folks, they attracted some different attention.

Some of it was positive, and some of it was not.

It's about protecting myself. There was a long time—and it changed towards the end of college—where I felt that, if somebody had a problem with me being gay, it was my problem, not theirs. And I needed to do something to fix that. I had to help them understand why it's not a bad thing. Whatever thoughts they had that made it an issue for them, what could I say or do to address those concerns, so that they would still want to be my friend and not resent me for my identity?

Part of that is that I believe in deep relationships… I have never been the person who has a whole lot of friends. I have a very small group of very close friends, usually. So, I'd feel a loss if this got in the way of a friendship

My thoughts have obviously changed over the years. Now I'm just like, "Oh, that's your problem." I am, of course, still available to help somebody understand. I actually still have to do that quite a bit now that I am active in a church. But that was my thinking process back then.

So, I didn't come out all over the place. I just went through and did what I needed to be doing.

Society has, I think, come forward a whole lot in the past 25 years. Same-sex marriage has been legalized throughout the country and in many other countries around the world. It's pretty amazing.

In representation, LGBT characters are present within media, especially movies and TV shows. I think that has created a greater exposure to the population at large to help dismiss some of those stereotypes that used to exist—whatever those were.

And some of the stereotypes are obviously going to be negative: "You are promiscuous. You sleep around. You can't have a stable relationship. You have no morals. You can't be religious," or any of those things. A lot of those have been dispelled, which is a really good thing.

The single biggest TV show that probably did that for a lot of the country was *Will and Grace*. I think that started in 1998. Before then, when there were gay characters on TV, they often played into those stereotypes. It wasn't until that show progressed that you saw someone like Will Truman. He's heteronormative, or a more masculine kind of guy. I think it just helped, in a comedic way, to be able to put that out for the larger society.

Being gay has never been the defining aspect of my identity. But it has been part of it. I have lived most of my life single. I don't go out to bars or clubs. I don't put myself out on dating apps. That type of experience doesn't really appeal to me. That's not to say that I'm asexual, because I'm certainly not. I would like to be in a relationship, I just tend to be a pretty shy person and don't put myself out there…

In 2014, I was thinking suicidal thoughts. This had nothing to do with my sexuality. It was just a really dark place that had to do with my life situation at the time.

I had some very good friends who were Christian, and these two guys… they were some of the nicest, most caring, giving people that I knew. I was like, "I want that. I don't have that, and I want that in my life." I was struck that the commonality between them was their faith.

I had pushed away faith for most of my life because I saw the hypocrisy. You would see news headlines of religions leaders having an affair or caught embezzling money.

So, I started engaging in a conversation with these guys about faith, and I let myself be open to it in a way that I never had before, and it meant hard conversations, and fraught conversations, letting them lead me by saying, "Hey you should read this in the Bible, and you know what, we can talk about it."

They both knew that I was gay, and that wasn't an issue for them in regard to having a conversation... Neither used religion as a cudgel. They built on our relationship and on friendship, and that was the focus.

And if they hadn't done that, I wouldn't be where I am today.

If someone had approached me with, "I need to pound the Bible into your head and convince you of how you are living your life wrong," I would've just been like, "Peace out. We are not going to be friends. I have no desire to do that."

My life is changed dramatically for the better. And it all started with them being my friends and caring for me and wanting to share their faith, and what that did in their own lives, with somebody else.

My mother, of course, was ecstatic when I told her that I was exploring faith. I hesitated to tell her for a very long time because I didn't want her to get her hopes up. I had people who were helping me in this journey, and I didn't want that to be her.

There is not a contradiction between being gay and having religious faith. I think people create contradictions and situations where, "Oh you can't belong because of XYZ reasons," and sexuality is just one of countless reasons that people use.

I believe firmly that God made me this way. I didn't choose to be gay. I had those thoughts a long time ago, way before I even knew what it meant.

I am not involved in PFLAG or any other organization like the Human Rights Campaign. I attend Mosaic Christian Church in Elkridge, MD. It is the church that my friend went to at the time and bought me to. And I have felt a whole lot of love from that place.

But Mosaic is not affirming, which creates some tension. A lot of my journey has been figuring out, "What does God call me to be in regard to my sexuality?" My church says that if you are gay, you are called to be celibate, and I wasn't really sure about that. I like conversations, and I like reading and absorbing information, so I read a lot about the topic of sexuality and especially about the debate between Side A and Side B.

Side A, within church lingo, or within the gay community, is affirming. It means that the Bible affirms same-sex monogamous, committed relationships. Side B is more the traditional view of the Bible that if you are gay, you are called to be celibate, or even in more extreme situations, that you are a sinner, and all of *those* things.

And at the end of my research, I came to a place where I'm like, *yeah, I don't feel like I am called to be celibate.*

I was meeting with my associate pastor monthly, and his reaction was basically, "Well, no shit." Like, it wasn't a surprise to him at all.

And that was one of the huge things that had kept me away from faith for so long.

I decided that I wanted to get baptized, but what they say at Mosaic is that you can't get baptized if you have "sin on the calendar." For instance, if you are living with somebody else, having sex with someone before you are married, we are not going to baptize you. You need to be living separately. That is the way my church moves forward.

I was not dating anybody or sleeping with anybody. But I couldn't commit to being celibate for the rest of my life. So, did that mean that sin was on the calendar? My associate pastor said, "Yeah, I don't think you can get baptized, but ask the pastor. He is the spiritual leader of this church."

And I did. I posed the same question to him, and he was like, "Yeah, absolutely, you can get baptized. You are being so thoughtful about this and committed."

One of the things that I struggled with, and this is part of the depression aspect, was, what is my purpose in life? Why am I important? Why should I be here? What does it matter? When I was going through this journey, as I call it, I was trying to find somebody else who is gay and Christian as well. Because I naturally wanted to be able to talk to somebody who's gone through this experience.

And nobody could find somebody for me. It was really, really challenging.

At some point, I was like, all right, I don't want other people to have to go through this situation.

There are people in the closet at my church. And I don't fit a lot of the stereotypes. Most people would say, "I didn't know that David is gay."

So, I wanted Mosaic to be able to put my story out there, so maybe I could be a re-source for those people. That's why I let them include a write-up of my story in one of their publications.

I see it as we were both helping each other, because Mosaic is using me to say, "Hey, look at how progressive we are. We have people who are gay at this church." And *I* want them to get the message out that it is okay to be Christian *and* gay at the same time; it's not mutually exclusive.

So many people think that they don't mix. And that included me for a long time. It took time to be able to get to this place. To know that you can be both of those things, gay and Christian—it's not one or the other.

My participation at Mosaic has caused their staff to have discussions that they hadn't had before. I am trying to do things that nobody else in my position has asked for. It's forced them to try to figure out, is this okay? Is it not?

They have said I can't be a leader... It is frustrating. I am hurt by it, but more frustrated than hurt. The nature of my vocation is that I can facilitate groups, and that's what a lot of small group work is about, facilitating dialogue and conversation.

After reading the book *Torn* by Justin Lee, which has recommendations on what churches should do, I asked if they had ever done a small group on this topic. They hadn't. And I said, *"You should."*

I pushed for about two years for Mosaic to have a small group for gay people.

Eventually, our church started doing a churchwide experience for small groups... They were letting anybody host a group. So, it wasn't the same vetting process as their typical small groups. And since anybody could host, anybody could host.

So, for six weeks, I had up to six other LGBT+ people here at my house, where I led them through the very, very prescribed stuff. But we added our own piece to it. I asked everybody to share their story. Some of these people had never shared their story before in a truly authentic way, where they talked about being gay and about faith. Some of them are not out to their families, or only out to only some of their family.

The six weeks was up, and I wanted that to keep going. I asked them, "What do you all want?" They said, "Yes, we want this!" And they wanted *visibility*. Because they feel alone. They feel isolated in some ways.

People want community. They need community. Obviously. They are missing that community within faith.

So, we have continued meeting as a group. Once again, that does not mean a rainbow flag is hanging in the church lobby, but the group is posted on the website. It's important that this group is listed.

Part of the challenge that exists right now is making sure that the group can continue. I am continuing to challenge staff at Mosaic, and I think that this experience has maybe allowed them to see that, "You know what, maybe we can let David do this because it needs to be out there."

There is still tension. However, I attend a church where everybody has only given me love. I am always on the lookout for the snide comment or for the look, and I've never found it. And I am hyper-vigilant about it. I wish I wasn't.

I think that if and when I start dating somebody, I will probably have to leave the church that I am at because I think it's too much of a mind screw to continue to go to a place that says you are called to be celibate and that your relationship is sinful.

Being shy and not wanting to go out and meet people is the biggest inhibitor to my being in a relationship, to be honest. My father is like, "David, why aren't you dating somebody?" I just don't put myself out there. That's okay.

But I would find a different faith community. My belief is that I need to find somebody who is Christian, and that there will not be sex before marriage, and it will be a marriage. That's what I am committed to.

What do people need to hear? Love your children. Love your family. People are not different based on their sexuality. Your children are still the same people that you raised, that you fed, that you instilled your own values into. Being LGBT+ doesn't make them any less those things.

The support of my family is integral to my success in life. It was instilled in my parents by their parents.

That is my grandparents' legacy...

So, love, love, *love*.

Addendum from David:

Since the interview, there have been some developments related to the opportunity to have a LBGT group at Mosaic. The LGBTQ+ group was added to the list of groups being offered by my church. The description of the group reads:

"If you are looking to have fun, grow in your relationship with Christ, and build community together as LGBTQ+ people, this group is for you. This group will be a welcoming space across theological differences seeking to worship together, explore challenging topics, and share stories with one another. Please join us! You will be welcomed and valued just as you are!"

An exception was made to allow me to be an official leader, and I have led that group for three semesters now. That exception was made because of the trust that has been developed over the years with church staff.

When people fill out the interest form to join the group, I have a short conversation with them over the phone to share what the group is about – connecting people to Jesus and providing a space for community for a group of people who often feel that they don't belong in a Christian environment. I also share how members may have different views on both religion and the Side A/Side B positions.

Each week, every member shares a check-in with how they've been, we share prayer requests, and someone shares their story/testimony.

Membership in the group has continued to grow each semester and there are now have 11 members who regularly attend.

There is a commitment from the church to continue this group, even if I don't lead it.

If I begin to date, which I plan to do soon, I am not allowed to lead, as a same-sex relationship doesn't align with church beliefs...

It is my sincere hope and prayer that the foundation has been laid for the successful continuation of this group and that it helps attract people who often feel excluded from the church community.

15: CLAY ADAMS——
I felt like I was starting to understand that I had dignity… that I didn't deserve to be treated that way.

Clay grew up in Maryland right outside of Washington, DC. He is the eldest of three siblings and was raised in a very religious family belonging to the Independent Fundamental Baptists (IFB). His story of familial rejection is painful: as a child, he loved and trusted his parents; he still thinks about family game nights and listening to audiobooks with his dad in the car.

At the time of his interview, Clay was 24 and had been estranged from his parents for several years, supporting himself with jobs as a dishwasher in a restaurant and as a temp at a grocery store.

Though Clay did not come out to himself until he was 18, he knew early in childhood that he was different. Adults in his community attempted a sort of intervention when Clay was ten, warning his mother that he presented as too effeminate. Her response was to admonish him, "Do you want to sound like a faggot?"

Clay was homeschooled and his parents had tightly controlled the family's access to film and media; he did not yet know how sexuality worked or exactly what that word was supposed to mean. This was a hurtful and confusing experience.

When they were finally forced to deal with the fact that he was gay, Clay's parents responded "with a lot of fear." Because his father was a pastor in a community that was overly hostile to LGBTQ+ people, the family experienced an especial urgency to hide and repress his identity. His mother told him that if he ever acted on his desires, she would "pray to God to kill him."

Afraid of what he might do without their constant surveillance, Clay's parents fostered his dependence on them until he finally left home in a very dramatic way at age 21.

Since then, he has struggled, often feeling very much alone, "to understand that I have dignity."

Clay's story offers a glimpse into the experience of a child and young person who does not have access to affirming, safe spaces or representations; he literally lacked the language to help him to process and understand his own experience until he was an adult. He has struggled on and off with depression, including suicidal ideation. Though he thinks a lot about forgiveness, his relationship with his family now is limited.

Thankfully, he has benefitted from the support of friends who have helped him to understand that the way his parents treated him was wrong... but healing is a long road.

Thinking about his experience, Clay advises parents, whatever background they come from, to be empathetic.

"If you are not empathetic, you could ruin your kid's life. My life is not ruined... but there were close calls. You risk losing the relationship. You risk losing the kid."

I was very curious as a kid, and I would ask questions a lot, but... what your parents tell you is just a fact of life, so I believed everything that my parents believed, just out of default. But I was always curious and would wonder things and ask questions about why we think this way and why we do this.

We wouldn't listen to most kinds of music. We would only listen to hymns, and I would ask questions about that. And they would give answers, but privately, the answers weren't very satisfying.

But when your parents say things, you think that's just how it is… my parents believe that it's a sin for women to wear pants, or for men to have earrings, and those things were always confusing to me. I just sort of accepted what they told me until I got older.

My siblings and I would get in fights a lot, but I think it was a normal relationship. I was sort of a stereotypical older brother. I was very bossy, and thought I had the right to tell them what to do. My parents—I would say they were very strict. They could be very harsh sometimes. My parents did practice corporal punishment.

When you are a kid, you think, "I must be very bad, I must deserve this."

Looking back, they were very harsh. So, there were tensions in our relationship. I would say it was a mixed bag, just like any parent-child relationship. There was love, and resentment and struggle, along with having fun together. We would play games sometimes. We would watch movies. There was an audio version of *Left Behind*, an evangelical "end of times" book series, and me and my dad would listen to that in the car all the time.

I knew I was not fitting in pretty early on. I think you might say I was a proto-gay kid, even before puberty or anything. Even though it was before puberty, I would have these romantic feelings about other boys… especially the older boys. Especially as a kid I was, I think I was often interpreted as obviously gay. I liked a lot of boy things, but I also had a lot of stereotypical *affects*. I sounded very gay. (I still think I sound gay.) But even more so as a kid, I sounded very gay.

I guess there's not really such a thing as sounding gay because gay people sound all kinds of ways, right? But I was very stereotypical-sounding feminine… People noticed this about me when I was very young. This was something people didn't like. The way I was perceived, the way I was interpreted by others… They spoke to my mom. Looking back, it's very irritating to me. It's kind of creepy in a way. Because you are projecting things onto a child and trying to control them in a sexual way; it's like you are trying to manipulate them. It's almost like what they claim gay people do, but it's the reverse.

I was ten. Some people came to my mom and said that they thought I sounded very gay, and she asked me (this is very crude), "Do you want to sound like a faggot?" And I said *no*. Honestly, I didn't understand. It was just the way I spoke. I didn't understand why people were upset by it, you know, the way my voice sounded. That would be the beginning of when I started to think there might be something about me people didn't like.

I was very upset. I knew it was a really bad thing to be, but I didn't fully understand. I didn't even know yet how heterosexuality worked at the time, so I had no idea what this "faggot" thing was. I knew it had something to do with men being together in a romantic way. I think that was the extent of my understanding then.

I think also at the time, I thought – a lot of fundamentalists think this – that gender and sexuality are the same. They confuse things like being trans and being gay; they think of them as the same thing. So, I think I also thought that it was, like, a boy who wanted to be a girl. And I knew I didn't want that. I was fine with being a boy, with my gender, with how I was assigned at birth. I just knew it was a really bad thing to be.

I was homeschooled mostly. A lot of kids at my church, I grew up with them, and there were little things, but most people liked me, which I am very grateful for. Nobody other than the adults expressed any issue with any way they were perceiving me.

When I was 13, I did go to a homeschool umbrella group. And that was my first experience in a school with other kids who I didn't grow up with… I remember being kind of picked on. … The teacher was very… *He knew.* He could tell. And he would behave, I think, in a very inappropriate way, trying to control the way I acted. He tried to shame me; he tried to make me feel less masculine. When the older kids would beat up on me, he wouldn't help.

I now believe he was gay himself. He was very flamboyant, even though he was married to a woman and he went to an IFB church. Being gay was such a bad thing to be that you would never say it out loud, maybe not even to yourself.

Looking back, I think he saw things about me that were similar to maybe himself and wanted in his own, perverse way, to help me. He thought he was toughening me up.

In terms of school, that was my only experience of bullying, and then after that, I went back to homeschooling.

Even before puberty, I had romantic, proto-gay feelings. But I didn't interpret my feelings as gay; I didn't think of myself as gay. I guess you could say I thought of myself as straight by default. Just because that's what you were if you were in the IFB. There was no other option.

And if you did think that you were something other than straight, then you are automatically outside of the group.

But I would have feelings towards other boys. I would either not think about it or ignore it. There were a few times where I thought, sort of, "Maybe this means I'm gay." But I would immediately repress that thought because that was just something you cannot be. You cannot be this where you are going to Hell, or you are a horrible person. I didn't want to be a horrible person.

It was pretty bad.

When I first put that label on myself, I was 18.

I finally had language for it. When I was younger, there wasn't a whole lot of language available for what I was experiencing. IFB culture is very much insular, but still, even if they're insular, they cannot completely insulate themselves.

I don't remember anything in particular that introduced me to the idea that you can be gay. For a long time, I thought being gay was about what you did. I guess eventually, at some point, I learned that being gay is about who you are attracted to, not how you behave.

I kept it secret for a long time. What led up to that was actually that I had feelings for a friend of mine. I had been attracted to boys before, but I'd never had, like, a real crush, real strong feelings for somebody. That crush lasted from 15 to 18, when I finally said, *there is no other way to explain this.* I told one person, a friend whom I knew had other LGBTQ+ friends. She went to public school, and she would get in arguments with the adults at church over it. So, I knew she was probably safe to say this to.

Because I needed to tell somebody, because I wanted to discuss it. So, I told her first.

She stopped going to our church shortly after, so she was not a big part of the story after that. But it was so cathartic to say it to somebody.

I had a best friend I grew up with. He was older than me, but not by a lot. He was sort of like an older brother. We spent a lot of time at each other's houses when we were growing up. My parents treated him like a son, and he was also the choir director at our church. He wasn't as moralistic as other people in the church and was always someone safe that you could go to. He was respected as a "prayer warrior." To explain that, he was somebody who is really good at prayer. It sounds silly, but he was respected; that's the point.

And I was with him one day, and I decided I wanted to tell him and see what advice he had. Because I wasn't quite sure what to do with it. I had feelings for this other friend of mine, and I knew I was supposed to think it was wrong, but it didn't feel wrong to me. And I was just not sure what to do with it. I still felt awkward around the language… I said, "Um, I don't like girls." And he said, "Do you think you like boys?" And I said, "I know I like *a* boy. So yeah, I think so."

He was very gentle, which was very good, because if it had been somebody else, and they had not been gentle, it would have probably been really bad.

He said to me that he understood but, "You can't act on it." It got really quiet, and he said, "Can I tell you something?" And I sort of perked up, and I looked at him, and we looked at each other, and I was like, "Are you...?" And he was like, "Yes."

Maybe subconsciously, I had thought, you know, that he was, and that's why it would be safe to tell him. We talked about it, and it made me feel kind of normal, almost. Right? To have somebody to speak to about these sorts of things.

Around that time, I ended up coming out to my dad by accident. It was not smart. We got in an argument about something unrelated because I was very... I don't know, I was just under stress, and feeling very emotional, and volatile. And he asked me, "Why are you so angry today?"

The thing we were in an argument over wasn't really that significant, but I was very upset. I ended up, in this sort of fit of emotion, telling him.

Immediately, when I told him, I could see the fear on his face. Like, he was *terrified*. And that didn't feel good. And I was like, *he doesn't know what to do*, which meant I certainly didn't know what to do. Also, of course, if you are a kid, you don't want to be the cause of that kind of fear in your parents.

I was just telling the truth... That made it feel worse. I was just telling the truth, and yet it caused this emotion in my dad. He said, "We are going to work through this." And I said, "I'm not sure it is wrong."

And that was *double* the fear.

At first, he was very empathetic. But he was also operating from a place of paranoia and fear. And he started to get worse and worse; he started to get very controlling, and when we would have conversations about it, he became more and more hostile, to a point where I just didn't want to speak with him about it anymore. I finally told him I was just confused. "I'm not really gay. I like girls. Never mind." Which he knew wasn't true, but he pretended with me.

They were always sort of helicopter parents. But now, he would check my phone a lot. One time, he caught me reading this article, because I was still trying to figure out how my faith and liking boys fit. I'd be reading an article, and he would find it. He would confront me, and it would be a big thing. And I would go back to, *"No, no, I'm just confused. It's fine."* That happened several times.

The choir director, my best friend, said, "You shouldn't have told your dad." He was still questioning himself and figuring out, like, what he thought about it.

My father wanted to keep it between us. He didn't want my mom to know, though there was a fight we had once where he threatened to kick me out, and he threatened to tell my mom, which I did not want.

Then the choir director came out. He had gotten a boyfriend, and people found out and told my parents. My dad is the pastor of the church. They came to my dad, and sort of overnight, this person, who had been very close to everybody in the church, and who had been looked up to and seen as a mentor, wasn't spoken about. In my friend group, nobody spoke about him.

He was, obviously, no longer choir director. I remember being really upset because this was the only person I could talk to. He was like my lifeline because the church I grew up in is very homophobic. Very.

At one point, my parents brought all three of us siblings into the room, and they told us why the choir director left. They asked my little sister to leave, and they asked my brother and me if he had ever touched us in a sexual way. That was very painful, because this is a person who was like our family, and I couldn't express it, but I just remember being so angry that they would ask that.

It also made me think, well, what do they think about me? If my dad is asking me this—and I had told him that I was gay—does he think that that is something I'm capable of?

It made me angry and sad and just made me want to be out of there. But I couldn't go because I was financially dependent. I was experiencing depression and anxiety. I thought, "I'm going to be trapped here *forever*. I'm just going to be stuck."

And so, it felt very hopeless.

I went to a college in New Jersey for a while. Then I went to a different college another year, and I was home during that time. It was an IFB college.

After I turned 20, my mom found out, and that was very dramatic. She said some really unkind things, like, "If you ever act on this, I am going to pray to God to kill you...."

There was a time when I might have thought, "This means I am bad. This means there is something wrong with me." But I was older now, more mature... it was more like, "I *know* this is wrong. I know this is abuse. I know this is emotional abuse."

And there was other stuff: they were being very controlling. They were monitoring my phone. My dad said he did not want to let me get a job because he did not want me to be financially independent because I might choose to sin.

There was a lot of that stuff, and I knew it was abuse at the time, but I couldn't do anything. Which was almost worse than thinking they were right because I felt so trapped. Suffocated.

That's when I decided that I was going to start making plans to leave.

After the Pulse nightclub shooting, there were people who were in my church saying horrible things. I first heard about it from the dad of one of my friends at church. And he said, "They deserved it; they are disgusting." There were things I heard from my youth pastor, things I heard from my friend group. The boy I liked, though secretly – and I knew I could never let him know I was gay – he said, "There was a shooting in Florida." Someone else said, "Oh that's terrible." And he was like, "Oh, but they were gay." As if to say, it's not that big of a deal because these people who got shot were gay. It's not as bad anymore.

They said things like that.

And I was really angry. I'm going to be honest... I kind of hated everybody there. I would arrive late and leave as soon as possible. But I was still the pastor's son, and I still had to do things like preach in the teen boys' class, and I had to lead Sunday school, and things like that. So, it was this profound cognitive dissonance... it was "double mindedness," to use Bible language for it. I had to pretend, to survive.

This whole time, I was saving money. I was still secretly in contact with the former choir director. Then one day, he messaged me on Instagram and said he was moving to Baltimore. I asked if I could come live with him and be his roommate, and he said yes. This is very dramatic...

I didn't want to be too obvious, so I would slowly meet up with him, and I would give him some of my clothes, and some of my things. But I didn't want to give him too much of my stuff because I didn't want my family asking, "Where's your stuff going?"

When I first moved out, I didn't have very many clothes. I had one pair of jeans, a few shirts, and some dress shirts. And a book bag, and a toothbrush. I was very paranoid. I was trying to be very careful that nobody would know what was going on.

One day, my parents were in school, and my little brother was home sick, but he was old enough to take care of himself. I told him I was going to the gym. I went to leave, and I tried to give him a hug before I left because I knew what was about to happen. He was like, "Why are you touching me? Get away from me!" So here I was, trying to have this moment. It's kind of funny, looking back. I was trying to be tender, to say goodbye, but he just thought I was being weird, I guess, or annoying.

I met my friend and we started driving to Baltimore. I sent an email to my dad saying, "I'm moving out. Here is a list of reasons why..."

I tried very hard to make him understand. But I was very immature, to be honest, and very naïve. I was 21, but I was so sheltered. I guess I thought I could make him understand or empathize. But all he saw was what he was afraid of, and all my mother saw was what she was afraid of.

I didn't think he would read it until later because he was at school. Almost immediately, I start getting calls from my parents and text messages saying, "Pick up your phone!" Because they were panicking.

They were terrified. What they believe... I don't want to try to justify the harmful things they did and said, and threatened to do, but on another level, I can understand the mindset, even if it is irrational.

I destroyed my phone. Very dramatic. We stopped at a gas station, and I literally smashed my phone and threw it away because I thought they had a tracker on it, which I'm now pretty sure they did.

I didn't tell anybody where I had moved. Not even the friends that had sort of, like, tacitly supported me, which were very few. I didn't want anybody to know. I changed my number.

They didn't find out where I was living until sometime later. I was worried they would show up and do something. It took me a while, after all the threats, to realize they couldn't do anything to me legally. They had no power to force me to do anything. They couldn't make me go to conversion therapy.

But I was still afraid that they would show up if they found out where I was living and do something. The first night... like I said, I was very sheltered and immature.... It took me a long time to realize that I couldn't be touched here. Like they couldn't get me. So, the first night, I remember sleeping in my new room. Whenever there would be a creak, I would jolt.

Eventually, everybody found out. I didn't have to make an announcement. I just stopped hiding. It was like a coming out, but without a coming out. I was free. I was saying whatever I wanted. I wasn't hiding anything.

During Pride month, I posted a rainbow picture on my Facebook, so people found out.

I go to an Episcopalian church now. I remember telling my new pastor, "I'm so angry that I just feel like I am being swallowed alive sometimes. Sometimes, the anger is just overwhelming, and I don't know what to do." She suggested that I read Desmond Tutu's *The Book of Forgiving*. That helped me a lot. The idea that forgiveness is empowering is a major theme in his book. Fighting apartheid in South Africa... there is a lot to forgive there. There is a lot of pain and suffering there.

Forgiveness might be interpreted as just another form of domination, as letting the people who have harmed you get away with it. I think I didn't want the people I grew up with or my parents to get away with the things they had done and said. Because I felt like I was starting to understand that I had dignity... that I didn't deserve to be treated that way.

And so, the idea that I would forgive them... felt like I was saying, actually that isn't this big of a deal, because *I'm* not that big of a deal.

But Tutu helped me to think about forgiveness as a way to liberate yourself, to set yourself free.

I remember, after leaving, there was a period where I tried to stop being a Christian. Which sounds funny...I was trying not to be gay when I was in my dad's church, and then I left, and I was trying to stop being a Christian, because that's just another way to give people power over me.

But I wasn't very good at that because I would still pray. It was automatic... I would still think about God.

I'm kind of a nerd. I like things like philosophy and theology. I found that I still loved Jesus, but in a complicated way. And then I just stopped resisting. I ended up visiting an Episcopal Church, and I felt like I fit in very well. That's where I go now. There are a lot of LGBTQ+ people in my church. I don't feel othered in any way, and I don't even feel like, fetishized, in any way, like "here is our gay."

Relations with my family are still strained. I think they recognize me as an adult now. A legal adult. So, they have become, over the years, better at respecting boundaries. Us speaking more is very recent. Maybe that started the end of last year. It was gradual... in the beginning, they were very hostile.

When I moved to Vermont, they would try to reach out, but I was still so angry that I would push them away. My mom would text me things like, "I just want you to know I'm praying for you," and I would be hyper-sensitive, and I would, you know, say something... I wanted to hurt them as much as they had hurt me, to even the scales... Anger comes from when you are in pain.

When I went to the hospital to say goodbye to my grandmother, that was the first time I saw them. Which was intense. We went to dinner, and my mom said some really unkind things.

They would apologize, and then they would do things like that. So, I did not take their remorse seriously. But I think at this point... they probably realize that they handled it very poorly.

When I first left, the possibilities of what I could do with my life were so many that it was kind of overwhelming. Almost as if you had lived your whole life in this tiny, enclosed space, and then you went out into the open air. It felt overwhelming in a way. It felt good in a way, but also anxiety-producing.

Gosh. I could do anything with my life. There is not a limit. I have no idea what to do with that.

Before, everything was laid out: these are your options. And so, I drank, which is very dangerous, especially when you grew up in a denomination where you never drank. It's a matter of temperance... You don't learn how to measure yourself. I drank a-lot-a-lot. There was a lot of depression.

At the same time, I felt very free. I was like, *you can do anything*. But then I realized, you need money to do things. I had to learn to feel cozy in my limitations again.

Now, I'm doing very good... I'm friends with all kinds of people. I tend to make friends with older people... I don't know why. Having older queer adults around me shows me the possibilities for my life. Having straight people who like me and love me for who I am, not in spite of how I love... having that is very good.

I live in a college town. There are a lot of guys here. Though dating has not gone very well... I'm in a place where I'm not worried about that anymore. I like myself. I am good being single for now.

It has taken me a long time to recover. Like I said, the drinking. I engaged in sexually risky behavior. That's pretty normal from what I've read for LGBTQ+ people who grow up in communities that other them, that make them feel abnormal, that treat them badly.

I have had suicidal thoughts for years.

Not right now... it's off and on. You don't need to worry about me. But it was really dark times.

And I didn't have my family. I had friends, and they were very helpful. They gave me advice and they comforted me. I would probably be dead if I did not have them.

I recognize that people have religious beliefs, and I can't really reach into their head and change that. I would just say to parents, *be empathetic*. Understand how your kid is probably feeling...

If you are not empathetic, you could ruin your kid's life.

My life is not ruined... but there were close calls.

You risk losing the relationship. You risk losing the kid. And being replaced by other people.

I remember one story in particular that is very meaningful. When I was still in Baltimore, I had this friend... we were in the car, and I was talking to him about issues with my parents and with people that I grew up with. I had never said it out loud before, but I said, *"I hate them."*

It was like an explosion of emotion.

All of this stuff that I didn't even know was there started emptying out. I was saying, "I grew up with them all my life, but they now look at me like I'm disgusting. They think I am immoral. They only see me as this one thing, and nothing else."

I'm just pouring out my heart, and *just sobbing*. And I didn't even know that that was inside of me. And I'm saying these things: "They think that I'm evil. They think that I'm gross."

And then he stops the car, and he looks at me, and he says, "They are wrong."

I don't know, it was just something about the way he said it. He said it with authority.

He said it over and over again:

"They are wrong. They are wrong. They are wrong."

16: CAROL CRANE—
Well, just give me time here.

Carol Crane has three sons, two of whom came out as LGBTQ+ while in eighth and ninth grade. A nurse who spent time on the front-line of Covid care, she grew up in New Jersey and raised her family in Howard County, Maryland. Raised Lutheran, she now belongs to a large, non-denominational church which was less accepting of her elder son, Scott, than of her younger son, David, possibly in part because of the pathway carved by the older brother.

Carol begins her narrative with an account of her family's struggles early on, when the boys were toddlers: they had to give up a beloved dog, her husband changed jobs, the family had to deal with illness, separation, and a move.

In her story, one can hear her asking herself, "Were any of these things causative?," a groove of thinking that many parents coming to terms with having LGBTQ+ children may find themselves revisiting.

The reality, of course, is that most families experience periods of hardship. A compassionate and loving parent, Carol ultimately cares less about the how and why than about the well-being of her children as they move through their lives.

Here, she shares her limited prior experience with LGBTQ+ people and describes being part of a culture where such things were not discussed. Her memory of her LGBTQ+ college roommate who struggled alone is important because of current trends that seek to seek to silence discussion and erase LGBTQ+ presence.

Sharing an account that will resonate with many, she also reflects on what it was like to come out as an LGBTQ+ parent. For her, as for many parents belonging to many kinds of communities, this experience was isolating. She remarks, "Truthfully,

I wasn't sure of how to navigate all of this without hurting relationships and being kind of lonely." By the time her second child came out, she realized, *"this is not going away."* She told herself, "I have to figure this out because it's a means of survival."

Carol emphasizes that her children were who they were early on. She recalls a pediatrician visit at age two-and-a-half where Scott reported, "I am a girl," his early fascination with dresses, and an aunt who wondered out loud, when he was a toddler, if he were gay.

School bullying is a big part of Scott's story: he was bullied by a neighborhood child starting in preschool after he wore a dress outside, and by sixth grade, he was suffering, both from bullying and because of "his internal struggle that I didn't know about."

The public school Scott attended was unhelpful, and between sixth and eighth grade, he was admitted to psychiatric hospitals four different times with suicidal ideation; at one point, he even fantasized about revenge on his bullies.

Carol shares other kinds of situations unique to parenting LGBTQ+ children. When another child came out to David during a church retreat, she feared he could be accused of "grooming," and when Scott participated in a youth program trip to Japan, she worried that things with his host family could become difficult (they did).

Now, her sons, young adults, are doing well, and Carol recognizes many of those challenging moments as important growth experiences.

Carol attends Pride events, sends out rainbow-themed Christmas cards, and enjoys seeing her children blossom into their individual talents and skills.

"It's just fun," she says, a reminder to parents of what they could miss if they choose not to support their children.

I grew up in a small town in New Jersey. My parents stayed together. I am the oldest of three children, and I would say it was kind of an average middle-class neighborhood. Not a huge amount of diversity, not a whole lot of hate or anything like that.

I was raised Lutheran. They didn't preach anything particular about LGBTQ+. I didn't even really think about gender stuff until late middle school, early high school, and it wasn't a huge topic for me, truthfully.

In fact, later in life, I found out about friends that I had in high school that came out later. I had no knowledge back then that they were thinking any of this. I think some of them purposely didn't bring it up because they were probably afraid of judgment, or it was just the typical "we keep it all in the closet" thing.

It wasn't something that got discussed in public much at all when I was growing up. I am 53, so we are talking late 70s, early 80s.

There was a kid in school who was very flamboyant, who used to get teased and mocked a lot. In fact, some of the very macho guys would do things like throw him into the girls' changing room, ...stuff like that.

I only learned a few years ago about another friend that later has transitioned to female. So, there were people in my life who were friends of mine that I had no idea about. It really didn't even cross my mind growing up in a Christian home that this would even ever be a topic to worry about. It wasn't something we ever really talked about.

Going to college was more enlightening for me. I had a roommate who was also Christian. In Christian belief, you are supposed confess your sin. There was an exercise people would do. They would write what was bothering them on a piece of paper and throw it away. She would be writing these little notes and throwing them in the trash all of the time. I never read them, but one day, I opened up my backpack to get work out and I un-crumpled this piece of paper. It was hers... She was experiencing a lot of shame about having feelings for another woman, and she didn't quite know where to go with that or how to process it.

I never really talked to her about it because a friend of mine who knew her well said, "I don't think you should go there. I think it would be harmful. If she's ready to share, then she's ready to share."

So, we never talked about it until a few years ago, because of my kids coming out. She is still very much in the closet. She is with a woman and they pretty much just live like roommates and don't share that part of their life with people for the most part. They pretty much stay quietly to themselves, and she doesn't even really like to talk about it.

At any rate, that's some of my background. I have younger sister who had a baby at a young age; she was in high school, and this was shocking to our family. Nobody knew she was pregnant until the baby was born, so that was *really* shocking.

When our oldest was born, everything was fine for a while. But we had a lot of changes that happened quickly in succession. After our second child was born, we had a very large and hyper dog, and we had to give it up. About four months after that, my husband took the job that bought us here to Maryland. He went ahead to start the job, and a few weeks after he left, both kids got very, very sick... the oldest had to be hospitalized.

So, there were a lot of successive changes, and our oldest had a really hard time with the transition. Scott was just about three, and David was a year-and-a-half. They had never shared a room, and when we moved to the apartment, their room had this huge bank of windows that were hard to cover to make the room dark. Now they were sharing a room, and my oldest got stressed and stopped napping, and his behavior got crazy. He expressed a lot of angst towards his younger brother. I guess he imagined that his younger brother was the reason for all the changes, I don't know.

And he just went off the chain.

We eventually got Scott into a preschool because the pediatrician thought that the consistency of seeing the same group of people on a regular basis would help. We kept moving forward and trying to get settled. He started dressing in girl's dress up clothes in pre-k and wearing my heels. We have a picture... all you see is his little feet and my heels. He seemed to have this fascination with this stuff.

We lived next door to a girl who was his age. We would get home, and he would be out the door to go play with her before we could even get David out of the car seat. They would play with the kitchen stuff, and that did not bother me one bit. I was never thinking that he thought he was a girl like her, or anything.

He had a pediatrician's visit at two-and-a-half years. She asked, "Are you a boy or are you a girl?," and he said, "I am a girl."

Oh, I wonder why he has that idea?

So, I said, "No, you're not a girl." I said, "Nana's a girl, I'm a girl, but you are a boy." He didn't have a context for that because he didn't understand physical development and all that kind of stuff.

The doctor said, don't worry. It's a question that we ask at age three, but he was here, and I thought I'd just start the conversation to see where he was at.

Okay, not worried.

But then, like I said, he did the dressing up... The pediatrician said, "Don't worry about any of this. When he is six or seven, the kids at school will help him understand. He will fall into line. He'll get it."

Okay, not worried about it.

One of the things the preschool teacher would do to encourage Scott to participate in activities at school was to, I guess you could say, bribe him with, "You can put the dress up dress on if you do this, or you can take it home for the weekend if you do that."

I was like, "Oh great. Just what I wanted, too."

We came home one day... There was one older kid who picked on the other kids sometimes. So, I said, "Can you wait until we get inside of the house to put that on?" Of course, he went into the house, put it on, and promptly ran outside, straight out the door. That did become the stimulus for getting picked on, which didn't help.

Scott seemed to be making friends. He went to kindergarten and he seemed to be doing okay socially. He's extremely talkative, and schoolwork became the issue for the next few years, until we finally had him tested and found out that he has a specific learning disorder. That meant that he qualified for an Independent Educational Plan (IEP). Things started to get better, and he had a really good year in third grade. He started to read, finally, and we thought, "Okay, we are getting past this really stressful point."

Then, at the end of fifth grade, Scott developed a heart arrhythmia problem that we eventually treated successfully. That was a huge blow to him... He was still getting picked on by kids. He felt very different from other kids because of all of these things. He wasn't tolerating the medicine well... It led to depression.

He started sixth grade, and he had a really hard time in middle school. Partly he was getting picked on, partly he just didn't want to be there. Things bothered him... He wouldn't go to school because they wouldn't let him wear his hat; he got mad. He threw his skateboard at the wall and made a hole in the wall. So, there were some significant issues going on. We had real trouble getting him to go to school...

By the end of sixth grade, he was trying to have a girlfriend. After the girl broke up with him, he started cutting. He said he wanted to die, and he told a teacher, so he had to be admitted to a psychiatric hospital.

That started just about two years of unbelievable challenges. Three, no *four*, psychiatric admissions.

I was thinking, *the kids are picking on him...* At one point, I made him file a bully report, but he didn't want to. And so, what he wrote on it was, "I want to kill..." and he *named* people because he was so mad at them for picking on him.

Mean names, pushing, all kinds of things. A lot on the bus, and not always the same kids. The school didn't consider it bullying because it wasn't always the same kids.

Part of this was also his internal struggle that I didn't know about.

He eventually went to an alternative school with good support programs. He got worse before he got better. But then, he finally settled down.

We were going to therapy... He finally told his therapist that he was gay and that this was really the internal struggle all along.

That was in eighth grade.

The therapist called me a couple of days after he confided in her, and she wanted to give him resources, PFLAG information and things like that.

I was like, *hold on*, because I knew from people that I had met that PFLAG doesn't really address the faith aspects. The impression I had was it didn't matter what your faith was, you (the parent) had to just go with the flow. Do whatever the kid said or did, and this is how they kind of operated. At that time, I was like, "That's not going to fit for me. I can't just deny everything I grew up with and let the kid be the leader."

That was the kind of thing I was thinking *then*.

We continued with therapy to work through things... Scott was doing better, but he very much, through that time, distanced himself from us. We would have family games or family meetings, and he wouldn't want to participate.

I didn't get the sense that I really knew who he was. I wanted him to be honest and to share, but I guess he'd been hurt so many times that he felt like he couldn't go there with anybody. I think that's just because he's been hurt so many times. More than we realized.

Stuff with his brother started to improve after that. His brother was having his own struggles. What's interesting is the thing that bought them together is the thing that was hardest for me as a parent to have to deal with... that they are *both* LGBTQ+, but we didn't know that until later.

Scott was very involved in youth group at church, but he didn't feel close with them. He wanted to try to write songs and be on the worship team and participate in youth service and things like that, but he wasn't getting good responses from the people involved. He felt very left out. Different and rejected.

He was trying to bring the issue into the church youth group... He would try to bring up topics at meetings that they weren't prepared to deal with. High-school aged boys tend to talk about their struggles with girls and things like that, and he would bring up his struggle with wanting to date a boy. They were like, we are *not* going to talk about that. He said, "They can talk about the girls, so how come I can't talk about this?"

Which is true.

At one point, the head of the high school-age group called a parent meeting to talk about some things that had been happening in the group. He wanted to "share" that this topic had come up. Interestingly, as conservative as our church is, one parent said, "Would we even be having this meeting if the situation was a guy interested in a girl in the group, as opposed to a guy interested in a guy in the group?"

After that, the family that hosted the youth meetings continued to let Scott come. They did not want to make him feel like he wasn't allowed to be there. So, he did continue to go for a while, which is surprising in a way. And pretty noble of him too, to keep going, and to trying to work out where faith worked in with his feelings and how he felt about himself.

When Scott had the opportunity to go to Japan as part of a church activity, we struggled... Should we really let him go? Because we weren't sure if he had feelings for the host family's son, whom he had been talking with, and we worried that the family would be kind of blindsided. We were asking: *Are we going to share this? What are we going to do?* Do we tell him he can't go if he doesn't tell the kid first?

Finally, he actually told the kid that he was gay, and the kid didn't seem to be bothered by it. But, as time went on, spending so much time with this kid, Scott shared that he had some feelings for him. That freaked this kid out. I mean, *it really freaked him out.* He wasn't able to maintain a relationship with him, and that was hurtful on both ends. Both of them really were hurt from that.

That's when Scott really started to eschew faith. He felt like, "These people. These people just don't really love people who aren't like them." That was a struggle, because he came back with the intention of, "I am going to change how all of these conservatives think."

And I was like, "That might not be quite so easy..."

He graduated in 2015. He did go to prom with a friend. And he wore a dress and heels. I don't know... I guess they had people looking out for him, because he really didn't seem to have any trouble. I guess everybody knew by then, so he didn't get picked on specifically at that point. And honestly, a lot of kids were coming out then, too. Over his whole high school career, it seems like more and more kids were coming out. So, I guess it became more of the norm in the community.

At that point, I knew where he was at, and I thought... *I am not going to deny him prom.* I just prayed that he wouldn't be abused or hurt.

He decided he was going to get a green dress. And he said, "I think I am going to get green heels to match with it." My mother doesn't talk a whole lot about these things, but he said this in front of her, and I was wondering, *"What is she thinking?"*

And she just said, "I think that would be a little too much green."

My dad, who was also there, isn't a real talkative guy, but he was also kind of the macho, military kind of guy. And I thought, "This will go over like a lead balloon." My dad didn't say a word. But at least he didn't criticize him and reject him.

My in-laws were also very loving and accepting of their grandkids. They didn't really have a lot of time to really process because they passed on soon after. But they knew about Scott's challenges… they knew something was inside him struggling.

Once, when the Marriage Equality vote was coming up, my father-in-law said, "This is ridiculous. I don't understand why they even need to go there." And Scott said, well, "What if the law said you couldn't be married to Nana and you loved her?" He didn't really argue with that, and he stopped saying anything.

They didn't have a lot of heart-to-heart conversation because Scott was sort of just deciding who it felt safe to talk with… I know they would have loved him right through it.

They have a saying: "The kid comes out of the closet, and the conservative Christian parent goes in." I really didn't share it with a lot of people at first. Truthfully, I wasn't sure of how to navigate all of this without hurting relationships and being kind of lonely.

Although it was kind of lonely anyway because I was isolating. I made the choice to not talk about it to a degree…

I spent a lot of time on my own, studying the Bible and doing research. I found Kathy Baldock, who explains the translation process that created modern day bibles. American words don't necessarily convey the actual meaning of words in a foreign language, especially Hebrew, and translators have always tailored translations to reflect what they thought at the time, especially about sexuality. That was eye-opening.

It took a long time before I came out to the small women's group that I was in. They didn't have LGBT+ kids, but some of our kids were in the youth group together. I didn't want them to restrict their kids from going to things that my kids were at, and I didn't want them to fear people that were LGBTQ+; I didn't want that group to become a hateful, horrible place.

Finally, I found another group of Christian moms whose kids were LGBTQ+, and that was very helpful. We did a lot of research and talked openly. At one point we discussed ex-gay therapy, which we agreed was not a good idea.

My husband and I knew that we were just going to be butting heads if we shoved faith stuff down Scott's throat... I could see that if we took that approach, we would lose him.

I can't imagine that you get rejected by your parents and then come closer to God, the father, when you have had such rejection. If you are so hurt by someone claiming to be a person of faith, are you even going to look for God? That *would* be quite the miracle.

Taking up this rejecting attitude towards people is like saying that somehow, you are less than fully human.

There is no changing people. All you can do is kind of guide them, direct your children as they are growing. But you're not going to change them. You just have to try to figure out how to tailor the person that they are and guide them to what they can use that for.

Scott has always been a very entrepreneurial kid. We would have a lot of yard sales when the kids were growing up. He would set up this table, and he'd be just *engaging* all of these customers.

So, I knew, early on, that that was his bent and that he'd be okay if he could figure out where to use those skills. Now, that's what he does at his job, a lot of day-to-day helping to run the business where he works.

He is very involved in PFLAG, and he has done a lot of work on Howard County Pride. He is trying to work on a drag gig. He is an organizer, getting volunteer groups together to get work done.

It's just fun. It's fun. I love seeing him succeed.

David is also doing well.

When he was in ninth grade, Scott kind of pushed him a little bit to come out. David was very open with his youth group leaders, and (unlike with Scott) they were very good supports to him. In fact, he is very close with one of them to this day. His mannerisms are so different than Scott's. He is much gentler about things, and he is lovable in so many ways that basically, the kids that knew, it didn't really faze most of them.

So, he has also had good support from friends, and it's kind of a generational thing, too. For youth today, this is not a big issue for many of them. There are one or two outliers that will say, "You're going to Hell for this." But for the most part, people actually care and still engage with people that are different.

One thing that was interesting is that when David came out as bi, we were like, "Oh, we didn't see that coming for you."

And Scott was looking at us like, "How come you are not having a fit?"

I was like, *"Well, just give me time here."*

If David doesn't have an active boyfriend, the church still lets him be a leader. He has been helping to lead summer camps and retreats. On one bus ride to a retreat, a kid came out to him. David didn't go into detail about his own story, but he was like, "This kid felt safe to come out to me because I'm here. He wouldn't have come out to just anybody."

I was glad he was there for that child. The only thing was, I was worried. I didn't want a parent to say, "You are trying to ruin my child." There are a lot of people that think it's only because someone has been groomed by some gay person that they "decide" to become gay. The idea is they have been led onto the path.

But yet, when you see a three-year-old putting on a dress, where did they get that idea? Nobody said, "Come dress up as a girl." I remember, my one aunt who is very conservative, speculated, when Scott was still tiny, that he might be gay. If you don't believe people are born gay, why would you even say such a thing?

For such a long time, it was kind of like *I do not want to share with people.* I remember, I felt like Scott was making me have to deal with something I didn't want to be made to deal with.

But then, after David, I was like, "I have to deal with it because this is not going away." I had to learn how to talk about this with people that don't agree with me. I have to figure this out because it's a means of survival.

You don't want to be alone in life.

I am proud of the things Scott has done. I share with my coworkers. "Hey, there is cool Pride event that my son is helping to run, if you want to come." In fact, my boss actually came to one of the events last year.

When we pick cards for birthdays and Christmas, I have cards that say something about having *Pride* in your kid.

The kids want us to champion them. They want us to be out there, changing the world for this…

We need to include people and not push them away. We can see what happens with divisiveness. Politically, things are the most divisive I have ever seen, and it has become very volatile.

In the end, you just want to protect your kids.

WORKS CITED

American Medical Association, Issue Brief 19-409200, 2019, pp. 1–5, *Sexual orientation and gender identity change efforts (so-called "conversion therapy")*, https://www.ama-assn.org/system/files/conversion-therapy-issue-brief.pdf

"Americans' Support for Key LGBTQ Rights Continues to Tick Upward: Findings From the 2021 American Values Atlas." *Public Religion Research Institute,* 14 Mar. 2022. https://www.prri.org/research/americans-support-for-key-lgbtq-rights-continues-to-tick-upward/

Baldock, Kathy. *Walking the Bridgeless Canyon: Repairing the Breach between the Church and the LGBT Community.* Canyonwalker Press, 2014.

Bittker, Bobbi M. "Pushing Against the Tide to Help At-Risk LGBTQ Youth THRIVE." *Human Rights*, vol. 47, no. 1, American Bar Association, 2021, pp. 24–25.

Carrasco, Maria. "Students Feel Pain of State Anti-LGBTQ+ Bills." *Inside Higher Ed*, 30 Mar. 2022, https://www.insidehighered.com/news/2022/03/30/state-anti-lgbtq-legislation-hurts-college-students?v2

"Children and Gender Identity, Supporting Your Child," *Mayo Clinic*, Mayo Foundation for Medical Education and Research, 23 Feb. 2022, https://www.mayoclinic.org/healthy-lifestyle/childrens-health/in-depth/children-and-gender-identity/art-20266811

Conron, K.J., and S.K. Goldberg. "Adult LGBT Population in the United States." Jul. 2020. *The Williams Institute*, UCLA, Los Angeles, CA.

Conron, K.J. "LGBT Youth Population in the United States." Sep. 2020. *The Williams Institute*, UCLA, Los Angeles, CA., https://williamsinstitute.law.ucla.edu/wp-content/uploads/LGBT-Youth-US-Pop-Sep-2020.pdf

Craig, Shelley L., et al. "Frequencies and Patterns of Adverse Childhood Events in LGBTQ+ Youth." *Child Abuse & Neglect*, vol. 107, 14 June 2020, p. 104623., https://doi.org/10.1016/j.chiabu.2020.104623

"Data on Family Research Reported by Researchers at University of Montreal (Parents' Journeys to Acceptance and Support of Gender-diverse and Trans Children and Youth)." *Psychology & Psychiatry Journal*, 14 Dec. 2019. pp. 1215-1235. *Gale Academic OneFile.*

Davidson, John W. "How the Impact of *Bostock v. Clayton County* on LGBTQ Rights Continues to Expand: News & Commentary." *American Civil Liberties Union*, American Civil Liberties Union, 15 Jun. 2022, https://www.aclu.org/news/civil-liberties/how-the-impact-of-bostock-v-clayton-county-on-lgbtq-rights-continues-to-expand

Deerwater, Raina. "GLADD's Where We Are on TV Report: Despite a Tumultuous Year in Television, LGBTQ Representation Holds Steady," *GLAAD.* 14 Jan. 2021, https://www.glaad.org/blog/glaads-where-we-are-tv-report-despite-tumultuous-year-television-lgbtq-representation-holds

"Despite Partisan Rancor, Americans Broadly Support LGBTQ Rights: Findings from the 2020 American Values Atlas" *Public Religion Research Institute*, 22 Mar. 2021 https://www.prri.org/research/despite-partisan-rancor-despite-partisan-rancor-americans-broadly-support-lgbtq-rights-broadly-support-lgbtq-rights/

"Facts about LGBTQ Youth Suicide." *The Trevor Project*, 22 June 2022, https://www.thetrevorproject.org/resources/article/facts-about-lgbtq-youth-suicide/

"Family Acceptance Project Launches National, Integrated Online Resource to Help LGBTQ Youth and Families Find Services, Increase Support for LGBTQ Youth during Mental Health Emergency." *Erie Gay News*, 2021. https://www.eriegaynews.com/news/article.php?recordid=202112faplaunch

"Family Acceptance of LGBT Adolescents Protects Against Depression, Substance Abuse and Suicidal Behavior." *Family Acceptance Project*, San Francisco State University, Dec. 2010, https://www.momsteam.com/successful-parenting/family-acceptance-lgbt-adolescents-protects-against-depression-substance-abuse-and-suicide-attempts

Gass, Henry. "With Roe in Peril, 'Slippery Slope' Looms Larger for LGBTQ Americans." *The Christian Science Monitor*, 09 May 2022, https://www.csmonitor.com/USA/Justice/2022/0509/With-Roe-in-peril-slippery-slope-looms-larger-for-LGBTQ-Americans

Giron, Robert L. Received by Esther Schwartz-McKinzie, *Thank You*, 21 June 2022.

Goodnight, Cameron. "Carroll County School Board to Develop New Policy on Political Symbols." Washington Post, 19Apr. 2022, https://www.washingtonpost.com/local/carrol-county-school-board-to-develop-new-policy-on-political-symbols/2022/04/19/6d17f19e-bf88-11ec-9b0a-38a983a2edcb_story.html

Gorse, Michael. "Risk and Protective Factors to LGBTQ+ Youth Suicide: A Review of the Literature." *Child and Adolescent Social Work Journal.* vol 39, 2020, pp. 17-28. https://link.springer.com/article/10.1007/s10560-020-00710-3

Haneshamah, Siddur Kol. "Asher Yatzar." *Ritualwell*, https://ritualwell.org/ritual/asher-yatzar

"Home." *National Network for Youth*, 20 Apr. 2022, https://nn4youth.org/

Issitt, Micah L. "Preface." *The Reference Shelf: LGBTQ in the 21st Century*. Salem, 2017. *Salem Online*, https://online.salempress.com accessed 22 May. 2022.

Jarrell, Zachary. "Overview of over 300 Anti-LGBTQ+ Bills in 2022." *Washington Blade: LGBTQ News, Politics, LGBTQ Rights, Gay News*, 22 Apr. 2022, https://www.washingtonblade.com/2022/04/22/overview-of-over-300-anti-lgbtq-bills-in-2022/

Jones, Jeffrey M. "LGBT Identification in U.S. Ticks up to 7.1%." *Gallup.Com*, Gallup, 10 June 2022, https://news.gallup.com/poll/389792/lgbt-identification-ticks-up.aspx

Kirchick, James. "The Struggle for Gay Rights is Over." *The Atlantic*. 28 Jun. 2019, https://www.theatlantic.com/ideas/archive/2019/06/battle-gay-rights-over/592645/

Kukla, Elliot Rose. "Blessings for Gender Transitioning." *Ritualwell*, https://ritual-well.org/ritual/blessings-gender-transitioning/

Lavietes, Matt, and Elliot Ramos. "Nearly 240 Anti-LGBTQ Bills Filed in 2022 so Far, Most of Them Targeting Trans People." *NBCNews.com*, NBCUniversal News Group, 22 Mar. 2022, https://www.nbcnews.com/nbc-out/out-politics-and-policy/nearly-240-anti-lgbtq-bills-filed-2022-far-targeting-trans-people-rcna20418

Lee, Justin. *Torn: Rescuing the Gospel from the Gays-vs.-Christians Debate*. Jericho Books, 2013.

"Legislation Affecting LGBTQ Rights across the Country." *American Civil Liberties Union*, American Civil Liberties Union, 24 Jun. 2022, https://www.aclu.org/legislation-affecting-lgbtq-rights-across-country

"LGBTQ Youth Are Living in Crisis: Key Findings from HRC Foundation ..." *Project Thrive*, Human Rights Campaign Foundation, 2021, https://hrc-prod-requests.s3-us-west-2.amazonaws.com/ProjectThrive_YRBSData_Exec-Summary.pdf?mtime=20210803150151&focal=none

Meanley, Steven et al. "The Interplay of Familial Warmth and LGBTQ+ Specific Family Rejection on LGBTQ+ Adolescents' Self Esteem." *Journal of Adolescence,* vol 93, 2021, 40-52.

Macbeth, Ashley J. et al., "Perceived Parental Religiosity as a Predictor of Depression and Substance Abuse Among LGBTQ+ Individuals: The Mediating Role of Perceived Familial Stigma." *Psychology of Religion and Spirituality*, vol 14, no. 1, 2022, pp. 140-147, https://doi.org/10.1037/rel0000411

Mallory, Christopher, N.T. Taylor and Brad Spears. "The Impact of Stigma and Discrimination Against LGBT People in Virginia." The Williams Institute at UCLA School of Law. 2020. https://www.jstor.org/stable/resrep35034.5#metadata_info_tab_contents

McConnel, Elizabeth A. et al., "Families Matter: Social Support and Mental Health Trajectories Among Lesbian, Gay, Bisexual, and Transgender Youth." *Journal of Adolescent Health*, vol. 59, no. 6, 2016. pp 674-680.

McShane, Julianne. "Adults Who Identify as LGBTQ Hit Record High." *The Washington Post*, 22 Feb. 2022. https://www.washingtonpost.com/lifestyle/2022/02/17/adults-identifying-lgbt-gen-z/

Miller, Kathleen K., Ryan J. Watson and Marla E. Eisenberg. "The Intersection of Family Acceptance and religion on the Mental health of LGBTQ Youth." Annals of LGB TQ Public and Population Health. Vol 1 no. 1 20202. Springer Publishing Company.

Mills–Koonce, W. Roger, et al. "The Significance of Parenting and Parent–Child Relationships for Sexual and Gender Minority Adolescents." *Journal of Research on Adolescence*, vol. 28, no. 3, Wiley Subscription Services, Inc, 2018, pp. 637–49, https://doi.org/10.1111/jora.12404

Milton, D.C. and Knutson, D. "Family of Origin, Not Chosen family, Predicts Psychological Health in a LGBTQ+ Sample." *Psychology of Sexual Orientation and Gender Diversity*, 30 Sep. 2021, https://doi.org/10.1037/sgd0000531

Morton, M.H., et al., "Missed Opportunities: Youth Homelessness in America. National Estimates." Chicago, IL: Chapin Hall at the University of Chicago. 2017, https://voicesofyouthcount.org/wp-content/uploads/2017/11/ChapinHall_VoYC_NationalReport_Final.pdf

Newcomb, Michael E., and Michael C. La Salsa, et al. "The Influence of Families on LGBTQ Youth Health: A Call to Action for Innovation in Research and Intervention Development," *LGBT Health,* vol. 6 no. 4. 29 May 2019. https://www.liebertpub.com/doi/10.1089/lgbt.2018.0157

"Observations & Recommendations." *GLAAD,* 15 July 2021, https://www.glaad.org/sri/2021/observations-recommendations

Powell, Laurel. "We Are Here: LGBTQ+ Population in United States Reaches at Least 20 Million." *Human Rights Campaign,* 9 Dec. 2021, https://www.hrc.org/press-releases/we-are-here-lgbtq-adult-population-in-united-states-reaches-at-least-20-million-according-to-human-rights-campaign-foundation-report

Pullen Sansfaçon, Annie, et al. "Parents' Journeys to Acceptance and Support of Gender-Diverse and Trans Children and Youth." *Journal of Family Issues*, vol. 41, no. 8, SAGE Publications, 2020, pp. 1214–36, https://doi.org/10.1177/0192513X19888779

Rafferty, Jason. "Gender Identity Development in Children." *HealthyChildren.org,* American Academy of Pediatrics, 11 May 2022, https://www.healthychildren.org/English/ages-stages/gradeschool/Pages/Gender-Identity-and-Gender-Confusion-In-Children.aspx

"Rainbow Railroad." *Rainbow Railroad,* 29 June 2022, https://www.rainbowrailroad.org/

Solomon, Andrew. *Far from the Tree: Parents, Children and the Search for Identity.* Scribner, 2013.

Ryan, Caitlin et al., "Family Acceptance in Adolescence and the Health of LGBT Young Adults" *Journal of Child and Adolescent Psychiatric Nursing*, vol. 23 no. 4, 15 Nov. 2010, https://doi.org/10.1111/j.1744-6171.2010.00246.x

"Support for LGBTQ Youth Starts at Home: An #AsYouAre Project." *YouTube*, The Institute for Innovation and Implementation at the University of Maryland, Baltimore School of Social Work in partnership with The Biden Foundation, 22 Jan. 2019, https://www.youtube.com/watch?v=fyXRwX3aeOU accessed 27 June 2022.

"Supporting Your LGBTQ Youth: A Guide for Foster Parents - Child Welfare." *Child Welfare Information Gateway*, U.S. Department of Health and Human Services, Administration for Children and Families, Children's Bureau, Jun. 2021, https://www.childwelfare.gov/pubpdfs/lgbtqyouth.pdf

"2019 Bi+ Youth Report." *Human Rights Campaign*, https://hrc-prod-requests.s3-us-west-2.amazonaws.com/files/images/resources/HRC-2019-Bi-Youth-_Report.pdf

"2019 YRBSS Results and Data Available Now." *Centers for Disease Control and Prevention*, Centers for Disease Control and Prevention, 27 Oct. 2020, https://www.cdc.gov/healthyyouth/data/yrbs/index.htm

"2021 Officially Becomes Worst Year in Recent History for LGBTQ State Legislative Attacks as Unprecedented Number of States Enact Record-Shattering Number of Anti-LGBTQ Measures into Law." *Human Rights Campaign*, 7 May 2021, https://www.hrc.org/press-releases/2021-officially-becomes-worst-year-in-recent-history-for-lgbtq-state-legislative-attacks-as-unprecedented-number-of-states-enact-record-shattering-number-of-anti-lgbtq-measures-into-law

RESOURCES FOR FAMILIES

American Civil Liberties Union:
https://www.aclu.org/

Bisexual Resource Center:
https://biresource.org/

Centerlink:
https://www.lgbtcenters.org/

Child Welfare Information Gateway:
https://www.childwelfare.gov/topics/systemwide/diverse-populations/lgbtq/lgbt-families/

Coming Out: Information for Parents of LGBTQ Teens (American Academy of Pediatrics):
https://www.healthychildren.org/English/ages-stages/teen/dating-sex/Pages/Four-Stages-of-Coming-Out.aspx

Family Acceptance Project:
https://familyproject.sfsu.edu/

Family Equality Council:
https://www.familyequality.org/

FIERCE:
https://www.fiercenyc.org/about

Find LGBTQ Services and Support, Searchable Map to Access Resources for LGBTQ Youth and Families (Family Acceptance project):
https://trainings-theinstitutecf.umaryland.edu/lgbtqfamily/map.cfm

Gender Diverse and Transgender Children (American Academy of Pediatrics):
https://www.healthychildren.org/English/ages-stages/gradeschool/Pages/Gender-Diverse-Transgender-Children.aspx

Gender Diversity:
http://genderdiversity.org/

GLAAD:
https://www.glaad.org/

GLMA: Health Professionals Advancing LGBTQ Equality (previously known as the Gay & Lesbian Medical Association):
https://www.glma.org/

GLSEN:
https://www.glsen.org/

HealthyChildren.Org (American Academy of Pediatrics):
https://www.healthychildren.org/English/ages-stages/teen/dating-sex/Pages/Four-Stages-of-Coming-Out.aspx

Human Rights Campaign:
https://www.hrc.org/

The International Lesbian, Gay, Bisexual, Trans, and Intersex Association
https://ilga.org/

Lambda Legal
https://www.lambdalegal.org/

Lesbian, Gay, Bisexual, and Transgender Health (Centers for Disease Control):
https://www.cdc.gov/lgbthealth/

LGBT Youth Resources (Centers for Disease Control):
https://www.cdc.gov/lgbthealth/youth-resources.htm

Matthew Shepard Foundation:
https://www.matthewshepard.org/

National Network of LGBTQ Family Groups
https://www.familyequality.org/family-support/national-network-lgbtq-family-groups/

Our Trans Loved-Ones (PFLAG):
https://pflag.org/sites/default/files/OTLO_2019.pdf

Parenting a Gender-Diverse Child: Hard Questions Answered (American Academy of Pediatrics):
https://www.healthychildren.org/English/ages-stages/gradeschool/Pages/parenting-a-gender-diverse-child-hard-questions-answered.aspx

PFLAG:
https://pflag.org/family

Rainbow Youth Alliance:
https://www.rainbowyouthalliancemd.org/

Safe Communities (PFLAG):
https://pflag.org/safe-communities

SMYAL:
https://smyal.org/

Support Resources for Families of gender Diverse Youth (American Academy of Pediatrics):
https://www.healthychildren.org/English/ages-stages/gradeschool/Pages/Support-Resources-for-Families-of-Gender-Diverse-Youth.aspx

The Trevor Project:
https://www.thetrevorproject.org/

Tips for Parents of LGBTQ Youth (Johns Hopkins Medicine):
https://www.hopkinsmedicine.org/health/wellness-and-prevention/tips-for-parents-of-lgbtq-youth

Trans Families:
https://transfamilies.org/

Transgender Law Center:
https://transgenderlawcenter.org/

Trans Lifeline:
https://translifeline.org/

Trans Justice Funding Project:
https://www.transjusticefundingproject.org/

Trans Women of Color Collective:
https://www.twocc.us/

Trans Youth Equality Foundation:
http://www.transyouthequality.org/

Whitman Walker Clinic:
https://www.whitman-walker.org/

GLOSSARY

*Unless otherwise indicated by footnotes, these definitions come from the Human Rights Campaign's "Glossary of Terms," located here: https://www.hrc.org/resources/glossary-of-terms

Ally: A term used to describe someone who is actively supportive of LGBTQ+ people. It encompasses straight and cisgender allies, as well as those within the LGBTQ+ community who support each other (e.g., a lesbian who is an ally to the bisexual community).

Bisexual: A person emotionally, romantically, or sexually attracted to more than one sex, gender or gender identity though not necessarily simultaneously, in the same way or to the same degree. Sometimes used interchangeably with pansexual.

Cisgender: A term used to describe a person whose gender identity aligns with those typically associated with the sex assigned to them at birth.

Coming Out: The process in which a person first acknowledges, accepts and appreciates their sexual orientation or gender identity and begins to share that with others.

Gay: A person who is emotionally, romantically, or sexually attracted to members of the same gender. Men, women, and non-binary people may use this term to describe themselves.

Gender binary: A system in which gender is constructed into two strict categories of male or female. Gender identity is expected to align with the sex assigned at birth and gender expressions and roles fit traditional expectations.

Gender diverse: An umbrella term to describe an ever-evolving array of labels people may apply when their gender identity, expression, or even perception does not conform to the norms and stereotypes others expect.[1]

Gender dysphoria: Clinically significant distress caused when a person's assigned birth gender is not the same as the one with which they identify.

Gender-expansive: A person with a wider, more flexible range of gender identity and/or expression than typically associated with the binary gender system. Often used as an umbrella term when referring to young people still exploring the possibilities of their gender expression and/or gender identity.

Gender expression: External appearance of one's gender identity, usually expressed through behavior, clothing, body characteristics or voice, and which may or may not conform to socially defined behaviors and characteristics typically associated with being either masculine or feminine.

Gender-fluid: A person who does not identify with a single fixed gender or has a fluid or unfixed gender identity.

Gender identity: One's innermost concept of self as male, female, a blend of both or neither — how individuals perceive themselves and what they call themselves. One's gender identity can be the same or different from their sex assigned at birth.

Gender non-conforming: A broad term referring to people who do not behave in a way that conforms to the traditional expectations of their gender, or whose gender expression does not fit neatly into a category. While many also identify as transgender, not all gender non-conforming people do.

Genderqueer: Genderqueer people typically reject notions of static categories of gender and embrace a fluidity of gender identity and often, though not always,

---

1   For this definition and other versions of definitions included here, see Jason, Rafferty. "Gender-Diverse & Transgender Children." *HealthyChildren.org,* American Academy of Pediatrics, 6 Aug. 2022, https://www.healthychildren.org/English/ages-stages/gradeschool/Pages/Gender-Diverse-Transgender-Children.aspx.

sexual orientation. People who identify as "genderqueer" may see themselves as being both male and female, neither male nor female or as falling completely outside these categories.

Heteronormative: Of, relating to, or based on the attitude that heterosexuality is the only normal and natural expression of sexuality.[2]

Homophobia: The fear and hatred of or discomfort with people who are attracted to members of the same sex

Intersex: Intersex people are born with a variety of differences in their sex traits and reproductive anatomy. There is a wide variety of difference among intersex variations, including differences in genitalia, chromosomes, gonads, internal sex organs, hormone production, hormone response, and/or secondary sex traits.

Lesbian: A woman who is emotionally, romantically, or sexually attracted to other women. Women and non-binary people may use this term to describe themselves.

LGBTQ+: An acronym for "lesbian, gay, bisexual, transgender and queer" with a "+" sign to recognize the limitless sexual orientations and gender identities used by members of our community.

LGBTQ+ Family: A family in which some people are lesbian, gay, bisexual, transgender, non-binary, or queer. This could include parents, guardians, foster parents, children, chosen family, siblings or grandparents who are LGBTQ+.[3]

Non-binary: An adjective describing a person who does not identify exclusively as a man or a woman. Non-binary people may identify as being both a man and a woman, somewhere in between, or as falling completely outside these categories.

---

2   See "Heteronormative Definition & Meaning." *Merriam-Webster,* Merriam-Webster, https://www.merriam-webster.com/dictionary/heteronormative

3   For this definition and other versions of definitions included here, see "LGBTQ+ Inclusive Family Diversity Definitions." *Welcoming Schools,* HRC Foundation, https://welcomingschools.org/resources/family-diversity-definitions.

While many also identify as transgender, not all non-binary people do. Non-binary can also be used as an umbrella term encompassing identities such as agender, bigender, genderqueer or gender-fluid.

Outing: Exposing someone's lesbian, gay, bisexual transgender, or gender non-binary identity to others without their permission. Outing someone can have serious repercussions on employment, economic stability, personal safety or religious or family situations.

Queer: A term people often use to express a spectrum of identities and orientations that are counter to the mainstream. Queer is often used as a catch-all to include many people, including those who do not identify as exclusively straight and/or folks who have non-binary or gender-expansive identities. This term was previously used as a slur but has been reclaimed by many parts of the LGBTQ+ movement.

Questioning: A term used to describe people who are in the process of exploring their sexual orientation or gender identity.

Sex assigned at birth: The sex, male, female or intersex, that a doctor or midwife uses to describe a child at birth based on their external anatomy.

Sexual orientation: An inherent or immutable enduring emotional, romantic, or sexual attraction to other people. Note: an individual's sexual orientation is independent of their gender identity.

Top Surgery: For transgender men and nonbinary people, top surgery is a procedure to remove breast or chest tissue (subcutaneous mastectomy). It's also called masculinizing chest surgery. This kind of surgery might be done as a step in the process of treating discomfort when gender identity differs from sex assigned at birth (gender dysphoria). The procedure can help transgender men and nonbinary people transition physically to their self-affirmed gender.[4]

---

4   For further explanation and discussion, see "Top Surgery for Transgender Men and Nonbinary People." *Mayo Clinic*, Mayo Foundation for Medical Education and Research, 13 Jan. 2022, https://www.mayoclinic.org/tests-procedures/top-surgery-for-transgender-men/about/pac-20469462.

Transgender: An umbrella term for people whose gender identity and/or expression is different from cultural expectations based on the sex they were assigned at birth. Being transgender does not imply any specific sexual orientation. Therefore, transgender people may identify as straight, gay, lesbian, bisexual, etc.

Transitioning: A series of processes that some transgender people may undergo in order to live more fully as their true gender. This typically includes social transition, such as changing name and pronouns, medical transition, which may include hormone therapy or gender affirming surgeries, and legal transition, which may include changing legal name and sex on government identity documents. Transgender people may choose to undergo some, all, or none of these processes.

Transphobia: Irrational fear of, aversion to, or discrimination against transgender people.[5]

---

5   See "Transphobia Definition & Meaning." *Merriam-Webster,* Merriam-Webster, https://www.merriam-webster.com/dictionary/transphobia.

ACKNOWLEDGEMENTS

I am indebted, in the making of this book, to many people. Foremost, I am humbled by those who trusted me to collect their stories and treat them with care. I have learned much from them; their words push back against silence, fear and misunderstanding and make me hopeful for the future. Speaking out is a form of activism, and it is an honor for me to play some part in that.

My daughter, Mac, and my husband, Matthew, have provided wise and thoughtful feedback, encouragement, and inspiration. I am profoundly grateful to them both.

I am indebted to the patience of my publisher, Robert L. Giron, who encouraged me to keep going through setbacks.

These people all played some role that deserves acknowledgement and gratitude: Noah McKinzie, Judy LaPrade, Stephanie Hartman, Angelica Rodriguez, Barbara Blitzer, Elizabeth Benton, Rita Kranidis, Greg Wahl, Deborah Taylor, Jerilyn Schweitzer, and Charmaine Weston.

Esther Schwartz-McKinzie earned her BA from Bard College and her PhD in 19th Century British and American literature from Temple University. Her scholarly work includes efforts to recover the voices of marginalized women writers who used literature as a way to expose injustice and to expand imaginative possibilities for their readers. As a professor of English, Literature and Women's Studies at Montgomery College, she has worked to promote access to the humanities, improve the well-being of student veterans, and to reduce violence against women and members of the LGBTQ+ community. Her chapter, "Keep 'Doing Good': Women's and Gender Studies Programs and VAWA Education Initiatives Against the Tide" appeared in *Theory and Praxis, Women's and Gender Studies at Community Colleges* in 2019. Also in 2019, she was among the first recipients of the College's Excellence in Equity Award, recognizing individuals who demonstrate a commitment to social justice, equity, inclusion, antiracism, and diversity. Her photography and poetry have appeared in the *Sligo Journal*.

Esther can often be found hiking the verdant parks and trails of Montgomery County with her husband, Matthew, and their two dogs.

Fiction/Nonfiction From Gival Press

Barrow's Point by Robert Schirmer

The Best of Gival Press Short Stories edited by Robert L. Giron

Boys, Lost & Found by Charles Casillo

The Cannibal of Guadalajara by David Winner

A Change of Heart by David Garrett Izzo

The Day Rider and Other Stories by J. E. Robinson

Dead Time / Tiempo muerto by Carlos Rubio

Dream of Another America by Tyler McMahon

Dreams and Other Ailments / Sueños y otros achaques by Teresa Bevin

The Gay Herman Melville Reader edited by Ken Schellenberg

Guess and Check by Thaddeus Rutkowski

Ghost Horse by Thomas H. McNeely

Gone by Sundown by Peter Leach

An Interdisciplinary Introduction to Women's Studies edited by Brianne Friel and Robert L. Giron

Julia & Rodrigo by Mark Brazaitis

The Last Day of Paradise by Kiki Denis

Literatures of the African Diaspora by Yemi D. Ogunyemi

Lockjaw: Collected Appalachian Stories by Holly Farris

Mayhem: Three Lives of a Woman by Elizabeth Harris

Maximus in Catland by David Garrett Izzo

Miss Lucy by William Orem

Middlebrow Annoyances: American Drama in the 21st Century by Myles Weber

The Pleasuring of Men by Clifford H. Browder

Riverton Noir by Perry Glasser

Redshift, Blueshift by Jordan Silversmith

Second Acts by Tim W. Brown

Secret Memories / Recuerdos secretos by Carlos Rubio

Sexy Liberal! Of Me I Sing by Stephanie Miller

Show Up, Look Good by Mark Wisniewski

The Smoke Week: Sept. 11-21. 2001 by Ellis Avery

That Demon Life by Lowell Mick White

Theory and Praxis: Women's and Gender Studies at Community Colleges edited by
   Genevieve Carminati and Heather Rellihan

Tina Springs into Summer / Tina se lanza al verano by Teresa Bevin

The Tomb on the Periphery by John Domini

Twelve Rivers of the Body by Elizabeth Oness

For a complete list of Gival Press titles, visit: www.givalpress.com.
Books available from Ingram, Brodart, Follett, your favorite bookstore,
on-line booksellers, or directly from Gival Press.

Gival Press, LLC
PO Box 3812
Arlington, VA 22203
givalpress@yahoo.com
703.351.007